WHAT PEOPLE ARE SAYING ABOUT

THE EARTH, THE GODS, AND THE SOUL

This is a very interesting, very useful and prospectively very important work, which summarises a great range of literature with crystal clarity, and makes a passionate personal argument that will contribute valuably to current debates over the nature and position of religion.

Ronald Hutton, Professor of History, University of Bristol, author of *The Triumph of the Moon*

History is usually written by the winners. This is as true for the history of philosophy as anywhere else. A thousand years of institutionalized monotheism decisively shaped how philosophy developed and remembered its predecessors. Yet as Brendan Myers demonstrates, often forgotten insights that had motivated early Pagan philosophical and wisdom traditions continue to speak to the human experience. Until recently no foundations beyond the brilliance of individual minds existed to develop these insights in a modern context. Today, as th~~~ ~~~~tion changes, we are all enriched by read~~~ ~~~~~ ~~~~~ ~ ory of philosophy written from a l~~~ ~~~~~~

Anyone wanting to place o ~~~~~~~~~~~~~ ~e grand history of Western tho ~~~~~~~~~~ ~s promise for the future, will be en~~~ ~~~~~~ ~y reading Myers' book.

Gus DiZerega, author of *Pagans and Christians* and *Beyond the Burning Times*

The Earth,
The Gods,
and The Soul

A History of Pagan Philosophy,
from the Iron Age to the
21st Century

The Earth,
The Gods,
and The Soul

A History of Pagan Philosophy,
from the Iron Age to the
21st Century

Brendan Myers

Winchester, UK
Washington, USA

First published by Moon Books, 2013
Moon Books is an imprint of John Hunt Publishing Ltd., Laurel House, Station Approach,
Alresford, Hants, SO24 9JH, UK
office1@jhpbooks.net
www.johnhuntpublishing.com
www.moon-books.net

For distributor details and how to order please visit the 'Ordering' section on our website.

Text copyright: Brendan Myers 2013

ISBN: 978 1 78099 317 1

A CIP catalogue record for this book is available from the British Library.

Design and cover: Stuart Davies

Printed and bound by CPI Group (UK) Ltd, Croydon, CR0 4YY

We operate a distinctive and ethical publishing philosophy in all
areas of our business, from our global network of authors to
production and worldwide distribution.

CONTENTS

Acknowledgments, Dedication, and a Preparatory Note

This book was informally commissioned by Trevor Greenfield of Moon Books, who originally wanted a short book to include in Moon Books' Pagan Portals series. Well, a short book grew into a longer one, and a long book grew into an even longer one. A year and a half later, this monster-length manuscript was complete; and I am grateful to Trevor for his patience.

I am also grateful to Greg Currie, Clara Blackwood, Natalie Evans, Allan Harrison, and Jane Trombley for the use of their private libraries, as I researched this book. And I am grateful to everyone who contributed a few words to the discussion of Living Voices, many of whom did so on very short notice. I also offer special thanks to my colleagues at the Cherry Hill Seminary who offered useful commentary on parts of the manuscript while it was in progress, especially Valentine McKay-Riddell, and Deirdre Sommerlad-Rogers. And I also thank several friends who kept my spirits up during the most difficult times in the writing and researching process, especially including Davina Kula, Idalia Nelson, Courtney Rheaume, Mj Patterson, Cassandra Boville, and Matt Clooney.

With the deepest friendship, I dedicate this work to Greg Currie, who has been my spiritual brother for all my adult life. And I dedicate this to the memory of Jane Estelle Trombley: may peace be upon her and all who knew and loved her.

As I wrote this book, I assumed that most readers know a little bit about the logical tools philosophers use when they work: tools like propositions, inferences, arguments, and the fallacies. I also assume that most readers know the main branches of the discipline of philosophy: metaphysics, epistemology, ethics, logic, phenomenology, and aesthetics. If these terms are unfamiliar to you, I have created a college-level textbook on logic and argumentation, called *Clear and Present Thinking*, which is available through my internet site, for free. And don't be afraid of logic! Most of it is actually quite easy, once you get the hang of it.

For researchers: a comprehensive index for this book, and my other books, is also available on my website.

Brendan Myers
Gatineau Quebec, Spring Equinox 2013
Web: http://brendanmyers.net

A heathen, consumably – but not, I hope, an unenlightened one.
–Lord Summerisle.

Overture

Philosophy was invented by pagans. Or to be more precise: it was invented by people who lived in pagan societies, many centuries before the foundation of the great monotheist religions of the Western world.

Yet most people do not associate the word 'pagan' with philosophy. The word began as a straightforward Roman Latin word for a villager, a *paganus*, a person who lived in a countryside district, a *pagus*, instead of in a city. We still get the word 'pagaent', from this root; it refers to a folkish theatrical performance associated with special times of year. A related word, 'heathen', began in roughly the same era, and referred to a civilian, a person not enrolled in the army, although it sometimes also referred to a poorly armed peasant-soldier. The modern word *peasant* comes from the same source. After the advent of Christianity, both words began to designate people who had not (yet) accepted Christianity. So, the association of pagan with a country dweller was natural perhaps, since the Christian message was first preached in cities, and then spread to the countryside later on. It may also have referred to a 'civilian' in the sense of someone who is not a Christian missionary, not a 'soldier for Christ'. (York, *Pagan Theology*, pg. 6) From there, both words eventually took on the association with ignorance and foolishness, as well as superstition, malicious magic, and evil. Actually, the exact origin of the word *pagan* is a point of some dispute, even inside the modern pagan community.

Today, despite efforts to raise the word to respectability, it is still regularly used as a term of abuse. It accuses someone of being a superstitious, unenlightened, or backwards person, or of practicing magic with fell purpose. Most especially, the word 'pagan' is associated with idolatry, that is, the worship of false gods, such as those which Old Testament writers warned against:

the sun and moon and stars, and various animal and human characters represented in figures of wood and stone. (c.f. Deuteronomy 4:15-24) The worship of such beings is specifically outlawed by the Second of the Ten Commandments.

But suppose we took the word in its simplest definition: a person whose religion is not Abrahamic; that is, a person whose religion is not Judaism, Christianity, or Islam. And suppose we limited this definition to the nations of the 'West', and their predecessor societies in Europe and the Mediterranean, just to keep things simple. What sort of people remain? In fact we do *not* find that everyone who could be classified as a pagan this way is an ignorant village idiot who fearfully gives offerings to malevolent gods, or who schemes to curse his enemies in the middle of the night. Instead, we find the people who built grand monuments like the Acropolis of Athens, Stonehenge, Newgrange, and the Pyramids of Egypt. We find the people who built complex astronomical instruments like the Antikythera Mechanism, the Nebra Sky Disk, and the Berlin Gold Hat. We find poets and scientists and literary intellectuals of every kind, especially including those who wrote some of the most important and influential books in all of Western history. Homer, Hesiod, Plato, Aristotle, and Cicero, just to name a few, are listed among the greatest writers in all Western civilization. *And they all lived in pagan societies.* We also find some of the greatest political and military leaders of all time: Alexander the Great, Pericles of Athens, Hannibal of Carthage, and Julius Caesar of Rome. These men were all pagans, or else living in a pagan society. Some took themselves for living pagan gods. And speaking of pagan societies: some of today's highest social and political values, like democracy, secular republican government, freedom of speech, and trial by jury, were invented by pagans. Even the Olympic Games were invented by pagans. Yet these facts are almost always ignored when people study the origins of Western civilization.

My full purpose in this book, however, is not simply, nor only, to draw attention to this often neglected and perhaps uncomfortable fact. It is also to examine what, if anything, is a distinctly pagan kind of philosophical thinking. It is to show that a pagan need not be an ignorant uncivilized person. I hope to show that a pagan can be a sophisticated, cosmopolitan, and enlightened person, and that a pagan culture can be artistically vibrant, environmentally conscious, intellectually stimulating, and socially just.

§ 1. Philosophy

To zoom in on what we're looking for more precisely, it's worthwhile to consider just what philosophy is, as an intellectual discipline, and also what it is not. Let us be clear from the beginning: philosophy does *not* mean having a certain 'mindset' (I hate that word). It does not mean that one must hold one particular belief about the meaning of life, or the nature of morality, or some such, instead of another. Someone who quotes a common saying, or a witty line from a pop song or a movie, and then says, 'That's my philosophy,' is simply not doing the work. Philosophy is both more complex and more simple than that.

Still, the question 'what is philosophy?' can be a surprisingly difficult one to answer. For the question itself is a philosophical one. To help understand this, let me take you to the ancient Mediterranean world, after the rise of the great city-states of the region, but before the invention of philosophy as we know it today.

At that time, and in that part of the world, the most important source of knowledge about the most important questions in human life was a religious institution called the Pythian Oracle of Delphi. The Oracle lived in a temple complex near the top of Mount Parnassus, in the middle of Greece. In the main temple, a priestess would sit on a tripod stool and perform a religious ritual which, people believed, would put her into direct

3

communication with the god Apollo. If you wanted to know about almost anything that was important to you, from practical questions about marriage or business deals, to the most abstract questions about the meaning of life, you could visit this priestess and pose your questions directly to Apollo himself. What better source of knowledge could there be than a god!

Petitioners had to undergo a ritual of their own in order to prepare themselves for their visit to the Oracle. The first major part of this ritual was the pilgrimage to Delphi itself. The second began when the petitioner arrived at the temple. There he would undergo various purifications, make offerings to the gods (and financial donations to the temple!), and consult with the priests to frame his question as best he could. It seems likely that this second part was in some way informed or inspired by the various proverbs carved over the entrance arches to the temple, several of which have been recorded for us by various writers. The most famous one is the first one: *Gnothi seautón* – know yourself. For many centuries thereafter, including well into our own modern time, this statement has served as the definitive motto of religious and spiritual seeking. Not that there is necessarily much consensus about what it means, of course! Polytheists, monotheists, atheists, and people who simply call themselves amorphously 'spiritual' all claim to follow it for their own purposes. The Gospel of Thomas reports that Jesus used this motto in his teachings as well. (*The Gospel of Thomas*, §3, as cited in Barnstone and Meyer, eds. *The Gnostic Bible*, pg. 45) But let us say in general that the statement 'know yourself' expresses a basic ethical demand to examine one's own character and habits and nature carefully and honestly, avoiding all fabrications and lies. The differences in opinion about the meaning of the statement tend to appear in different claims about what one can expect to find in that self-examination. Let us also add that since the statement is carved into the stones of the most important temple of its time, it may have the force of a scripture, that is, a divine revelation cast into written words.

This basic ethical demand, know yourself, is to my mind the first stirring of the philosophical impulse. For self-knowledge is not like ordinary, practical knowledge. Someone who examines himself will chop wood and carry water the same way as someone else who doesn't. Yet self-knowledge puts into question something you are probably inclined to take for granted, namely, your own existence, your identity, your being. The very words of the statement presuppose that the self is something that can be *known*. Yet the statement is phrased in the imperative – as an ethical command – and therefore it also presupposes that you can be ignorant about yourself. You can go through life *not knowing* who you are, and you must *find out* who you are. (Such an interesting and thought-provoking proposition – that a human being can be a mystery to herself!) That kind of knowledge can benefit every area of your life. Yet there's something special and spiritual about it, apart from any practical usefulness it may have. For self knowledge heals, enlightens, and empowers – and sometimes, it judges and condemns. The seeking of self-knowledge lifts the self up from the practical life and into the realm of the very highest and deepest things. It's fitting, perhaps, that someone must undertake this kind of soul-searching and self-seeking before being allowed into the presence of the god. And the philosophical theme of self-examination echoes down the ages, in the works of thinkers who couldn't be more different from each other, from Socrates to Nietzsche, from Plato to Sartre.

Several other mottos were carved into the stones of Delphi. A second, also widely credited to the god Apollo himself, is *medén ágan* – nothing in excess. Like the first motto, this one expresses an ethical demand, but this time a rather more practical one: it calls for the virtue of temperance. In its original meaning, temperance had to do with the use and regulation of one's emotions, especially one's taste for bodily pleasures like food, drink, and sex. It calls upon the seeker to guide his life not with instinct, intuition, or emotional intensity, but instead with calm and sober rationality. Many people today associate temperance with the suppression or the denial of the emotions, or with abstinence from things like alcohol. But that's not it at all. The idea is that one must learn to enjoy the pleasures of embodied life without becoming addicted to them. The Greeks knew that intensity of passion could be both a benefit to you, and at the same time a profound liability. So, temperance allows people to enjoy the pleasures of the flesh, but without becoming a slave to them. This insight, expressed in the second Delphic motto, is also a stirring of the philosophical spirit. And again, it is appropriate preparation for an encounter with a god like Apollo, the god of high culture and civilization.

But once we are properly prepared like this, what happens when we enter the holy of holies, and meet the Oracle herself? We find that her tripod stool stands directly above a fissure in the floor, from which strange vapors waft into the air. The priestess ascends her throne, breathes in these vapors, invokes the god, and speaks. What does she say? Gibberish, mostly. For she is in a mild drug-induced trance, and so she is no longer herself, and no longer in complete control of her own mind. Her ramblings are translated by the priests who sit around her throne in a circle; sometimes they turn her gibberish into poetry. And this they offer to the petitioner as the god's answer to the question.

Alas, here in the holy of holies, the spirit of philosophy has not yet appeared. For we are relying upon a divine communication to answer our questions. Not that the gods cannot be wise. But the point of a philosophical spirit is to rely primarily upon *one's own thinking*. The philosophical spirit is not satisfied to simply accept what it is told, no matter how much prestige the teller seems to have. This is true even if the teller is a god. The philosophical spirit looks within itself, regards the world with wonder but also with curiosity and skepticism. It poses serious questions, and makes a serious attempt to find answers. Nor does it settle for the quick and easy answer, unless it is also the *best* answer.

Now philosophy is not science, not social science, not religion, not poetry, and not theology. But it overlaps with all those disciplines. We could define it in terms of the Greek roots of the word: the *philia* of the *sophia*, the love of wisdom, the friend of knowledge. But that might not be fully satisfying, because we might not know what love is, or what wisdom or knowledge are, or what it means to be a friend. Even among professional philosophers there is disagreement about the meaning of their own discipline. I define philosophy as the investigation of the highest and deepest questions by means of systematic critical reason. But my definition is not the only one, and perhaps not even the best one. Here's how British philosopher Bertrand Russell defined it:

> Philosophy, as I shall understand the word, is something intermediate between theology and science. Like theology, it consists of speculation on matters as to which definite knowledge has, so far, been unascertainable; but like science, it appeals to human reason rather than to authority, whether that of tradition or that of revelation. All *definite* knowledge – so I should contend – belongs to science; all *dogma* as to what surpasses definite knowledge belongs to theology. But between theology and science there is a No Man's Land, exposed to attack from both sides; this No Man's Land is philosophy. (Russell, *History of Western Philosophy*, pg. 13)

Russell then presents a long list of typical philosophical questions, such as questions about the nature of the world, or human life, or the cosmos, or the soul. Then he finishes with this thought:

> To such questions no answer can be found in the laboratory.

Theologies have professed to give answers, all too definite; but their very definiteness causes modern minds to view them with suspicion. The studying of these questions, if not the answering of them, is the business of philosophy. (Russell, *ibid*, pg. 13-4)

Russell was, of course, a committed atheist, and probably can't be expected to say all that many kind words about theology. However, suppose we took at face value the idea that philosophy occupies a middle ground between theology and science. I think he means that philosophy seeks answers to the ultimate questions about 'life, the universe, and everything', like a theologian, but uses systematic critical reason to do so, like a scientist. Philosophy is the study of what is *a priori* about the highest and deepest things. Imagine a scientist doing a theologian's work: that is the way of a philosopher.

We can also define the philosopher as Friedrich Nietzsche did: 'a terrible explosive, endangering everything...' (Nietzsche, *Ecce Homo*, III.2.3) And this is because philosophers often have the most inconvenient habit of questioning everything – yes I mean everything – and putting all of our beliefs on the table for close examination. She exposes the inconsistencies, irrationalities, and the plain silliness, which often dominates people's thinking. She will not let you believe the gratifying lie, or the comfortable illusion. She doesn't care if you feel 'invalidated' by her work. She taps on your thoughts and beliefs with tuning-hammers to hear which ones resonate sweetly and which ones jar with discordant noise. That's what Nietzsche meant by 'How to Philosophize With A Hammer.' The philosopher lays out your very soul on a medical table, prepped and ready for exploratory surgery, and finds out what's really in there. And then she cuts out the conceptual tumors and epistemic infections that you did not know you had. And this is painful, let there be no doubt. People hate it, when it's done to them by others. No one likes to have their deepest and most intimately treasured beliefs questioned, doubted, criticized, or even identified as crap and thrown out with the trash. But in the long game, this is healthier and better for you. No one is served or benefitted by believing in false or faulty ideas. So a philosopher who is good at her job is not necessarily a 'safe' person to hang around. But at the same time, if she is good at her job, then she will have healed you of your faulty beliefs and dispelled your ignorance, and you will be better off, and you will thank her for it.

§ 2. Pagan Philosophy?

Is there such a thing as a pagan philosophy? Our question is thus something like this: if we set aside the ideas of the Western world that are not obviously Abrahamic, then what remains? Or, to put it another way: if there is a philosophical or spiritual idea in the Western tradition which is *not* clearly Abrahamic, then what kind of an idea is it? And must it be defined by what it is not, or can it be defined for what it is? Let us see if we can understand it in terms of own qualities, whether they be merits or flaws. Here are some of the places where I will look for an answer.

- Writers who professed to be pagans.
- Writers who lived in pagan societies.
- Writers who professed ideas that they characterized as pagan ideas.
- Writers whose ideas influenced the present-day pagan movement.
- Writers who attempted to synthesize pagan ideas with mainstream Abrahamic ideas, or secular ideas.
- Writers who sought philosophical and spiritual truths in real or imagined ancient pagan civilizations.
- Finally, writers attacked as 'pagans' by their opponents.

A study like this may take us to people who might not consider themselves pagans, and who might be horrified to be included in a study like this one. But while many, perhaps most, of the philosophers to be studied here would not think of themselves as pagans, nonetheless I've included them here because they had pagan thoughts, at least for a while. There are many more writers who fit that criteria who I could have included here; I've chosen the ones who seem to me the most outstanding and influential.

The last criteria on this list, although easy to use, is also notoriously frustrating. For sometimes people use the word 'pagan' to mean something threatening and dangerous but otherwise imprecise and vague. In June of 2009, for instance, the American politician Newt Gingrich told an assembly of church-goers in Virginia, 'I think this is one of the most critical moments in American history. We are living in a period where we are surrounded by paganism.' (Nicholas Graham, 'Newt Gingrich: Americans 'Are Surrounded by Paganism'' *The Huffington Post*, 7 June 2009) It's likely he was thinking of atheists, Catholics, Mormons, and a host of other people who certainly don't think of themselves as pagans. But what this offhand remark does tell us is that, at minimum, paganism is that which isn't Christian – or, in Gingrich's case, it's that which isn't *his* kind of Christianity. For our purposes, that definition is too broad, and too much *determinatio est negatio* – that is to say, paganism is defined by what it is not. If that was all we had to go with, then the search for a pagan philosophy would be over before it began.

But let us not give up too soon. There might not be a systematic and definitive category which clearly and unambiguously shows what is and what isn't a pagan way to think. But, as I hope to show, there are a cluster of ideas and arguments which bear a certain 'family resemblance' to each other, to borrow Wittgenstein's term. These ideas have almost nothing to do with ritual, or spellcraft, or magic. But they have a lot to do with reality, truth, nature, art, beauty, knowledge, the gods, right and wrong, life and death, fate and freedom, and the ultimate destiny of the soul, and other similar themes besides. In other words, they have to do with all the major themes of philosophy. And they have to do with taking a certain kind of stand toward those themes, and embodying a kind of world view, and living one's life in a certain way. Writers inside the contemporary pagan community offer various descriptions of what that world view is like. In 1979, pagan writer and NPR journalist Margot Adler wrote that paganism means animism, pantheism, and polytheism. (Adler, *Drawing Down the Moon*, pg. 25) This is the simplest definition I've ever seen, and I think probably the most frequently quoted. More recent research conducted by theologian Christine Hoff Kraemer produced a slightly longer list of pagan religious concepts: pantheism, panentheism, animism, polytheism, ecotheology, ritual practice, personal gnosis, magic(k), virtue ethics, and pluralism. (Kraemer, *Seeking the Mystery*, from the introduction to the e-book edition) Theologian Michael York wrote that we probably cannot create a definitive list of what ideas count as pagan. 'At best,' he said,

...we can determine a range of possibilities that we might expect to find in any bona fide pagan example. These include polytheism, animism, idolatry, corpospirituality, local emphasis, recognitions of geosacred concentrations, percep- tions of soul duality, and either nature worship or nature as chief metaphorical register expressive of the divine. If paganism is humanistic in essence, it is simultaneously never far from exalting the natural cycle of birth-death-rebirth. (York, *Pagan Theology*, pg. 13)

By the way, this strange word, corpospirituality, which I've never seen elsewhere, apparently means the spirituality which holds that things of the embodied world, like the earth, or the human body, are spiritually valuable, a source of spiritual knowledge and blessing in their own right. (Why he didn't just say 'pantheism', I don't know.)

There are also a few writers from outside the pagan community who treat the word with respect, although such treatments emphasize pagan moral and political values rather than pagan religious concepts. British journalist Cole Moreton, reporting on how pagan ideas in Britain were becoming more and more mainstream, wrote that, 'Everyone's a pagan now':

> All you have to believe to be a pagan... is that each of us has the right to follow our own path (as long as it harms no-one else); that the higher power (or powers) exists; and that nature is to be venerated. If you asked everyone in Britain if they agreed with those three statements, millions would put their hands up. At its loosest, paganism is beginning to look like our new national faith. (Cole Moreton, 'Everyone's a pagan now', *The Guardian*, 22 June 2009)

Moreton also observed that in Britain there are a quarter of a million practicing pagans, which makes for more pagans in Britain than Buddhists, and almost as many pagans as Jews.

Here's a final example. American journalist Robert D. Kaplan, in *Warrior Politics: Why Leadership Demands a Pagan Ethos* (2003), described pagan ethics as public rather than private, requiring self-interest rather than self-sacrifice, and concerned with 'manly vigor, that is, but usually in the pursuit of the general good. [Pagan] Virtue presupposes ambition, but not only for the sake of personal advancement.' (pg. 55) And these virtues, he said, are necessary for contemporary politicians, especially in the field of international relations. Therefore Kaplan treated writers like Niccolò Machiavelli, and Sun Tzu, as pagan writers. So, as I surveyed the whole of Western intellectual history from ancient Greece to the end of the twentieth century, I looked for, and found, ideas like those ones. But I found much more besides, as you shall see in the pages to come.

It is reasonable to ask: is a project like this one *possible?* Can one speak of a history of pagan thought, as one can speak of a history of, say, Christian theology, or German romanticism, or American pragmatism? Many to whom I described this project said that it is impossible. There has not historically been a continuous pagan community, or continuous pagan intellectual tradition, or the like, which lasted long enough to permit the development, evolution, or even the mere transmission, of pagan ideas. When I point out the proposition with which this overture began, that philosophy (in the Western world anyway), was invented by pagans, it is often replied that those ideas were 'not truly pagan' because they were associated with people in organized urban civilizations, or because their ideas were too easily assimilated into Christianity. 'And anyway,' said one associate of mine at a formal academic reception, 'doesn't the word *pagan* inherently mean someone who is uncivilized and uneducated, and therefore by definition couldn't be a philosopher?' I pointed out how much this sounded like the fallacy of question-begging, and I pointed out how many well-respected Greek and Roman philosophers invoked pagan gods by name right in their books. Indeed, Socrates himself invoked the pagan god Asclepius in his dying breath! My associate laughed, and then excused himself to find more wine.

Philosophy might also seem to lean away from paganism, and away from religion in general, for other reasons. A passage in one of the letters of St Paul advises believers to avoid philosophers. (Colossians 2:8) The Biblical definition of faith itself, which appears in the letter of Paul to the Hebrews, states that faith is the belief in something *without* evidence, without rational argument, without logical support: 'Faith is the substance of things hoped for, the evidence of things not seen.' (Hebrews 11:1) But there does not need to be a strict dichotomy between the religious spirit and the philosophical. For one thing, it's easy to see how those two mottos at Delphi can be important for both religious and philosophical streams of thought. Furthermore, back in the Roman Empire, as observed by historian James Rives, 'philosophy' was one of the four main ways that people were religious. (The other three were cult, myth, and art.) This is partly because philosophy involved contemplation of the nature of the gods and of 'the divine' in general. Philosophy did not offer new rituals to perform, nor spells to cast, nor did it 'worship' the gods in the usual sense of that word. Rather, philosophy offered:

> ...an integrated way of life in which one's moral values and everyday behavior was grounded in a particular view of the cosmos and of its relationship to human life. In modern Western culture, philosophy is often regarded as an abstract intellectual pursuit, remote from and often irrelevant to people's actual lives. In Graeco-Roman antiquity the situation was very different: 'philosophy' would for many people have suggested first and foremost a whole way of life. (Rives, *Religion in the Roman Empire*, pg. 40)

That, according to Rives, was what ancient philosophers did for religion, which cult, myth, and art, could not do. (Those other modes of religion were intended to provoke mystical feelings, or to secure the favor of the gods for one's endeavors.) And, as teachers of a way of life, philosophers could compete with seers, diviners, priests, mystics, and the like, on an equal footing. Successful philosophers in the Roman era opened their own schools and made a comfortable living from their students' tuition fees, and from donations from wealthy patrons. Rives notes that very successful philosophers like Apuleius and Dio Crysostom, 'were celebrities who could attract large crowds to their lectures and command sizable fees for their appearances.' (Rives, *ibid*, pg. 40) Aristocratic families in Rome sometimes hired a household philosopher, who served as the family's educator, spiritual advisor, and 'life coach', and sometimes as intermediary in political or commercial negotiations. And the philosophers themselves often thought these jobs quite prestigious; at any rate, they often paid very well. (Liebeschuetz, *Continuity and Change in Roman Religion*, pp. 112-133)

One might ask, what did this philosophical way of life look like? Judging by the utterances of the philosophers who promoted it, it involved peace of mind, inner harmony, a way of thinking and living that enabled people to lead worthwhile and meaningful lives, no matter what their circumstance or situation. This is exemplified, of course, in Socrates' famous statement that 'The unexamined life is not worth living.' Numerous other philosophers have made similar bold claims about the benefit of philosophical thinking. Here's one from Cicero that is typical of the genre: 'Philosophy will ensure that the man who has obeyed its laws shall never fail to be armed against all the hazards of fortune: that he shall possess and control, within his own self, every possible guarantee for a satisfactory and happy life.' (Cicero, *Discussions at Tusculum*, ch.V, cited in *On the Good Life*, pg. 63) Philosophy, at least in the ancient Roman and Greek world, sought out and addressed itself to the highest and deepest things – 'things in the sky and below the earth' as Socrates would say. (*Apology* 19b) And they thought that they could thereby help people overcome debilitating emotions like excessive passion, overcome the fear of death, and reach a sustainable and truly worthwhile kind of happiness. Between the abstract contemplation of the divine, and the practical ordering of the soul, we have two arms of a singular practice, one pointing above and one pointing below. And that, let there be no doubt, is a spiritual practice.

But philosophy is not just a matter of believing what Plato said, or what any other philosopher said. Actually, philosophy does not have a list of 'beliefs' at all, which one must accept in order to be a philosopher. Rather, it has a set of methods and skills, by which it asks questions and solves problems. That method is called systematic critical reason. Plato's discussion of the well-ordered soul is a conclusion he reached by applying that method; it is not a dogmatic statement of faith which the method cannot question. Thus other philosophers, employing the same method, reached different conclusions. So as I search for a pagan philosophy, I am *not* calling for a wholesale, uncritical revival of the beliefs of ancient philosophers. That would be impossible, and also rather silly. But I *am* calling for a revival of the orientation, guided by reason, toward the above and the below, for the sake of the health of the soul, and the justice of the body politic. I am convinced that this is a *spiritual* task, and I hope to convince you too, my friends, that it is so.

The trouble with a project like this one, it seems to me, is not only in the aura of primitivism which still surrounds the word 'pagan'. It's also the assumption that a philosophical tradition has to be associated with an *institution* of some kind to be viable. It's certainly the case that some of the world's great systems of thought, like Confucianism, or Judaism, or Vedic Hinduism, achieved greatness because libraries, universities, churches, governments, and similar institutional resources were available to their thinkers. At least since the year 590 CE, when Emperor Justinian ordered the Platonic philosophy schools to close, pagan philosophy had no institutions to foster or protect it. After that time, pagan philosophy, as a distinct tradition of thought, dwindled and disappeared. The philosophers themselves, being only human, within a few generations migrated to other traditions of thought, which could offer them better lodgings. I can't find it in my heart to condemn them for it.

But ideas don't need institutions. Ideas only need *people*. In principle, therefore, ideas can survive and evolve and flourish any place where there are two or more people who can talk to one another. Institutions can help, but they might not be strictly necessary; and ideas might be able to flourish just fine without them. This is because ideas in some sense belong to the world.

They can be created, discovered, examined, criticized, developed, and promoted, or in general worked upon in any way, by anyone who can follow the logic. Philosophy and its method belongs to everybody: one could call it the world's first 'open source OS'. This book is a history of a family of ideas, born in ancient times, which survived to the present day *without* the patronage of institutions. Indeed there are three ideas in this family which, it seems to me, consistently emerge as the dominant intellectual themes in any discussion of paganism. Any given philosophy which could be called pagan is a variation of one of these ideas, or a combination of two or all three of them. They are:

- *Pantheism*, the idea that the natural world is in some sense the body of a deity, or of several deities; the belief that the world itself bears the immanent presence of the divine. A common variation is called panentheism, which holds that the natural world reveals the presence of the divine and yet the divine is more than just its revelation in the natural world.
- *Neo-Platonism*, the idea (derived from Plato and his heirs) that God and the natural world are separate from each other, but that God is an impersonal and impartial force, which can be contemplated by reason as well as by spiritual experience, and which creates the world in an on-going process with no beginning and no end.
- *Humanism*, the idea that there's something special and spiritual about being human; that each human being shares in, or participates in, some kind of divinity; and that we can achieve something like enlightenment, however that might be defined, by means of our own efforts.

These three themes correspond to three great immensities which any system of thought worthy of being called 'theology' must confront: the Earth, the Gods, and the Soul. When I speak of pagan philosophy, then, I speak of a philosophy which addresses itself to one or more of these three immensities, and which reasons about these immensities in a unique way, as the course of this narrative shall show.

But can an idea, or family of ideas, which does not possess the support of institutions, flourish as brilliantly and completely as another idea which does possess such support? This is the philosophical-historical question of this book. In a way, I'm using pagan ideas as the case study with which to examine this question. Did that family of pagan ideas not only survive, but also evolve and thrive as a full-fledged *developing critical tradition*, even without its own churches, schools, and political patronage? Let's find out!

First Movement: Brainy Barbarians

Before philosophy, there was poetry. Not all poetry is philosophical, of course. But philosophical ideas often appear in poetry. To find a philosophical statement in a poem, or in any kind of narrative literary art, one may need to sort through the deliciously murky waters of metaphor and emotive expression. And it isn't likely that one will find arguments, counter-arguments, and analysis of concepts, as one could expect in a normal philosophical text. Nonetheless, you do often find strongly-expressed propositions, and those propositions can prompt philosophical thinking and discussion. It is probably in poetry that people first expressed their philosophical thoughts in words, and shared them with others.

§ 3. The Wanderer

In an ancient text called the *Codex Exoniensis*, 'The Book of Exeter', we find a large collection of poetry written in Anglo-Saxon, the very oldest form of the English language. The book was donated to the Exeter Cathedral collection by Bishop Leofric of Exeter, in or around the year 1050. Many of its poems are clearly Christian in character, so we cannot assume that the poets whose work appears in its leaves were card-carrying pagans. But neither can we assume that all of them were all fully-converted Christians either. Several of the poems in its pages include direct references to Germanic and Anglo-Saxon pagan mythology, which presuppose that the reader knows a few things about the pagan heroic culture of his or her recent past. For example, a short poem from the book called 'Deor' mentions pagan characters such as Weyland the Smith and King Ermanaric. But the best known poem from the book is 'The Wanderer'. In lines famously paraphrased by JRR Tolkien, 'The Wanderer' positively laments the loss of that heroic pagan culture:

Where is the horse gone? Where the rider?
Where the giver of treasure?
Where are the seats at the feast?
Where are the revels in the hall?
Alas for the bright cup!
Alas for the mailed warrior!
Alas for the splendour of the prince!
How that time has passed away,
dark under the cover of night,
as if it had never been! (92a-96b)

Nor are these the only lines where the speaker describes the life of the hero-warrior in Anglo-Saxon England, and how miserable he feels at being thrust out of that way of life. In that very lamentation, 'The Wanderer' is one of those rare ancient poems that opens for us the mind of the pagan. We see what was important to him through what he is sorrowful for having lost. Here we find a very thoughtful man, driven by certain unexpected events into exile, far from his clan and kinsmen and the way of life he knew and loved. The opening lines of the poem speak of how solitude brings one into the grace of God, but that one:

... must for a long time
move by hand [i.e. row one's boat]
along the waterways,
along the ice-cold sea
tread the paths of exile.
Events always go as they must! (3a-5b)

The main character of the poem is apparently an old man, contemplating his past, and also the nature of the world. He describes how important it is to keep one's unhappy thoughts to oneself, because *'the weary spirit cannot / withstand fate / nor does a rough or sorrowful mind / do any good.'* (15a-16b) But after a lifetime of concealing his thoughts, he can contain them no longer. It's the transience of things which aggrieves him the most: not the changing but the *passing* of things, which saddens him. In this lamentation we find an implied metaphysical proposition, that is, a proposition about the nature of reality and the ways of the world: *all things are transitory.* This proposition is confirmed in other Anglo-Saxon poems, such as 'Deor', which also appears in the *Book of Exeter.* Deor mentions various historical and mythological events, and then caps them with the refrain '*þæs ofereode, þisses swa mæg!*' '*That passed away, this may [pass away] too.*' A favorable comparison may be made with the Persian Sufi proverb about hope, humility, and temperance: 'This too shall pass.'

'The Wanderer' is most philosophical, I think, when the poet contemplates not just his own sad state, but also '*when I ponder on the whole / life of men / throughout the world.*' That's a philosophical move! It brings us out of the ordinary and into the realm of the higher and deeper things. The author also asserts a few moral propositions, and also speaks about what it really takes to become wise.

Therefore man
cannot call himself wise, before he has
a share of years in the world.
A wise man must be patient,
He must never be too impulsive
nor too hasty of speech,
nor too weak a warrior
nor too reckless,
nor too fearful, nor too cheerful,
nor too greedy for goods,
nor ever too eager for boasts,
before he sees clearly.
A man must wait

21

when he speaks oaths,
until the proud-hearted one
sees clearly
whither the intent of his heart
will turn. (64a-72b)

We do not see arguments or explanations or any of the other usual features of philosophical writing in this selection. But we do see strongly asserted propositions, which are the basic building blocks of argumentation. We see them in the manner of presentation, that is, the poet's use of simple declarative sentences. More than that, we also see these building blocks in the selection's content, which has to do with ethics. The poet describes some of the character-virtues of the wise man. Such a man, according to the poet here, is patient, strong, well tempered, and self-aware. The poet also asserts that it takes a long time, *'a share of years in the world'*, to acquire these qualities. These are propositions about ethics because they assert the praiseworthiness of certain forms of human life.

Despite the romantic title of the poem, there is no glorification of the 'lone wolf' here. This poem was written at a time when people believed that exile was the very worst thing that could happen to anyone. Indeed exile was often used as a punishment for certain criminal offenses, and as such it was considered worse than death. Overall, the poem gives me the impression of a weary old man who lost his home and family for reasons he doesn't understand, and who needs to unburden himself of his sorrows and find some kind of peace before he dies. In the last lines of the poem, he makes one last moral proposition:

...a warrior must never speak
his grief of his breast too quickly,
unless he already knows the remedy–
a hero must act with courage.

22

It is better for the one that seeks mercy,
consolation from the father in the heavens,
where, for us, all permanence rests. (112b-115b)

Thus although the last three lines here are generally Christian in character, I trust the pagan character of the previous four lines is clear. A wise man is a man of action: *'he must act with courage'*. And he should look to the gods for help only when he cannot do something about his situation on his own. Most interpreters assume that The Wanderer calls for help from the Christian God. There are, of course, plenty of pagan Father Gods dwelling in the sky who the writer could also be turning to. But suppose that the writer is indeed turning to Christ, instead of to Odin. Still we see that for most of the poem he does so as a pagan would do: for his condition is that of a lonely man seeking companionship, *not* a sinful man seeking redemption. Only the last three lines of the whole piece are unambiguously Christian.

All these various ideas are presented in the poem (and my interpretation of it) only as propositions, not as arguments. So we are not yet 'doing philosophy' in the strict sense of the word. But the propositions concern some of the highest and deepest problems in human life. Thus we certainly do have the *beginnings* of a philosophy, and that I think is worth acknowledging.

§ 4. The Hávamál, or, The Lay of the High One

Another Germanic text which deserves philosophical attention is *The Poetic Edda*, also known as *The Elder Edda*. It is a collection of poems written in Iceland around the twelfth century, although some of the older poems in the collection may have been composed elsewhere in Scandinavia. They cover a wide range of details about the mythology and history of the Germanic people. There's also a *Prose Edda*, which covers the same fields, and was written about a century later. These two books are often treated as the core texts of Norse heathen mythology and religion.

Now the most important social and religious event in early European pagan culture was the feast (in Irish, the *tarb feis*; in old Norse, the *Sumbel*). A prominent person in the community would invite his friends, associates, relatives, the members of his tribe or his war-band (in Anglo-Saxon, his *wer-guild*), possibly his debtors and creditors, and certainly any higher-ranking persons who he hoped to impress. A little bit of ritual surrounded the occasion, for instance in the distribution of mead by the lady of the house, and the arrangement of the seating plan. The feast might also include a *flyting*, a kind of argumentative provocation issued by a figure called the *thyle*, a spokesperson for the host in matters where the host himself might not want to do the provoking personally. Poems such as those which appear in *The Elder Edda* would have been recited by professional artists (in Irish, the *fili* or the *bard*; in old Norse, the *scald*). Gifts would be distributed from host to guest, and the guests in turn would swear oaths of loyalty or friendship to the host. And, of course, there was lots of mead-drinking, and offerings to various gods, and boasting of heroic deeds recently done or planned for the near future. The whole point of the heroic feast was to reinforce the cohesion and solidarity of the community, demonstrate the social and economic power of the host, and of course to enjoy the good things in life. With all the eating, drinking, storytelling, debating, boasting, and noise, heroic feasts must have been boisterous affairs! And just to remind you: it is precisely this exuberant and celebratory culture that The Wanderer had lost.

The *Hávamál* is the best known part of *The Elder Edda*, and to my eyes it's the most philosophical. The first four verses (called *strophes*) describe the arrival of a guest in a feasting-hall, and the uncertainty that the guest might feel:

§1. *Have thy eyes about thee when thou enterest,*
Be wary alway, be watchful alway,
For one never knoweth when need will be

to meet hidden foe in the hall.

But food and drink and dry clothes and a warm seat by the fire are quickly offered, which diffuses the tension and creates trust. Guest and host can then speak freely to each other. And so the next strophes of the poem attest to the importance of independent thinking, clear speaking, critical observation of one's situation, and respecting those who are wise, even if only to avoid being counted among the foolish:

> § 5. *Of his wit hath need, who widely fareth–*
> *a dull wit will do at home;*
> *a laughingstock he who lacketh words*
> *among smart wits when he sits.*

> §6. *To be bright of brain let no man boast,*
> *But take good heed of his tongue:*
> *The sage and the silent come seldom to grief*
> *as they fare among folk in the hall.*
> *[More faithful friend findest thou never*
> *than shrewd head on thy shoulders.]*

> § 7. *The wary guest to wassail who comes*
> *listens that he may learn,*
> *opens his ears, casts his eyes about;*
> *thus wards him the wise man 'gainst harm.*

With statements like these, so it seems to me, the *Hávamál* lays the groundwork for a kind of critical rationality, an essential part of philosophical method. Strophes 22-27, for instance, paint a kind of portrait of the 'unwise man', whose main fault appears to be a lack of self-knowledge:

> § 22. *The ill-minded man who meanly thinks,*

flees at both foul and fair;
he does not know, as know he ought,
that he is not free from flaws.

And in addition to these epistemic topics, the *Hávamál* also advances various claims about ethics. Most of them have to do with the goodness of friendship and generosity, the foolishness of boasting, the moderation of one's eating and drinking, and the importance of preserving a good reputation. Here are a few examples:

§ 44. *If a friend thou hast whom faithful thou deemest,*
And wisest to win him for thee:
ope thy heart to him, nor withhold thy gifts,
and fare to find him often.

§ 48 *He who giveth gladly, a goodly life leadeth,*
and seldom hath he sorrow;
but the churlish wight is chary of all,
and grudgingly parts with his gifts.

Interestingly, there's a mention of the goodness of having one's own home, and the wretchedness of exile and loneliness, which reminds me strongly of The Wanderer:

§ 36. *One's home is best, though hut it be,*
There a man is master and lord;
Though but two goats thine and a thatched roof,
Tis far better than beg.

§ 47. *Young I was once, and went alone,*
And wandering lost my way.
When a friend I found, I felt me rich.
Man is cheered by man.

And the *Hávamál* offers a few statements about what rewards await those who follow its precepts, such as this one:

> § 69. *All undone is no one, though at death's door he lie:*
> *Some with good sons are blessed,*
> *and some with kinsmen, or with coffers full,*
> *and some with deeds well-done.*

> § 76. *Cattle die and kinsmen die,*
> *Thyself eke soon wilt die;*
> *But fair fame will fade never,*
> *I ween, for him who wins it.*

Now I don't wish to give the impression that the whole poem is philosophical. The strophes from §138 to the end the poem (§165) deal with rune-magic and spellcraft, and we're out of the realm of philosophy. Moreover, some of the practical advice on human relations is too misogynist for modern eyes. Strophes §83 to §110 offer instructions on how to entice a woman into one's bed: these instructions portray women as deceitful and untrustworthy, as well as rather gullible. (How the author thought these qualities could exist in the same person, I don't know.)

This prompts what might be called 'the problem of reconstruction'. Those who wish to revive certain ancient pagan ideas, or who find inspiration in pagan writings, often land in the difficult position of having to study the sources very selectively, to avoid committing themselves to values or practices that conflict with modern values and practices. No one, or almost no one, treats these texts as untouchable, in the sense that one who edits or alters them risks eternal damnation, even though the words of the *Hávamál* are said to have come from the Norse god Odin. So such cherry-picking is not, in principle, ethically wrong. But it is certainly epistemically problematic. For if we read certain sources selectively, we can protect our modern values and sensibilities, but we may end up with an improper understanding of those sources. If we don't cherry-pick the sources, and try to revive their ideas and practices as accurately as possible, then we could lay claim to a more 'authentic' revival, if that is one's aim. But we would likely run afoul of our modern values. This problem is regularly debated by members of the Norse heathen revival community, and to my knowledge there's no consensus about how to solve it. But the most prevalent response to the problem usually goes like this: we should revive the values, religious practices, ideas, etc., within certain limitations. Those limitations may vary from one individual or local group to another, but they usually involve the rejection of things that our pagan predecessors used to do which clearly have no place in the modern world: honor-killing, misogyny, excessive superstition, and tribal racism, for instance. Some might have stricter limitations: for example, they might reject meat-eating, or wearing synthetic fibers in their clothes. Wherever the line is drawn, it is usually argued that the point of studying these sources is not to uncritically revive everything our pagan predecessors believed. The point of studying them is to be inspired by them, and having been inspired, to live more enlightened and empowered lives today. So let us be honest about what we're doing. And let us remember Nietzsche's warning against using history as 'a storage room for costumes.' (Nietzsche, *Beyond Good and Evil*, §223)

§ 5. The Druids

The Celtic speaking societies that lived in western and central Europe in the Bronze and Iron Ages had a class of intellectual professionals called the Druids. Virtually all documented accounts of their organization describe the services Druids performed with reasonable consistency: they were astrologers, magicians, prophets, lawyers, peacemakers, medical doctors, teachers, and sometimes warriors. It is perhaps obligatory to mention that 'not much is known about the Druids': this phrase, or something like it, appears in probably every book written about the Druids in the last three hundred years, from the most scholarly academic monogram to the most popular new-age trade paperback. But of the things that are definitely known about the Druids, a consistent theme is that they were philosophers. The Roman observer Strabo wrote that there were three classes of educated persons in Celtic societies:

> The Bards composed and sung odes; the Uatis [Ovates] attended to the sacrifices and studied nature; while the Druids studied nature and moral philosophy. So confident are the people in the justice of the Druids that they refer all private and public disputes to them; and these men on many occasions have made peace between armies actually drawn up for battle. (Strabo, *Geographica*, IV,4)[1]

Diogenes Laertius also presents the Druids as philosophers, and claims they were just as good at it as their peers in other societies:

> Some say that the study of philosophy was of barbarian origin. For the Persians had their *Magi*, the Babylonians or the Assyrians the *Chaldeans*, the Indians their *Gymnosophists*, while the Kelts and the Galatae had seers called *Druids* and *Semnotheoi*, or so Aristotle says in the 'Magic', and Sotion in the twenty-third book of his 'Succession of Philosophers'. (Diogenes Laertius, *Vitae*, Introduction, I,5)

Pomponius Mela wrote that the Druids '...profess to know the size and shape of the world, the movements of the heavens and of the stars, and the will of the gods. They teach many things to the nobles of Gaul in a course of instruction lasting as long as twenty years, meeting in secret either in a cave or in secluded dales.' (Pomponius Mela, *De Situ Orbis*, III,2,18) I find this fragment interesting as it attributes to the Druids scientific, astronomical, and theological knowledge. It also reminds me of the way Socrates was described as one who 'busies himself studying things in the sky and below the earth' (*Apology* 19b), that is to say, one who studies basically absolutely everything. To Socrates, however, this claim was one of the accusations put against him by his enemies. It implied not a wise man but a blasphemer; one who busies himself studying useless things, or even forbidden things, and who might be a little bit crazy. In that respect the fragment can be compared to the line in Lucan's *Pharsalia*, which says of the Druids: 'To you alone it is given to know the truth about the gods and deities of the sky, or else you alone are ignorant of this truth.' (Lucan, *Pharsalia*, I,450-8) This fragment, like many others, affirms the Druidic reputation for expert theological knowledge. Yet there is some irony in this gesture of respect. For Lucan is actually saying the Druids are either in possession of the wisdom of the gods which no one else knows, or else they are entirely barking mad.

Among the best sources of information about the ancient Druids is a war propaganda book written by Julius Caesar entitled *The Conquest of Gaul*. In it, he describes the role of the Druids as follows:

The Druids officiate at the worship of the gods, regulate public and private sacrifices, and give rulings on all religious questions. Large numbers of young men flock to them for instruction, and they are held in great honour by the people. They act as judges in practically all disputes, whether between tribes or between individuals; when a crime is committed, or a murder takes place, or a dispute arises about an inheritance or a boundary, it is they who adjudicate the matter and appoint the compensation... (Julius Caesar, *The Conquest of Gaul*, pg. 140)

Some of what Caesar said here is confirmed in other sources: for instance, the Táin Bó Cúailnge, one of Ireland's great heroic tales, says that 'he had one hundred studious men learning druid lore from him – that was always the number that Cathbad taught.' Strabo also wrote that the Druids were called in to handle murder cases. And Cicero, the famous Roman statesman and Stoic philosopher, described meeting a Druid named Divitiatus the Aeduan, who: '…claimed to have that knowledge of nature which the Greeks call 'physiologia' [natural science, physics], and he used to make predictions, sometimes by means of augury and sometimes by means of conjecture.' (Cicero, *De Divinatione*, I,41) So, although Caesar's book is a work of political propaganda, it's probably a reliable source of information nonetheless.

From passages like these, it's safe to infer that the Druids were the educated and intellectual class of their society. In further support of this, we also know from other fragments that the Druids held annual conferences to discuss matters of interest to them, just as modern university professors attend academic conferences today. One such meeting was described in the story of the Táin Bó Cúailnge, where the aim of the meeting was to reach a consensus about the content of the story itself. Another, as described by Caesar, took place in a holy site in the territory of the Carnutes, a Gaulish tribe; anecdotal evidence suggests that the actual site of the meeting is now the site of Chartres Cathedral. But, alas, history has not bequeathed to us the minutes of those meetings.

Well then, if the Druids were such great thinkers, what were their thoughts? On this point, the classical sources leave us only scraps and fragments. But piecing them together is no less fruitful a task than, say, piecing together the fragments of Pythagoras, Heraclitus, and a dozen other early Greek philosophers who are studied respectfully in universities around the world. Several of the Roman and Greek writers drew parallels between Druidic and Pythagorean thinking. Hyppolytus, for instance, wrote that:

> ...the Keltic Druids applied themselves thoroughly to the Pythagorean philosophy, being urged to this pursuit by Zamolxis, the slave of Pythagoras, a Thracian by birth, who came to those parts after the death of Pythagoras, and gave them opportunity of studying the system. And the Kelts believe in their Druids as seers and prophets because they can foretell certain events by the Pythagorean reckoning and calculations. (Hyppolitus, *Philosophumena*, I,XXV)

Clement of Alexandria went so far as to claim that the direction of influence was the other way around, and that Pythagoras learned his letters from the Druids:

> Alexander, in his book *On the Pythagorean Symbols*, relates that Pythagoras was a pupil of Nazaratus the Assyrian... and will have it that, in addition to these, Pythagoras was a hearer of the Galatae [the Celts of Galatia] and the Brahmins... Thus philosophy, a science of the highest utility, flourished in antiquity among the barbarians, shedding its light over the nations. And afterwards it came to Greece. (Clement of Alexandria, *Stromata*, I,XV,70,3)

Although this parallel with Pythagoras is attested in more sources than just these examples, it does not necessarily follow that all Druidic thinking was Pythagorean. Historian Stuart Piggott speculated that the comparison was probably drawn to make Druidic thinking, otherwise radically different from Roman thinking, easier for Roman audiences to understand. It was not a perfect fit, but it was the nearest fit. (Piggott, *The Druids*, pg. 114)

Given that all our primary sources are fragments like these, how much can be known with certainty about ancient Druidic philosophical thinking? The subject-matter of Druidic thinking is made fairly clear: it covers mostly natural science, mathematics, astronomy, theology, and ethics. If they inherited anything from their Neolithic predecessors, whose monuments can be found everywhere in the traditional Celtic territory, then they would have been expert timekeepers and calendar makers. An artifact called the Coligny Calendar, attributed to Druidic manufacture by archaeologists, attests to this likelihood. Some literary fragments state that they count the seasons by nights instead of by days, and months starting on the sixth day of the moon – again, suggesting a Druidic interest in timekeeping. A number of other literary fragments (not included here just to save space) suggest the Druids had expert knowledge of the medicinal properties of various plants, and that they studied their possible magical qualities too.

We also know the Druids were interested in moral philosophy. For instance, here's Diogenes Laertius again: 'They say the Gymnosophists and Druids make their pronouncements by means of riddles and dark sayings, teaching that the gods must be worshipped, and no evil done, and manly [honourable] behaviour maintained.' (Diogenes Laertius, *Vitae*, Introduction, I,5) But aside from this single fragment, the Classical sources have nothing at all to say about the content of Druidic moral teaching. And in most other fields where the Druids apparently had an interest, such as astronomy and mathematics, we are shown almost nothing of the content of their beliefs, or the arguments they advanced in favor of them. Such is the lot of those who compete with the philosophers of big empires, and lose.

One teaching, however, looms very large in the fragments: the doctrine of the immortality of the soul. Ammianus Marcellinus wrote: 'Between them [the Bards and Ovates] came the Druids, men of greater talent, members of the intimate fellowship of the Pythagorean faith; they were up-lifted by searchings into secret and sublime things, and with grand contempt for mortal lot they

33

professed the immortality of the soul.' (Ammianus Marcellinus, *Works*, XV,9,4-8) Lucan, in a poetic fragment, wrote: 'And it is you who say that the shades of the dead seek not the silent land of Erebus and the pale halls of Pluto; rather, you tell us that the same spirit has a body again elsewhere, and that death, if what you sing is true, is but the mid-point of long life.' (Lucan, *Pharsalia*, I, 450-8) Diodorus Siculus wrote: 'The Pythagorean doctrine prevails among them (the Gauls), teaching that the souls of men are immortal and live again for a fixed number of years inhabited in another body...' (Diodorus Siculus, *Histories*, V.28) Julius Caesar provides probably the best description of the Druidic doctrine of immortality:

> A lesson which they [the Druids] take particular pains to inculcate is that the soul does not perish, but after death passes from one body to another; they think that this is the best incentive to bravery, because it teaches men to disregard the terrors of death. They also hold long discussions about the heavenly bodies and their movements, the size of the universe and of the earth, the physical constitution of the world, and the power and properties of the gods; and they instruct the young men in all these subjects. (Caesar, *The Conquest of Gaul*, pg. 141)

Although this teaching is very prominent in almost all the primary sources, none of those sources provide *arguments* for it. And this is perhaps hardly surprising, as the classical authors were writing reports on Druidic ideas for anthropological or propaganda purposes. They were not engaging the Druids in a debate between equals. This is a disadvantage because these fragments alone do not constitute a philosophy 'proper', although, like the ideas expressed by the unknown author of 'The Wanderer', they do constitute the *beginning* of philosophy. This shortage of information has also allowed just about anyone to create their own arguments upon similar themes, and then retroactively attribute them to the ancient Druids, in order to paint those ideas in the glamour of an ancient heritage. For better or worse.

Another main problem with studying the philosophy of the Druids is that for every quotation that depicts them as wise and learned intellectuals, perhaps in possession of an ancient gnomic wisdom, there's another quotation which depicts them as screaming bloodthirsty madmen. There's Julius Caesar's account of the famous Wicker Man, in which the Druids ritually propitiate the gods and avert natural disasters by building a giant wicker effigy, stuffing it full of living people, and setting it on fire. Condemned criminals were the preferred victims: 'but when they run short of criminals, they do not hesitate to make up with innocent men.' (Caesar, *The Conquest of Gaul*, pg. 141-2) Tacitus wrote that the Druids 'deemed it, indeed, a duty to cover their altars with the blood of captives and to consult their deities through human entrails.' (Tacitus, *Annals*, XIV, 30) Even if these statements served Roman propaganda purposes, still they should not be dismissed. Indeed much archaeological evidence supports them. Human bodies, preserved in peat bogs, have been discovered all over Western Europe, bearing various signs of ritual murder. The most famous of them is the Lindow Man, who was killed in three different ways: strangulation, blunt force trauma to the head, and drowning. The 'problem of reconstruction', which I mentioned in the discussion of the *Hávamál*, also affects those who wish to revive Celtic pagan values and practices. For no one in the modern Celtic pagan community is seriously committed to reviving the practice of human sacrifice. And the solution has turned out to be broadly similar: revive the values and practices of the 'old ways' but within certain limits. And while there is no consensus about exactly where those limits should be, the principle is mostly the same.

But to return to the main narrative. There are other sources of

Celtic philosophical expression which come to us not from Roman or Greek outside observers, but from Celtic native insiders. So let's turn to:

§ 6. The Irish Wisdom-Texts

When Christian missionaries arrived in Ireland some time in the third to the fourth centuries, they brought with them a new and radical form of information technology that had almost no precedent in Irish society at the time: literacy. Of course the Irish had an alphabet called the Ogham, which consisted mainly of scratches on the edges of stones or logs, and was used to indicate things like property boundaries and burials. But they had nothing like ink on a parchment page, which could record much more information on much less physical space, and with less physical effort. It therefore could do much more than the Ogham could do. For instance, you can use it to write business accounts, or history, or poetry. Greek and Latin letters were readily adopted for Irish words, which were first used to spell out the Gospels, in fabulously illustrated manuscripts. And soon thereafter, the written word was used to write down mythologies, poems, songs, laws, historical accounts, jokes, and basically anything that seemed interesting enough to write about. Irish monks wrote in their own language, and they wrote in a time when Irish people still had a mostly heroic-age society. So the accounts of pre-Christian mythology and religion which were put to writing are fairly accurate and trustworthy. Historian Stuart Piggott, whose well-respected book *The Druids* (1968) had surprisingly few kind words for Druids, wrote that:

> ...the Irish vernacular sources, especially the hero-tales, are the product of a primitive, illiterate, heroic society with a warrior-aristocracy, and were composed in accordance with the values and code of manners of this social class. They represent a non-Christian, pagan, world which seems to have

been remarkably unaltered in its presentation even though the final redaction and first transference from oral to written form was the work of Christian clerics. (Piggott, *The Druids*, pg. 100)

Piggott also observed that the social functions which one would expect Christian censors to remove from their written works were precisely what those works emphasized. We read of Druids performing magical spells such as divinations, performing battle-magic to confound enemies, and providing policy advice to chieftains. (Piggott, *ibid*, pg. 112) Thus, when contemporary pagans work to revive ancient Druidic practices and beliefs, they have a reasonably trustworthy body of mythology and folklore to consult. A few major principles have emerged from the pagan community's study of those sources: principles like *imramma* ('sea journey', a euphemism for spirit-flight), *imbas* or 'the fire in the head' (for poetic inspiration), and *firinne* or 'the sacred truth' (having to do with integrity and justice). There isn't precise universal agreement about the meaning of these terms, but there is enough general agreement that the community can debate them productively.

Seven of these early works, known as the Irish Wisdom Texts, are of interest for the current purpose. The great scholar of early Irish manuscripts, Fergus Kelly, identified them as 'those texts which contain precepts, proverbs, and gnomic statements bearing on human behaviour, society, nature, and other topics. All wisdom-texts contain material of relevance to early Irish law...' (Kelly, *A Guide to Early Irish Law*, pg. 284) The seven Irish wisdom-texts are:

- the *Audacht Morainn*, 'The Testament of Morann';
- the *Tecosca Cormaic*, 'The Instructions of Cormac';
- the *Trecheng Breth Féne*, 'A Triad of Judgments of the Irish', also known as the Irish Triads;

- the *Bríatharthecosc Con Culainn,* 'The Precepts of Cú Chulainn';
- the *Tecosc Cuscraid,* 'The Instructions of Cuscraid';
- the *Senbríathra Fíthail,* 'The Ancient Sayings of Fíthal';
- and the *Aibidil Luigne maic Éremóin,* 'The Alphabet of Luigne mac Éremóin'.

Most of these texts are very short: a few paragraphs, or a few pages. They usually take the form of a kind of speech in which an elderly person offers moral teachings to a younger person. They describe the kind of behavior and personal habits that are expected of a grown mature adult in Iron Age Celtic society. And like the poetic fragments already studied, they offer these teachings in the form of bold propositions without much supporting argument. But still, they are worth looking at in detail, as the beginning of a systematic philosophy.

Of the seven Wisdom Texts, the best known to modern Celtic pagans is probably *The Testament of Morann.* Dating from the ninth century, it is a record of the teachings of a Druid named Morann son of Móen, to a young aristocrat named Feradach Find Fechtnach, apparently a survivor of a genocide attempt against Irish nobles in Scotland. Here's one of the most often quoted passages:

Let him keep my advice which follows here.
Tell him before every [other] word,
Bring him with every word this lasting advice.
Let him preserve justice, it will preserve him.
Let him raise justice, it will raise him.
Let him exalt mercy, it will exalt him.
Let him care for his tribes, they will care for him.
Let him help his tribes, they will help him.
Let him soothe his tribes, they will soothe him.
Tell him, it is through the justice of the ruler that plagues [and] great

lightnings are kept from the people.

It is through the justice of the ruler that he judges great tribes and great riches.

It is through the justice of the ruler that he secures peace, tranquility, joy, ease, [and] comfort.

It is through the justice of the ruler that he dispatches (great) battalions to the borders of hostile neighbours.

It is through the justice of the ruler that every heir plants his house-post in his fair inheritance.

It is through the justice of the ruler that abundances of great tree-fruit of the great wood are tasted.

It is through the justice of the ruler that milk-yields of great cattle are maintained.

It is through the justice of the ruler that there is abundance of every tall, high corn.

It is through the justice of the ruler that abundance of fish swim in streams.

It is through the justice of the ruler that fair children are well begotten. (Audacht Morann, §4-21)

To my mind, this passage suggests that the ruler is involved in an ongoing substantial relationship with the people, and the land. Thus when the ruler is just, the people and the land flourish. The word translated here as 'justice' is *fírinne*, which can also be translated as 'truth', and is related to the word *fíor*, which has to do with truth, correct-ness, and reality. *The Testament of Morann* doesn't say much about the precise definition of *fírinne*. But as is customary in a lot of heroic-age literature, it gives a short description of the personality and character of the ruler who possesses *fírinne*. And we can infer the meaning of *fírinne* from that description:

Tell him, let him be merciful, just, impartial, conscientious, firm, generous, hospitable, honourable, stable, beneficent, capable, honest, well-spoken, steady, true judging.

For there are ten things which extinguish the injustice of every ruler. (Beware that you do not do it, beware of everything, o all rulers.) Announce from me the ten: rule and worth, fame and victory, progeny and kindred, peace and long life, good fortune and tribes. (Audacht Morann, §55-6)

We can infer from this list an answer to the question of what a just ruler is: the just ruler is one whose laws and decisions are merciful, impartial, generous, and so on. A list of characteristics is not the same as a formal definition, but for most practical purposes it's good enough. And we can infer from this that *fírinne*, as a philosophical concept, is the name for the right relationship between a ruler and the land and people; a relationship founded upon justice, truth, and various moral qualities.

We can also consult other Irish wisdom-texts to fill in more details of the moral character expected of rulers, and indeed the moral character expected of anyone in Celtic society. For instance, *The Precepts of Cú Chulainn* is a good choice here because, like *The Testament of Morann*, the young person being advised by the older person is about to become a king. In this case, the older man is Cú Chulainn, the great Red Branch hero. And the younger man is a charioteer named Lugaid of the Red Stripes, who had been selected for the High Kingship of Ireland by a seer. Here is the entire text, as it appeared in Lady Gregory's *Cuchullain of Muirthemney*:

Do not be a frightened man in battle; do not be light-minded, hard to reach, or proud. Do not be ungentle, or hasty, or passionate; do not be overcome with the drunkenness of great riches, like a flea that is drowned in the ale of a king's house. Do not scatter many feasts to strangers; do not visit mean people that cannot receive you as a king. Do not let wrongful possession stand because it has lasted long, but let witnesses be searched to know who is the right owner of land. Let the tellers of history tell truth before you; let the lands of brothers and their increase [their children] be set down in their lifetime; if a family has increased its branches, is it not from the one stem they are come? Let them be called up, let the old claims be established by oaths; let the heir be left in lawful possession of the place his fathers lived in; let strangers be driven off it by force.

Do not use too many words. Do not speak noisily; do not mock, do not give insults, do not make little of old people. Do not think ill of any one; do not ask what is hard to give. Let you have a law of lending, a law of oppression, a law of pledging. Be obedient to the advice of the wise; keep in mind the advice of the old. Be a follower of the rules of your fathers. Do not be cold-hearted to friends; be strong towards your enemies; do not give evil for evil in your battles. Do not be given to too much talking. Do not speak any harm of others. Do not waste, do not scatter, do not do away with what is your own. When you do wrong, take the blame for it; do not give up the truth for any man. Do not be trying to be first, the way you will not be jealous; do not be an idler, that you may not be weak; do not ask too much, that you may not be thought little of. Are you willing to follow this advice, my son? (Gregory, *Cuchulain of Muirthemney*, pg. 639-670)

Another wisdom-text, in which the elder speaker is already a king and the younger character is the king's grandson, is called *The Councils of Cormac*. As in *The Precepts of Cuchullain*, the emphasis tends to be on treating others with respect, being generous and hospitable, being firm and strong, upholding one's own dignity, and occasionally demanding that others uphold it too. But *The Councils of Cormac* offer us a much more comprehensive picture than all the other wisdom-texts. Its thirty-seven chapters cover a wide variety of topics, from specialized advice like what is expected from kings and leaders, to more ordinary topics like mead hall etiquette, health and nutrition, and growing up. One of its most memorable passages describes a general principle of temperance, as follows:

§ 29. 'O grandson of Conn, O Cormac', said Carbre, 'I desire to know how I shall behave among the wise and the foolish, among friends and strangers, among the old and the young, among the innocent and the wicked.'
'Not hard to tell', said Cormac.
'Be not too wise, be not too foolish,
be not too conceited, be not too diffident,
be not too haughty, be not too humble,
be not too talkative, be not too silent,
be not too harsh, be not too feeble.
If you be too wise, one will expect (too much) of you;
If you be too foolish, you will be deceived;
If you be too conceited, you will be thought vexatious;
If you be too humble, you will be without honour;
If you be too talkative, you will not be heeded;
If you be too silent, you will not be regarded;
If you be too harsh, you will be broken;
If you be too feeble, you will be crushed.'

§ 30. 'A question,' said Carbre, 'how shall I be?'
'Not hard to tell,' said Cormac.
'Be wise with the wise, lest anyone deceive you in wisdom,
be proud with the proud, lest anyone make you tremble,
be humble with the humble when your work is being done,
be talkative with the talkative... [?]
be silent with the silent when a recital is being listened to,
be hard with the hard lest anyone slight you,
be gentle with the gentle lest everyone [?] you. (Meyer, *The*

Instructions of King Cormac Mac Airt § 29-30)

On the surface, this passage looks like a simple list of decent character qualities which a good person should possess. But there's an *argument* here: Cormac offers his protégé *reasons* why he should behave as he's being asked to behave. We have to infer for ourselves what the general principle is, since Cormac doesn't give it directly; but that inference is not hard to tell. Carbre's question asks about how he should behave no matter where he is or who he's with. And Cormac's answer is to list a few basic character qualities: thoughtfulness, pride, amiability, strength. These qualities are listed in terms of the problems that can befall someone who has too much or not enough of them. In this way Cormac's teaching is comparable to Aristotle's Doctrine of the Mean, or even to the Buddha's Doctrine of the Middle Path.

Rationality plays a prominent place in the text. Proverbs like 'Knowledge deserves to be honoured' (§15), and 'do not be a wrangler against truth, take no cognizance of falsehood' (§19) appear in teachings concerning the duties of a chieftain. Several chapters offer what could be called procedures for sound argumentation, when participating in parliamentary assemblies, or arguing criminal justice cases. These procedures are offered in the form of logical fallacies to avoid. Here's my favorite one:

§ 22. O grandson of Conn, O Cormac,' said Carbre, 'What is the worst pleading and arguing?'
'Not hard to tell,' said Cormac. 'Seventeen signs of bad pleading, vis.:
Contending against knowledge,
Taking refuge in bad language,
Much abuse,
Contending without proofs,
A stiff delivery,
A muttering speech,

Hair-splitting,
Uncertain proofs,
Despising books,
Turning against customs,
Talking in too loud a voice,
Shifting one's pleading,
Inciting the multitude,
Fighting everybody,
Blowing one's own trumpet,
Shouting at the top of one's voice,
Swearing after judgment.' (*ibid* §22, pg. 41)

But *The Councils of Cormac* is also a product of its time, and not all of its teachings are worthy of our admiration today. In §16 Carbre asks his grandfather, 'How do you distinguish women?', and Cormac's answer is a torrent of misogyny: over 120 lines of it. I won't quote any of it here; it's too ugly. And we have already seen the problems that can arise when we cherry-pick ancient literary sources to suit modern sensibilities.

But I'd like to end this section on a friendlier note. So let's take a look at a few selections from *The Triads of Ireland*, one of the most popular wisdom-texts. The *Triads* are a collection of proverbs and sayings which were preserved in several manuscripts, the oldest of which dates to the fourteenth century. Thematically, their subject matter ranges from lists of place-names, almost like a tourist agenda, to legal statements, practical moral advice, and even satire. It's their poetic structure which unites them: almost all the 256 canonical triads list three things each (hence why they are called triads). Oftentimes the third item on the list is ironic, unexpected, or even anticlimactic. One gets the impression that people competed with each other to create new, more clever, and more memorable triads, much as people today compete to create inspirational quotations or witty one-line jokes. Although the earliest collection of triads dates, as mentioned, to the fourteenth century, the style of the triad can be found in much older manuscripts. The translator, Kuno Meyer, dated them to the late ninth century, on the basis of evidence like noun stems and verb declensions. (pg. xi)

Here are the ones which seemed to me the most philosophical. I invite the reader to find her own inspiration in them.

77. Three things which justice demands: judgment, measure, conscience.

78. Three things which judgment demands: wisdom, penetration, knowledge.

80. Three things for which an enemy is loved: wealth, beauty, worth.

81. Three things for which a friend is hated: trespassing, keeping aloof, fecklessness.

82. Three rude ones of the world: a youngster mocking an old man, a healthy person mocking an invalid, a wise man mocking a fool.

84. Three fair things that hide ugliness: good manners in the ill-favoured; skill in a serf; wisdom in the misshapen.

86. Three things that kindle love: a face, demeanour, speech.

90. Three ungentlemanly things: interrupting stories, a mischevious game, jesting so as to raise a blush.

93. Three fewnesses that are better than plenty: a fewness of fine words; a fewness of cows in grass; a fewness of friends around good ale.

96. Three ruins of a tribe: a lying chief, a false judge, a lustful priest.

97. Three preparations of a good man's house: ale, a bath, a large fire.

98. Three preparations of a bad man's house: strife before you, complaining to you, his hound taking hold of you.

110. Three maidens that bring love to good fortune: silence, diligence, sincerity.

111. Three silences that are better than speech: silence during instruction, silence during music, silence during preaching.

112. Three speeches that are better than silence: inciting a king to battle, spreading knowledge, praise after reward.

113. Three impossible demands: Go! Though you cannot go, bring what you have not got, do what you cannot do.

115. The three chief sins: avarice, gluttony, lust.

119. Three things that constitute a physician: a complete cure, leaving no blemish behind, a painless examination.

122. Three things that constitute a harper: a tune to make you cry, a tune to make you laugh, a tune to put you to sleep.

123. Three things that constitute a poet: 'knowledge that illumines', 'teinm laeda', improvisation.

162. Three on whom acknowledgment does not fall in its time: death, ignorance, carelessness.

166. Three ranks that ruin tribes in their falsehood: the falsehood of a king, of a historian, of a judge.

173. Three doors of falsehood: an angry pleading, a shifting foundation of knowledge, giving information without memory.

174. Three doors through which truth is recognised: a patient answer, a firm pleading, appealing to witnesses.

177. Three glories of speech: steadiness, wisdom, brevity.

178. Three ornaments of wisdom: abundance of knowledge, a number of precedents, to employ good counsel.

179. Three hateful things in speech: stiffness, obscurity, a bad delivery.

182. Three excellences of dress: elegance, comfort, lastingness.

192. Three signs of wisdom: patience, closeness, the gift of prophecy.

193. Three signs of folly: contention, wrangling, attachment (to everybody).

194. Three things that make a wise man foolish: quarreling,

anger, drunkenness.

197. Three signs of a bad man: bitterness, hatred, cowardice.

200. Three rocks to which lawful behaviour is tied: a monastery, a chieftain, the family.

201. Three candles that illume every darkness: truth, nature, knowledge.

204. Three keys that unlock thoughts: drunkenness, trustfulness, love.

242. Three things that are best for a chief: justice, peace, an army.

243. Three things that are worst for a chief: sloth, treachery, evil council.

245. Three things that ruin wisdom: ignorance, inaccurate knowledge, forgetfulness. (Meyer, *The Triads of Ireland*, pp. 8-35)

§ 7. The Pelagian Heresy

To finish this tour of early Celtic philosophy, let's look at an unorthodox form of early Christianity. Named for its chief promoter, a British philosopher named Pelagius, it grew in popularity in Britain and Ireland around the same time that Roman Christianity was spreading there. I've no doubt that it was a form of Christianity, and not a form of paganism, but there is some evidence which suggests that it inherited some of the teachings of the Druids. Pelagius' opponents described his teachings as 'full of Irish porridge', and accused him of attempting to revive 'the natural philosophy of the Druids'. This of course is not unequivocal proof of paganism, but it certainly suggests the possibility. Pelagius' use of triads, in the old Druidic fashion, to explain some of his core teachings, is also not definitive proof. But it is another potential indicator. A stronger way to detect the pre-Christian thinking in the Pelagian world view is by looking at which of its teachings most enraged the Catholic bishops from the continent. Here's one that stands out:

47

In the year of our lord 394, Arcadius, son of Theodosius, forty-third in line from Augustus, became joint-emperor with his brother Honorius, and ruled for 13 years. In his time, the Briton Pelagius spread far and wide his noxious and abominable teaching that man had no need of God's grace... (Bede, *Ecclesiastical History of the English People*, pg. 56)

I think one cannot stress enough the enormous importance of the idea that 'man had no need of God's grace'. It is the idea that you can achieve salvation, however defined, by means of one's own effort, and without direct assistance from God. This is an affirmation of spiritual freedom, and also enormous personal responsibility. In fact I dare say it is an affirmation of spiritual humanism. A few fragments of Pelagius' own letters to his friends have survived history, and we can learn a little bit of his mind with them. Here's a place where Pelagius specifically rejects the claim that we human beings are too weak to achieve salvation on our own:

Nothing impossible has been commanded by the God of justice... No one knows better the true measure of our strength than he who has given it to us nor does anyone understand better how much we are able to do than he who has given us this very capacity of ours to be able; nor has he who is just wished to command anything impossible or he who is good intended to condemn a man for doing what he could not avoid doing. (Rees, *The Letters of Pelagius and his Followers*, pg 53-4)

The leading intellectual competition at the time, so to speak, was Bishop Augustine of Hippo, author of *The City of God* and the main architect of the doctrine of Original Sin. Augustine's view was that human beings are naturally predisposed to act badly toward one another, a disposition we supposedly inherited from Adam and Eve. But through God's grace, and *only* through God's grace, this natural disposition can be cleansed away. Pelagianism denies that we have any such natural disposition. As Pelagius himself said:

> And lest, on the other hand, it should be thought to be nature's fault that some have been unrighteous, I shall use the evidence of the scripture, which everywhere lay upon sinners the heavy weight of the charge of having used their own will and do not excuse them for having acted only under constraint of nature. (Rees, *ibid*, pg 43)

And one of his cheekier statements pokes fun at people who want their salvation without having to do the work to earn it: 'Those who are unwilling to correct their own way of life appear to want to correct nature itself instead.' (Rees, *ibid*, pg. 39) Think of contemporary people who believe they can achieve enlightenment just by visualizing it, but without changing their lifestyles in any other way.

The Pelagian view of human nature is that we mortals are born *non pleni*, 'without character', that is, without a disposition either to good or to evil. What becomes of us in our lives is a product of three things: ability, will, and actions. The first, ability, flows from nature and is given to us by God. But the other two flow from human freedom, and are up to us to decide. (Peter Ellis, *The Druids*, pg. 185) The historian Peter Ellis speculated that Pelagius developed this radical idea while visiting Rome. There he observed first-hand the excesses of the Roman rich, including the Roman Church leadership, who were confident they could do whatever they wanted because God had already decided whether they were destined for heaven or hell. And, as Pelagius himself says, the Augustinian idea of predestination causes the whole notion of morality to collapse. For if people believe they are not responsible for their own actions, of if they believe they are already favored by God, then nothing will hold them back from doing anything they want, no matter who gets hurt (including themselves).

> Under the plea that it is impossible not to sin, they are given a false sense of security in sinning... Anyone who hears that it is not possible for him to be without sin will not even try to be what he judges to be impossible, and the man who does not try to be without sin must perforce sin all the time, and all the more boldly because he enjoys the false security of believing that it is impossible for him not to sin... (Rees, *ibid*, pg 168)

Other sources, such as the near-contemporary writer Julian of Eclanum, go into more detail about the foundations of the Pelagian faith. Pelagians believed, according to these sources, that the saints of the Old Testament were not consigned to purgatory just because they lived and died before the time of Christ. Rather, that they purified themselves of sin and thus attained to eternal life in heaven. The Pelagians believed there is nothing inherently evil in the sexual impulses, and indeed that sexual desire is ordained by God. Most of all, they believed that all human beings are endowed with free will and that the original sin of Adam did not wipe this freedom away, nor bestowed upon us any kind of natural disposition for goodness or evil. Pelagians did, however, affirm that the grace of Christ is still necessary for a blessed life. That last point is what made them Christians, after all.

Pelagianism seems to have been so widespread and popular in Britain that in the year 429 the Church in Rome sent their best preachers to put the Pelagians down. A public debate was organized, in which representatives of both sides would make arguments and be judged by the audience. The occasion, as described by Venerable Bede, must have been quite the festive affair:

An immense gathering had assembled there with their wives and children to watch and judge, but the contestants were greatly dissimilar in bearing. On one side human presumption, on the other divine faith; on one side pride, on the other piety; on one side Pelagius, on the other Christ. The holy bishops gave their adversaries the advantage of speaking first, which they did at great length, filling the time, and the ears of their audience, with empty words. The venerable bishops then fed the torrents of their eloquence from the springs of the Apostles and evangelists, confirming their own words by the words of God, and supporting their principle statements by quotations from the scriptures. The conceit of the Pelagians was pricked, their lies exposed, and unable to defend any of their arguments they admitted their errors. The people, who were acting as their judges, were hardly restrained from violence, and confirmed their verdict with acclamation. (Bede, *ibid*, pg. 66-7)

And just in case the intellectual debate was not enough to silence the Pelagians, Bishop Germanus of Auxerre, who headed the Roman delegation, miraculously cured the son of a local aristocrat of blindness. Venerable Bede, on whom I have relied for an account of this occasion, also described how Germanus quelled a sea-storm that held up his trip to Britain before the debate took place. Supernatural propaganda is a very effective way to influence people, and at that time it was one of the Roman Church's most powerful and most regularly deployed tools. (Read the text yourself and you'll see.) Yet though Germanus and his entourage won the day, Bede writes that Pelagianism flared up again several times in the following years. In 634 Pope John IV sent an ecclesiastical letter to the bishops in Britain and in Ireland ordering them to suppress it. Part of the letter said:

We learn also that the pernicious Pelagian heresy has once

again revived among you, and we strongly urge you to expel the venom of this wicked superstition from your minds... For who can do other than condemn the insolent and impious assertion that *man can live without sin of his own free will* and not of God's grace? In the first place, it is blasphemous folly to say that any man is sinless; for no one can be sinless save the one mediator between God and man, the Man Jesus Christ... (Bede, *ibid*, pg. 139, emphasis added)

Historian Peter Ellis argued that by rejecting the doctrine of Original Sin, Pelagius would have been seen by his fellow Christians as returning to a pre-Christian way of thinking. As he observed, the notion of sin doesn't even appear in the Celtic languages:

In both Old Irish and Welsh the word for sin, *peccad* (Irish) and *pechod* (Welsh), is borrowed from the Latin *peccatum*, and is always used in its Christian sense as opposed to the Old Irish *cin* or *lochtach* meaning guilt or culpability, or the Welsh *euogrwydd*. The new concept of the Christian idea of sin seems very alien to the Celtic world and, I believe, this is underscored by the Pelagian arguments. (Ellis, *The Druids*, pg. 182)

Ellis also pointed out that Pelagianism may have differed from Roman Christianity in its social and political views. Other philosophers of Irish or British origin who were called 'Pelagian' by their critics were concerned not only with personal sinfulness, but also with poverty, and corruption among the ruling classes. Various records exist in which Celtic 'Pelagian' bishops lambast their Roman counterparts for their material excesses. An unnamed Celtic philosopher branded as 'Pelagian' by his critics wrote that if you 'overthrow the rich man and you will not find a poor man... for the few rich are the cause of the many poor.' (c.f. Ellis, *ibid*, pg. 186) A statement such as that would find a welcome place in today's 'Occupy Wall Street' movement! Nor is this the only example of left-wing thinking attributed to the Pelagians. It would seem that the Pelagians inherited Celtic social values, which were characteristically tribal, and less individualist, than the dominant Roman social values. The Celts were also generally more democratic and less hierarchical than the Romans (although with a few notable exceptions), and in economics they were more communal and much less profiteering. Thus the excessive wealth of the Roman patricians and the crushing poverty of the Roman plebeians would probably have horrified them.

I have said that the Pelagian heresy may have inherited some of the earlier Druidic ideas. This statement should be qualified, since the Pelagians were Christians and there should be no confusion on that point. In fact it is possible that the Pelagians saw themselves as more orthodox than the Roman Christians who believed that that salvation is possibly only through the grace of God. To the Pelagians, the Roman way of Christianity would have looked like a throwback to Mediterranean pagan beliefs about fate and the uselessness of any attempt to overcome fate. However, there do appear to be various interesting fragments of evidence to suggest that Pelagius himself maintained Celtic cultural and metaphysical ideas, and perhaps used them to support his Christian teachings. As Ellis concludes, it is '...a supportable argument that Pelagius had not evolved a new philosophy but was a representative of Celtic culture whose philosophy was already established before Christianity by none other than the Druids and what Rome saw as the teachings of Pelagius winning converts in Ireland and Britain was no more than the Celts abiding by their own social and cultural order.' (Ellis, *ibid*, pg. 186)

The argument that Pelagianism preserved aspects of Druidic thinking might be only circumstantial or anecdotal. But I think the idea itself, that we human beings are responsible for our own enlightenment, is a pagan one. It falls into what I call the third branch of pagan philosophy: humanism. And I think that it deserves attention in its own right.

Second Movement:
Philosophy and the City

Most history books state that philosophy began in ancient Greece. This is of course not the whole story. Philosophy began independently in various places around the world. But it is certainly true that the thinkers who began the Western tradition of philosophy began in the Greek speaking world some time from the sixth to the third centuries BCE. In fact we could pin it on the city of Miletus, on the coast of the Aegean Sea, in what is now Turkey. It was somewhere in that time when a small but very influential collection of people found themselves very unsatisfied with mythological explanations for the origin and the nature of the world. It is probable that this change in their thinking was prompted by the increasing variety of foreign cultures and ideas which Greeks were discovering, as the trade routes that enriched their cities reached more distant places. Traveling merchants bring not just trade goods, after all; they also bring customs, languages, religions, traditions, and ideas. And as people are exposed to new and different ideas, so they find themselves (and others!) challenging their own ideas. The Greeks of the time had never really encountered cultural change before; or if they had, it wasn't something that they thought was worth worrying about. But in the halcyon days of high classical Greek civilization, the notion of cultural change suddenly became very important. One of the signs of this appears in the writings of the earliest philosophers. Plato's *Republic* opens with a street scene where Socrates and some of his friends are on their way to observe a new religious festival recently introduced to the city by visiting Thracian merchants. (The ceremony involved a horseback relay race at night, using firebrands as the relay baton. It must have been an impressive sight!) So it is perhaps not an exaggeration to say that the first philosophers were people who began to seriously attend to the way that things in the world are always changing. Again, it's not that no one had ever noticed that before, but these Greek philosophers were among the first to really try to make sense of change in a systematic and non-mythological way. For the most part, their investigation was largely to do with metaphysics. They asked questions like, 'Is the world a unity of One Big Thing? And if so, then what is that thing? Or, is it a diversity of Lots of Different Things? And what are those?' 'By what process do things come into being, remain in the world, and pass away?' 'What is the soul?' And, 'What happens to us when we die?'

§ 8. The Pre-Socratics

The Pre-Socratics are grouped together in perhaps the most arbitrary of ways: they are simply the philosophers who were active before the life and career of Socrates. Why Socrates? Because he is the first philosopher about whom we have a reasonably complete idea of his life and teachings, as we do for most philosophers who came after him as well.

The famous theory of the four elements, the theory that the world is composed of earth, air, fire, and water, appeared during the time of the Pre-Socratics. This theory has a place in the history of science, as is well known; it also has a place in modern occultism. Mediaeval occultists used them to create magical correspondences with things like zodiac signs, alchemical substances, and bodily fluids (the 'four humours'). Twentieth century occultists expanded the correspondences to include cardinal directions, colors, Tarot cards, the months and the seasons, and so on. Those who study the occult philosophy might be interested in the origin of one of their most treasured and ancient ideas.

- Thales of Miletus (~600 BCE) wrote that everything is water. Since most things appear to have water inside them, including the earth itself (as it springs up from wells and caves, etc.), he thought that therefore water was the essence of everything. A fragment in Aristotle's *De Anima* states that Thales thought 'all things are full of gods', which suggests that Thales had a very well developed sense of wonder! As befits a philosopher, of course.

- Anaximenes of Miletus (~550 BCE) said everything is 'aer', a word normally translated into English as 'air'. But he was not referring to the gases of our atmosphere. Rather, he had in mind something better translated as 'mist', or possibly as 'ether'. As he saw it, mist is a singular, unifying substance that can account for the apparent diversity of materials in the world while allowing us to claim that the world is 'one'. Mist could condense to form water and solid things, and disperse to form clouds and wind.

- Heraclitus of Ephesus (~500 BCE) wrote that everything was fire. But unlike the other thinkers mentioned so far, Heraclitus was not just suggesting that the world is made of a different kind of 'stuff'. Rather, he used the word 'fire' to describe a process or an event, such that all things are undergoing near-perpetual transformation.

- Empedocles (490-435 BCE) is the first philosopher to put the four elements together, and probably the first philosopher in recorded Western history to suggest that the world is made of more than one kind of substance. Empedocles also associated each of the elements with certain Greek gods: fire was Zeus, 'aer' was Hera, Aidoneus was earth, and Nestis was water. These four elements are irreducible and indestructible; what we perceive as motion and change in the world is but the re-arrangement of their combinations. Empedocles also thought that motion and change were caused by two primordial cosmic forces, Love and Strive. Think of the

Love and Strife that characterized the married life of Zeus and Hera. In the same way, the four elements both attract and repel each other. Anecdotal accounts suggest he was a rather flamboyant character: 'rich purple robes, a golden diadem, and bronze shoes'. He also claimed to possess magical powers. After helping to cleanse a town in Italy of a plague, by diverting two nearby streams, the grateful people said that he was an immortal god.

§ 9. Pythagoras of Samos (~570 to ~495 BCE)

Pythagoras was born and educated on the Greek island of Samos. He was very widely travelled, and had some of the most famous philosophers of his time for his teachers, including the aforementioned Thales of Miletus. He developed a great reputation as a wise man fairly early in life; one fragment about him attested:

> There was a certain man among them who knew very holy matters
> who possessed the greatest wealth of mind,
> mastering all sorts of wise deeds.
> For when he reached out with all his mind,
> easily he would survey every one of the things that are,
> yea, within ten and even twenty generations of humans. (Porphyry, *Life of Pythagoras*, cited in Curd & McKirahan, *A Presocratics Reader*, pg. 19)

Some time in his early 40s he fled to Croton, a city on the coast of southern Italy, apparently to escape from Polycrates, ruler of Samos, who had become something of a tyrant. In Croton, Pythagoras founded a community to develop and teach his philosophical, political, and religious views. But some twenty years later, for reasons unexplained, there was an uprising against him. So he had to escape to the sea again. As the story goes, he sought sanctuary in a temple in Metapontum, just across the Gulf of Tarentum. There, again for reasons no one knows, he met his death by starvation.

We have already seen some of Pythagoras' ideas when we were looking at the Druids: the teaching that the soul is immortal, for instance. As reported by Porphyry:

First he [Pythagoras] declares that the soul is immortal; then that it changes into other kinds of animals; in addition that things that happen recur at certain intervals, and nothing is absolutely new; and that all things that come to be alive must be thought akin. Pythagoras seems to have been the first to introduce these opinions into Greece. (Porphyry, *ibid*, pg. 19)

As evidence for the truth of this theory of the soul, Pythagoras claimed to have complete knowledge of his various past lives. Indeed he claimed that this knowledge was a gift from the god Hermes, who he said was his father in a past life. (Curd & McKirahan, *A Presocratics Reader*, pg. 19) This claim of divine patronage wasn't very unusual for the time. After all, the great poets Hesiod and Homer both confirm that the gods have mortal offspring and descendants. What's interesting here is that Pythagoras also reasons about what exactly the soul is. To understand his thoughts about the nature of the soul, we have to look at his thoughts about the nature of mathematics.

Just about everyone knows the Pythagorean theorem concerning triangles: it is still taught to primary school children today. But his teachings concerning mathematics also involved religious and metaphysical matters. Aristotle reported that he was the first to make a serious philosophical study of mathematics:

...the so-called Pythagoreans, in their interest in mathematics, were the first to bring these in and, being involved in them, they thought that the principles of mathematical entities were the principles of all entities... Since then all other things seemed to be assimilable to numbers in their nature, and the numbers were primary of the whole of nature, they assumed that the elements of the numbers were the elements of things as a whole, and they thought that the whole heaven was a harmony and a number. (*Metaphysics*, 985b-986a)

To give you an example of what is meant here by the harmony of numbers, consider this diagram of ten dots:

This shape is called a tetractys. It contains a three-fold symmetry, such that whichever of the three corners you start from, you can count the first four natural numbers in each row. This diagram was used by Pythagoras and his followers as a teaching tool: they thought the whole of the universe had this same kind of symmetry and elegance. 'This number [ten] is the first tetractys, and is called the source of ever flowing nature since according to them [the Pythagoreans] the entire cosmos is organized according to *harmonia*, and *harmonia* is a system of three concords – the fourth, the fifth, and the octave...' (Sextus Empiricus, *Against the Mathematicians*, cited in Curd & McKirahan, *ibid*, pg. 19) Not only the whole universe: Pythagoras thought that the human soul is also a concord of elements (the body, the mind, and their various dispositions and habits) which relate to each other in this mathematically harmonious and elegant way.

A critic might object that if the soul is only a harmonious relation among the elements of one's body and mind, then there is no point in saying that the soul reincarnates. It may be replied that Pythagoras had two camps of followers, who believed different things about the soul: one believed in reincarnation, the other did not. Both camps held in common the idea that understanding things in terms of mathematical ratios, such as musical scales, could help people make sense of the world. But one camp, called the Akousmatikoi (from *akousmata*, 'things heard'), followed Pythagoras' teachings about reincarnation and religion. The other camp, the Mathematikoi (from *mathema*, 'study' or 'learning'), held that the soul is a harmony of elements, as just described, and that it does not reincarnate. Perhaps because of this difference, the Akousmatikoi did not acknowledge the Mathematikoi as true Pythagoreans! Furthermore the Mathematikoi were also a secret society: they were more interested in astronomy, music, and philosophical investigation, and they may have been among the first to discover the number *pi*. (They thought it was the fraction 22/7.) And they didn't think much of religion. This might be the oldest recorded case of a religious community splitting itself into dogmatically opposed factions! But leaving that aside for now, the philosophical ideas of Pythagoras and his various followers turned out to have huge influence on the philosophical developments which followed. In addition to his well known contributions to mathematics, Pythagoras is possibly the first philosopher in the Western world to reason about the nature of the soul, not just assert its existence on the basis of mystical experience. Even Plato, who rejected some of Pythagoras' ideas about the soul, inherited some of his ideas about musical and mathematical relations within the soul. And as we shall soon see, Plato and his teacher Socrates involved themselves in a critical dialogue with Pythagorean teachings. But first:

§ 10. Heraclitus of Ephesus (~535 to ~475 BCE)

We should take another look at the madman of Ephesus, who gave up the rule of a petty kingdom he inherited, so that he could remain a philosopher. And now his philosophy of fire still warms Western thought in surprising ways. Aristotle wrote that

Plato as a young man was deeply influenced by Heraclitus' ideas (c.f. *Metaphysics* 987a); closer to our own time he was frequently praised by Friedrich Nietzsche. His most lasting contribution to philosophy is the notion of *Logos*. It has a long list of English near-equivalents: an account, a report, an explanation, a reason, a principle, a saying or speech. The Will. The Word. You've seen the *logos* in any English word that ends with the suffix -ology. You've seen it in the first line of the Gospel of John: '*en arche en ho logos, kai o logos ho pithos to Deos, kai Deos en ho Logos.*' – 'In the beginning was the Word, and the word was with God, and the word was God.' In fact Heraclitus and the unidentified author of the Gospel of John were both from Ephesus, suggesting that the gospel was influenced by a tradition of Greek thought which by then would have been around five-hundred years old.

As is the case with other Pre-Socratic thinkers, we must put together Heraclitus' ideas from fragments – that is, from single sentences or short passages quoted from other authors. He wrote a book called *On Nature*, of which no copies exist anymore. But Sextus Empiricus quoted the entire opening paragraph for us, and here it is:

> Although this account [logos] holds forever, men ever fail to comprehend, both before hearing it and once they have heard. Although all things come to pass in accordance with this account, men are like the untried [i.e. the inexperienced] when they try such words and works as I set forth, distinguishing each according to its nature and telling how it is. But other men are oblivious of what they do awake, just as they are forgetful of what they do asleep. (Kahn, *The Art and Thought of Heraclitus*, pg. 29)[2]

A short and simple way to translate this would be to say, 'The *logos* is true forever. But people don't get it, because they're just not paying attention!'

From here, the job of understanding Heraclitus is a bit like putting together a jigsaw puzzle. We don't know the sequence in which the fragments appeared in the original text, and we probably don't have all the pieces. But the longer you look at the pieces, the more interesting they become (well, so it seems to me). Here's my partial attempt to assemble the picture.

Heraclitus says that whatever the *logos* may be, it can be grasped by reason: 'Whatever comes from sight, hearing, learning from experience: this I prefer.' (XIV) Even so, the logos can be difficult to see, because 'nature loves to hide' (X) Therefore 'men who love wisdom [i.e. philosophers] must be good inquirers into many things indeed.' (IX) But most people are very bad inquirers because (as already noted) they aren't paying attention. And those who do see the *logos* sometimes still don't understand it properly, because: 'Eyes and ears are poor witnesses for men if their souls do not understand the language [literally: 'if they have barbarian souls']. Not knowing how to listen, neither can they speak.' (XVI-XVII) So, to understand the *logos*, you need to pay attention, and you need to be prepared.

So to prepare yourself, you have to know yourself. 'It belongs to all men to know themselves and to think well.' (XXIX) Most people go searching for knowledge in the teachings of poets like Hesiod (XIX), but they are foolish to do so, because 'in taking the poets as testimony for things unknown, they are citing authorities that cannot be trusted.' (XII) In fact 'Homer deserved to be expelled from the contests and beaten with a staff' (16) for misleading everyone – I'm sure that comment won Heraclitus lots of friends.

Instead of going to those popular sources of knowledge, Heraclitus says, 'I went in search of myself' (30).

Now, when you are properly prepared, and paying attention, what will you find? Most of all, you will find that everything is in motion and nothing is still: 'Cold warms up, warm cools off, moist parches, dry dampens.' (XLIX) And 'The same [thing is] living and dead, and the waking and the sleeping, and young and old. For these transposed are those, and those transposed again are these.' (XCIII) In fact things in the world change so rapidly that, 'As they step into the same rivers, other and still other waters flow upon them. One cannot step twice in to the same river, nor can one grasp any mortal substance in a stable condition, but it scatters and again gathers; it forms and dissolves, and approaches and departs.' (L-LI) Change is the normal activity of the world: 'It rests by changing.' (LII)

The name for this condition of perpetual change is 'fire'. 'The ordering [the cosmos], the same for all, no god nor man has made, but it ever was and is and will be: fire everliving, kindled in measures and in measures going out.' (XXXVII) And, 'All things are requital [exchange] for fire, and fire for all things, as goods [exchanged in the market] for gold and gold for goods.' (XL) Fire is not a substance, like the water or the 'aer' which his predecessors said was the basis of the material world. Rather, it is a process, an activity, an event. Fire isn't something that 'is'; Fire *happens*. But just as 'the beginning and the end are shared in the circumference of a circle' (XCIX), so it is that all these changes are governed by a single principle. 'It is wise, listening not to me but to the report [*logos*], to agree that all things are one.' (XXXVI)

To understand the *logos* which governs the movements of this fire, we need to adopt the perspective of the gods. From an ordinary human perspective, everything looks chaotic and disorganized, and it may appear that the highest truth of things is relativism: 'the sea is the purest and foulest water: for fish drinkable and life-sustaining; for men, undrinkable and deadly. Asses prefer garbage to gold. Swine delight in mire more than in clean water; chickens bathe in dust'. (LXX-LXXII) But among all this apparent relativism, there's actually a hidden *logos*. 'They [ordinary people] do not comprehend how a thing agrees at variance with itself; it is an attunement turning back on itself, like that of the bow and the lyre. The name of the bow is life; its work is death.' (LXXVIII-LXXIX) The hidden *logos* reveals itself when we adopt a divine perspective. For, 'The most beautiful of apes is ugly in comparison with the race of man; the wisest of men seems an ape in comparison to a god. A man is found foolish by a god, as a child by a man.' (LVI-LVII) And at the highest possible perspective, all is one: 'For god all things are fair and good and just, but men have taken some things as unjust, others as just.' (LXVIII) From that divine perspective it is possible to claim without contradiction that 'the fairest order in the world is a heap of random sweepings.' (CXXV)

There's a bit more I could try to extrapolate from Heraclitus' hundred and twenty-five surviving fragments, such as his moral and political views. But I'll leave it here in case I've already hung myself. For my account (my *logos!*) of the fragments of Heraclitus could be objectionable on various grounds. I might have got the interpretation of some of the fragments wrong. Or, it could be accepted as an accurate reconstruction, but criticized at face value. Why, for instance should anyone take a 'divine perspective' on things? And what is that perspective, really? But I trust there's enough here to give a general idea of what Heraclitus is all about, and why he proved so influential over the centuries to come.

§ 11. Plato (428 BCE-328 BCE)

And at last we come to Plato, the son of Ariston, almost certainly the most important and influential philosopher ever to have lived in the history of Western civilization. It's simply not possible to under-estimate his influence on almost everything that followed him. In his praise Alfred North Whitehead wrote that, 'The safest general characterization of the European philo-sophical tradition is that it consists of a series of footnotes to Plato.' (Well, until Wittgenstein perhaps, but that's another story.) All the works of Plato are written in the form of dialogues between Socrates and his friends and associates, and sometimes his adversaries. Plato's early works are generally agreed to be accurate accounts of the life and thought of Socrates, and the later books present Plato's own ideas. But the later books retain the conversational style, with Socrates as the main speaker; it seems this was Plato's way of honoring his friend and teacher.

In the Overture, I mentioned that philosophers of the ancient world sometimes acted like personal councilors or 'life coaches'. The practice of philosophy in the classical world was not just an academic exercise: it was an integrated spiritual way of life. One of the best, although also among the most cryptic, statements of the benefits of philosophy as a spiritual activity comes from Plato. He says that the philosophical person:

...isn't concerned with someone's doing his own externally, but with what is inside him, with what is truly himself, and his own. One who is just does not allow any part of himself to do the work of another part or allow the various classes within him to meddle with each other. He regulates well what is really his own, and rules himself. He puts himself in order, is his own friend, and harmonizes the three parts of himself like three limiting notes in a musical scale – high, low, and middle. He binds together those parts and any others there may be in between, and from having been many things he becomes entirely one, moderate and harmonious. Only then does he act. And when he does anything, whether acquiring wealth, taking care of his body, engaging in politics, or in private contracts – in all of these, he believes that the action is just and fine that preserves this inner harmony and helps achieve it, and calls it so, and regards as wisdom the knowledge that oversees such actions. (*Republic* 443d-444a)

Plato's idea is that the philosophical person unites all the different parts of her mind and soul into a single, well-ordered, harmonious unity. Plato wrote of three 'souls' each of us have: the appetitive, which wants material wealth and pleasure; the spirited, which wants honor, love, and glory; and the rational, which wants knowledge and wisdom. Today we might speak of Jungian archetypes, or the Freudian trio of id, ego, and superego. But the principle is the same: the philosophical person achieves inner peace by arranging these psycho-spiritual forces properly. Actually, Plato's philosophy guided people toward the above as well as the within: one can seek inner peace in the stars in the sky, for 'there is a model of it in heaven, for anyone who wants to look at it and to make himself its citizen on the strength of what he sees.' (*Republic* 592b) Thus, philosophy offered an inner peace obtained by arranging one's soul in accord with the arrangement of the cosmos itself. In all the works of the modern day new-age teachers or pop-psychology self-help gurus, you will *never* find a more eloquent, original, and powerful statement of spiritual fulfillment than this. (And yes, I've looked.)

Plato is probably best known today as the author of the Parable of the Cave. It originally appears in Book 7 of *The Republic*, Plato's masterwork. Here's how it begins, in his own words:

> Compare the effect of education and of the lack of it on our nature to an experience like this: Imagine human beings living in an underground, cave-like dwelling, with an entrance a long way up... They've been there since childhood, fixed in the same place, with their necks and legs fettered, able to see only in front of them, because their bonds prevent them from turning their heads around... (*Republic* 514a)

And from there Plato describes how puppeteers stand on a platform behind the prisoners, and project the shadows of their puppets on the wall. The prisoners can see these shadows, and hear the voices of the puppeteers echoing off the cave wall. But because they are not able to turn their heads, these shadows and echoes are all that they can see and hear. The conclusion we are to draw from the story is that the shadows and echoes become the only reality that the prisoners know. Indeed they believe that those echoes and shadows constitute the whole of reality. They are wrong about the true nature of reality, but they do not know that they are wrong; they are prisoners of their false beliefs, but they do not know that they are prisoners.

Historically, the parable is often interpreted metaphysically; that is, the parable is making a point about the nature of reality. Theologians and mystics have compared the life of the prisoners to the life of unbelievers, or to the life of we mortals on earth prior to the life after death, or to the life of those who have never beheld a mystical experience of God, for example. Atheists, of course, have compared the cave to the life of religious people who, from the atheist perspective, worship nothing but shadows, and who know almost nothing of the sunlight of reason. Today, pop-culture variations of Plato's Cave appear everywhere: *The Matrix* series of films is perhaps the best known example. Such interpretations are interesting: but on reading the actual text it's reasonably clear that Plato's main point had to do with *education*, more than metaphysics. The point Plato is making is that the life of a person who has not studied philosophy is exactly like the lives of the prisoners in the cave. The uneducated person thinks that he knows all that he needs to know to understand the world and get on with life. He may think he is free, and may even enjoy something resembling pleasure and happiness. But Plato's argument is that there are much better sources of happiness and freedom to be had in life, and that only the philosophically educated person can experience them. This point is emphasized in the parable itself, as well as in several places elsewhere in *The Republic*. Near the end of the book, for instance, Plato argues that the philosopher leads the happiest kind of life, because the philosopher understands and experiences all the pleasures of life, including the pleasures of food and wealth and a gainful reputation, but also understands intellectual pleasures which the money-loving or glory-loving person can never experience and never understand. (cf. 582b-583a, for example.)

This leads me to another of Plato's parables, which belongs together with the Parable of the Cave. It is called the Parable of the Sun, and it concerns the nature of the knowledge which the prisoners in the cave are supposedly missing. Here's how part of the argument goes:

> We say that there are many beautiful things and many good things, and so on for each kind, and in this way we distinguish them in words. And what is the main thing, we speak of beauty itself and good itself, and so in the case of all the things that we then set down as many, we turn about and set down in accord with a single form of each, believing there is but one, and call it 'the being' of each. (*Republic* 507b)

To understand Plato's point here, try the following exercise. Make a list of thirty things in the world that you consider beautiful, and then ask yourself what is this thing called 'beauty' that they all have in common. Plato's idea is that what they all have in common is a kind of universal essence, with its own independent existence. Today we might say that beauty is a kind of intellectual abstraction. But Plato's point is metaphysical: *beauty*, itself, exists, as a kind of metaphysical presence, apart from any of the particular things in the world that might be called beautiful. Beauty somehow *comes first* in the order of things: and the things on your list share in its presence. The word Plato uses for this essence is *eidos*, traditionally translated as 'Form'. These Forms are not seen by the eye, but rather grasped or perceived by the reasoning mind. How can this be? To explain it, Plato uses an analogy, like this:

> You know that, when we turn our eyes to things whose

69

colours are no longer in the light of day but in the gloom of night, the eyes are dimmed and seem nearly blind, as if clear vision were no longer in them.

Yet whenever one turns them on things illuminated by the sun, they see clearly, and vision appears in those very same eyes.

Well, understand the soul in the same way: When it focuses on something illuminated by truth and what is, it understands, knows, apparently possessing understanding, but when it focuses on what is mixed with obscurity, on what comes to be and passes away, it opines and is dimmed, changes its opinions this way and that, and seems bereft of understanding.

So that which gives truth to the things known, and the power to know to the knower, is the form of the good. (*Republic* 508c)

Plato's idea is that just as we can see properly when sunlight illuminates the world for us, so too can we *know* properly when the Forms *in-form* our thinking. Chief among these Forms is '*to agathon*', a word normally translated as 'good', but can also mean 'beauty'. This Form is somehow responsible for the existence of good things, and also endows people with the ability to recognize good things in the world.

You'll be willing to say, I think, that the sun not only provides visible things with the power to be seen, but also with coming to be, growth, and nourishment...

Therefore, you should also say that not only do the objects of knowledge owe their being known to the good, but their being is also due to it... (*Republic* 509b)

Thus we find that the Theory of Forms, although mainly about education, also has a metaphysical aura. For the Sun represents the knowledge of the Form of the Good (*to* Agathon) which Plato says the prisoners in the cave lack. This idea has turned out to be incalculably powerful and influential over 2,400 years to the present day. Curiously, however, the Sun is often missing from pop-culture versions of the Cave, but it is arguably more important and more influential.

In one of Plato's early books, the *Phaedo*, there's a conversation between Socrates and two of the secret-society Pythagoreans, Simmias and Cebes, on the question of the immortality of the soul. The Pythagoreans argued that when the body dies, the soul, which was only a harmony of the relations of the elements of a living body, dissipates into nothing. 'Our soul is a mixture and harmony of those things when they are mixed with each other rightly and in due measure,' said Simmias. 'If the soul is a kind of harmony or attunement, clearly, when our body is relaxed or stretched without due measure by diseases or other evils, the soul must immediately be destroyed, even if it be most divine, as are the other harmonies found in music and all the works of artists...' (*Phaedo* 86c) Plato, with Socrates as his spokesperson, replies with several arguments about why the soul is a thing of a different sort, and so could survive death after all. We are born with some knowledge of things like numbers, which suggest that we were able to perceive the Forms of such things before we were born. He also argues that the soul participates in the reality of the Forms, which are eternal, and not subject to death. And he also offers an elaborate tale of what happens to the soul when the body dies, and where its guardian spirit takes it, and the nature of the world and the underworld. And he concludes his tale with this curious conclusion:

No sensible man would insist that these things are as I have described them, but I think it is fitting for a man to risk the belief – for the risk is a noble one – that this, or something like this, is true about our souls and their dwelling places, since the soul is evidently immortal, and a man should repeat this to himself as if it were an incantation... That is the reason why a man should be of good cheer about his own soul, if during life he has... seriously concerned himself with the pleasures of learning, and adorned his soul not with alien but with its own ornaments, namely, moderation, righteousness, courage, freedom and truth, and in that state await his journey to the underworld. (*Phaedo*, 114d)

It's worth noting that Plato set the scene of this discussion in Socrates' jail cell, as he awaited execution for the crime of being a philosopher. Plato had a flair for the dramatic!

One other thing should be mentioned about Plato before moving on. In his view, knowledge and reality can be measured on a scale of intensity: some things are 'more' real than others; and some claims of knowledge are more true than others. The specifics are explained in another Platonic parable called the Divided Line, which I will not discuss here because it's been done to death everywhere else. But this idea, among the rest, was given special attention by the lineage of philosophers who developed Plato's metaphysical ideas further, over the next half-dozen centuries or so. These philosophers were called Neo-Platonists. We'll see more about them soon. But first, let's meet one of Plato's teachers.

§ 12. Diotima of Mantinea (4th century BCE)

There are very few women among the canonical philosophers of the ancient Greco-Roman world. For that matter, there are very few philosophical women getting their names known anywhere, prior to the early twentieth century. So when one appears, one should pay attention. Diotima of Mantinea is one such philosopher, and we know about her thought from only a few short pages in just one text: The *Symposium* by Plato. And Plato's treatment of her ideas is remarkably respectful; in the presentation of her argument, Socrates describes her as one of his most influential teachers.

If Diotima's philosophy had a single motto, it would be: 'love desires immortality'. (*Symposium* 207a). This proposition is presented first of all in practical terms. Animals seek mates to produce children, and then will nurture and protect those children, possibly at the cost of their own lives. It is love, seeking a kind of immortality, which drives this behavior. Observing this in the natural world, as well as among human beings, she then leads to the conclusion: '...mortal nature seeks so far as possible to live forever and be immortal. And this is possible in one way only: by reproduction, because it always leaves behind a new young one in place of the old.' (*Symposium* 207d)

More than this, however, Diotima also argued that Love, not Reason, is the means of grasping the Platonic Forms and thus understanding the highest and deepest things.

'...One goes always upwards for the sake of this Beauty, starting out from beautiful things and using them like rising stairs, from one body to two and from two to all beautiful bodies, then from beautiful bodies to beautiful customs, and from customs to learning beautiful things, and from these lessons he arrives in the end at this lesson, which is learning of this very Beauty, so that in the end he comes to know just what it is to be beautiful. And there in life, Socrates, my friend,' said the woman from Manitea, 'there if anywhere should a person live his life, beholding that Beauty... In that life alone, when one looks at Beauty in the only way that Beauty can be seen – only then will it become possible for him to give birth not to images of virtue, because he's in touch with no images, but to true virtue, because he is in touch with the true Beauty. The love of the gods belongs to anyone who has given birth to true virtue and nourished it, and if any human being could become immortal, it would be he.

(Symposium 211d-212b)

The core of the argument, if I understand it correctly, is that Love seeks out beautiful things, and in that seeking Love can lead you to the *eidos* of Beauty itself. The philosopher might start out by falling in love with people for the shape of their bodies, but if he is wise, he will also fall in love with their souls. And from there he will learn to love other, more abstract and immaterial things, like customs and laws and ideas, in a sequence which eventually leads to the *Agathon*, the Beautiful Good itself.

§ 13. Aristotle (384 BCE-322 BCE)

Earlier I wrote that the most influential philosopher in the history of Western civilization was Plato. It happens that perhaps the *second* most influential philosopher in that way was Plato's apprentice Aristotle.

As a young man, Aristotle had a privileged life: born the son of the personal physician to King Amyntas of Macedon, he studied under Plato at the famous Academy of Athens for twenty years. He then moved around Asia Minor for a while, then settled on the island of Lesbos to start a family. Then he was appointed by Philip of Macedon to head the Royal Academy of Macedon, where he taught several future kings, including the boy who would grow up to become Alexander the Great. Eight years later, at the age of fifty-one, he returned to Athens where, unhappy with the way things had changed at Plato's Academy in his absence, he founded his own school: the Lyceum. Tradition holds that he hired a thousand research assistants and sent them all over the known world to gather information about everything. He sent them to collect mineral and botanical specimens, make records of foreign customs and laws, make accounts of historical events, and so on. The idea, it seems, was to create what would have become the world's very first comprehensive database of scientific, philosophical, and anthropological knowledge. But the project was not completed in Aristotle's lifetime. Twelve years after founding the Lyceum the political winds in Athens changed, and Aristotle was compelled to flee for his life back to Macedonia. He bequeathed his Lyceum and its library to his student Theophrastus, who passed them on to a series of others until they eventually landed in The Museum, the 'home of the Muses', another philosophy school founded by Ptolemy I (Soter) in 310 BCE, a dozen years after Aristotle's death.

I'll focus here on what Aristotle made of Plato's theory of Forms. Being a more practical person, Aristotle first pointed out some absurdities in Plato's teaching: that there could be a Form of something in the metaphysical world, for instance, but no object in the visible world which embodies it. For example there could be a Form for some device or gadget which has never been invented and never will be. And this is clearly an absurdity. So, instead of following a line from observation to intellectual abstraction, Aristotle follows a line from observation to empirical generalization. It goes like this. When you look at anything, you see it has material, and a shape. The material is the 'stuff' that it is made of: wood, stone, metal, and so on. And the physical shape which the substance has taken on, or has had imposed upon it, is its Form. On my desk, for instance, is a volume of ceramic material shaped in the Form of a teacup. As you can see, this is simple enough: indeed Bertrand Russell described the idea as 'Plato diluted by common sense'.

The theory gets slightly weirder when Aristotle says that the Form of the thing, the empirically observable shape which the matter has taken on, is in some sense the *essence* of the thing. 'Essence', here, means what something naturally 'is'; the essence of a thing is its *sine qua non*, the attribute or the property which, if changed, would render it something else. Now much of this is still common sense. The ceramic which my teacup is made of could have been used to make a bowl or a candlestick or a lamp stand. Or, my teacup might have been made of glass, or wood,

75

instead of clay. But the teacup-shape imposed on it by the potter is what makes it a teacup and not a candlestick, or anything else. Long ago, it was only a mass of clay in the earth, not yet separated off from the rest of the clay deposit from which it was drawn. In that state, it was perhaps 'potentially' a teacup, although potentially many other things too. The potter gathered the clay, sculpted it into the present shape, fired it, and thus gave it form. To use the Aristotelian language, the form imposed on the clay also bestowed upon it 'actuality': it is now *actually* a teacup, and no longer *potentially* a teacup or anything else. It's the Form that makes it what it is. Change some 'accidental' qualities like its size or color, and it would still be a teacup; but change the form, and it would be something else. That may seem like common sense too: the weird part is in the next move, where he declares that the Form of the thing is the soul.

Actually, the soul is more than just the Form. It's also that in virtue of which something is an organic unity. A thing's Form has a lot to do with it, but not everything. For instance, look at one of your hands. It has a certain form which enables it to grasp things, point at things, make rude gestures, and so on. It also has various materials it was made from: flesh, bone, blood, and so on, all of which took on the shape of a hand when your body first started growing, before you were born. A hand severed from its arm would still be a hand, as it would still have the same materials, and the same form. But it would not be able to do anything. What's missing, so the Aristotelian reasoning goes, is its membership (!) in the organic unity which we call the human body. So the soul is distinct from the sum of a body's various parts, but still it is a product of the right relation between those parts. As Aristotle says in his book, *De Anima* [On the Soul]:

It must be the case that soul is substance [*hypostasis*] as the form of a natural body which potentially has life, and since this substance is actuality, soul will be the actuality of such a body... And since knowledge is in the individual case prior in origin, soul is the first actuality of a natural body which potentially has life. (*De Anima* II.1)

And by the way, the word here translated as 'substance' is *hypostasis*; and it doesn't refer to another material or 'stuff', but rather to 'essence'. Thus Aristotle elaborates his definition like this: 'We have then said what soul is in general, substance [*hypostasis*] in accordance with the account [*logos*] of the thing.' (II.1) In other words, he's saying that the soul is the essence of something as accounted for by means of reason. So, if you put matter and form together, you've got an actual thing; and if the actual thing has an organic unity about it, then it's got soul. 'So just as pupil and sight are the eye, so in our case, soul and body are the animal.' (II.1)

From this line of thinking emerged the conclusion that 'the soul is not separable from the body'. (II.1) And this conclusion turned out to be one of the biggest problems in all of Western philosophy. It's a problem because it appears to reject the ancient teaching that the soul is immortal. Instead, it suggests that when the body dies, the soul dies too. Let's take another look at Aristotle's argument:

For substance [*hypostasis*, essence] is, as we have said, spoken of in three ways, as form, as matter, and as the composite [of the two], and of these matter is potentiality, form actuality, and since the composite is in this case the ensouled thing, it is not that the body is the actuality of the soul but that the soul is the actuality of some body. And for this reason they have supposed well who have believed that the soul is neither without body nor a kind of body. For it is not a body but belongs to a body, and for this reason is present in a body and a body of the appropriate kind... (*De Anima* II.2)

Clearly, Aristotle says that souls and bodies go together. And for centuries people have supposed that this means the soul dies when the body dies. However, the only conclusion that logically follows from the preceding argument is that the soul is not separable from the body *while the body is still alive.* Nothing in this argument leads to any conclusion of any kind about what happens to the soul after death: whether it dissipates into nothing, or whether it reincarnates, or travels to an Otherworld, or whatever.[3]

In fact Aristotle's metaphysics provide for the possibility that Forms can exist independently of the things in which they are exemplified. And this, in turn, opens the possibility that one can accept Aristotle's view of the soul as belonging to a body, and also preserve the claim that the soul is immortal. Exactly how that might be possible, and exactly in what way the soul survives death (if at all), remained unexplained: and that's what caused all the trouble.

We've already seen how, in this system, the more Form something acquires the more actual it becomes. In the *Metaphysics* Aristotle argues that God is a kind of pure Form, a pure Actuality, whose movements are the 'first cause' of all other movements in the observable world:

> Our discussion has, in fancy, established that there exists a kind of eternal, unmoved substance that is separate from sensible things. It has further been shown that it is impossible for it to have any magnitude but that it is without parts and indivisible. The reason is that it is a source of movement for infinite time, and nothing that is finite has an infinite capacity... (*Metaphysics* 12.7, pg. 375)

And this infinite eternal essence can have no other concern but itself, lest it sully its own perfection: 'that is why it must think itself, if it is to retain supremacy, and absolute thinking is the thinking of thinking.' (*ibid* 12.9, pg. 383) God, then, is pure thought, thinking about thinking itself.

By the way, this argument will be picked up in the thirteenth century CE by St. Thomas Aquinas who, with a few intelligent modifications, will re-brand it as The Argument from Motion, and the first of the Five Ways to prove the existence of Christianity's God. But in the shorter term of history, Aristotle's Lyceum preserved an oral tradition which mainly concerned various teachings about the nature of God and of the soul. An early text of Aristotle's called the *Eudemian Ethics* appears to have recorded some part of that oral tradition. It offers a story which he says was related to him by his then-deceased friend and student, Eudemus of Rhodes. In that dream, a messenger from the divine assured him that the soul is indeed immortal, thus conferring a quasi-mystical side to Aristotle's philosophy. It's actually a rather non-philosophical moment in the history of philosophy, but at least it's a poetic one.

Aristotle's metaphysics, while more practical and empirical than Plato's, is also strangely similar to Plato's, and various commentators have observed the advantages and the problems that arise from this similarity. It's a little beyond the scope of this book to describe them in detail, but I'd like to draw attention to one more implication of the argument that souls and bodies go together, at least while bodies remain lively. It's that there's more to your Form than just your bodily shape. Your Form is also your physical activity habits. It's the way you 'hold' or 'carry' yourself, the way you walk and speak, the way you eat and exercise and care for your health, and the way you sleep and rise again in the morning. It's also your personality habits like whether you tend to be late for things, or whether you regularly cook your own food, or whether you are excitable, patient, impulsive, or thoughtful. And the whole catalogue of moral virtues can be added here: your Form is also the extent to which you are courageous, or generous, or a good friend to others. And it's your vices too: it's your selfishness, or your coldness, or your excessive pride, or whatever. It's by habitually acting in these ways that we take on, or come to embody, certain Forms, and not others. So, just as the Oracle asks you to know yourself, Aristotle asks you to pay attention to your habits [*hexis*], and to whether your habits are healthy [*euhexia*; good habited-ness], and leading you towards happiness and to full human flourishing [*eudaimonia*]. Your habits, taken together, form (!) your way of being in the world. And your way of being in the world is your soul.

§ 14. Three Branches of Pagan Philosophy after Aristotle

From its earliest days, philosophy was taught using a combination of written and verbal teachings: students examined texts as well as attended lectures and participated in debates. This had the effect of producing 'lineages', so to speak, of teacher and student. And these lineages had names. Words like 'cynic' and 'skeptic', which today denote people who are critical, disbelieving, and perhaps misanthropic and annoying, began as names for philosophy schools and their associated lineages. By the second century BC, around two-hundred years after Aristotle, the three most prominent lineages were Stoicism, Epicureanism, and Neo-Platonism.

I want to make it clear what a 'lineage' here is. It's only partly a matter of transferring knowledge from a teacher to a student who becomes a teacher and who transfers the knowledge to the next generation of students. It is also a developing critical tradition of philosophical teaching and enquiry. In a developing critical tradition, students are also expected to contribute meaningfully to the community of philosophers. They can do this by correcting errors or clarifying ambiguities in whatever they received from their tradition. Or they can identify new variations, implications, and conclusions which can be drawn from its premises. In the twenty-first century this notion of a lineage continues at the Masters and Doctoral levels of university education, when a student becomes a direct apprentice to a professor. (As it happens, my own doctoral lineage includes prestigious names like Heidegger and Husserl, and my master's lineage includes John McMurtry. But as a philosopher I am still expected to do my own homework, and not merely repeat every-thing uttered by someone in my lineage.) The point of mentioning this fact is to remind the reader that one cannot expect a branch of philosophy to remain permanently unchanged after its creation. And although many traditions have a prominent founder, and may even have been named for that founder, no single person is responsible for all of it on his or her own. Every tradition of thinking, if it is a developing critical tradition and not a historical curiosity, moves and changes and adapts itself over time, as it is worked over by hundreds, maybe thousands, of others. Indeed, inside a given tradition people may disagree as much as they agree. They will argue with each other over what its core concepts mean, how best to apply them to life, or even what the tradition is supposed to be all about.

With that out of the way, let's talk about those three main branches of Greco-Roman pagan philosophy, and what they are all about.

§ 15. The Stoics

This tradition began when one of its founders, Zeno of Citium (334-262 BCE), was not allowed to play with the popular kids in Plato's Academy. They told him his ideas were too weird, and invited him to leave. So he decided to teach his students in front of one of the public monuments in the Agora of Athens, a building which had a covered outdoor porch – the *Stoa Poikile* – which was open to the public but also sheltered from sun and wind and rain. The Stoic tradition got its name from this building. Stoicism eventually rose to become probably the most important and influential of the three branches of Roman thought. Emperor Marcus Aurelius (121-180 AD) counted himself a Stoic, as did important philosophers like Posidonius, Chrysippus, and Seneca. The renowned Roman politician of the first century BCE, Marcus Tullius Cicero, is sometimes counted as a Stoic, partly because he did the most to introduce Greek thinking into the Roman world. In my view the best primary sources on Stoicism are the *Discourses* and the *Enchiridion* of Epictetus (55-135CE), and the *Meditations* of Marcus Aurelius, and I shall draw upon those texts in the notes to follow.

Like the members of any philosophical tradition, Stoic thinkers were interested in all the major branches of philosophy. They were also interested in developing techniques of systematic reasoning: for instance they invented a form of propositional logic which is still used by philosophers to this day. But Stoicism is best known for its moral teachings, and I will focus on those teachings here.

First of all, Stoicism begins with a premise similar to the one that Aristotle began with: what we all ultimately want is to lead a fulfilling, worthwhile life. Then the argument asks the practitioner to face the world honestly, and also to face one's own position in the world honestly. And from this direct look at things, the Stoic draws an important conclusion: there's really nothing you can do about a lot of what's going on in the world. You just have to accept that certain events will affect you which you cannot avoid or change. For this reason, perhaps, the word Stoicism has today come to mean something like unemotional, indifferent fortitude, or even resignation, in the face of bad fortune. But this impression is only half-right; Stoicism does not teach that the emotions are bad, but it does teach that there's no point getting upset or afraid of that which you can neither affect nor avoid. Stoicism teaches that we are all responsible for our own happiness: we cannot blame our circumstances or surroundings for how we feel. As Epictetus wrote, 'It is not the things themselves which disturb men, but their judgments about these things.' (Epictetus, *Enchiridion*, §5) In relation to other people, you should not let yourself feel hurt by gossip or slander. 'It is not the man who reviles or strikes you that insults you, but it is your judgment that these men are insulting you. Therefore... be assured that it is your own opinions which have irritated you.' (*ibid* §20) Even in the face of tragic loss such as death, one should preserve a state of mental equanimity. Marcus Aurelius wrote: 'Do not despise death: welcome it, rather, as one further part of nature's will.' (*Meditations* 9.3) And similarly, Epictetus wrote: 'Never say about anything, 'I have lost it', but only 'I have given it back.' Is your child dead? It has been given back. Is your wife dead? She has been given back...' (*Enchiridion* §11) Being responsible for our own happiness, therefore you should concern yourself with what is within your range of realistic choices.

If you make it your will that your children and your wife and your friends should live forever, you are silly; for you are making it your will that things not under your control should be under your control, and that what is not your own should be your own... If, however, it is your will not to fail in what you desire, this is in your power. Wherefore, exercise yourself in that which is in your power. Each man's master is the person who has the authority over what the man wishes or does not wish, so as to secure it, or take it away. Whoever, therefore, wants to be free, let him neither wish for anything, nor avoid anything, that is under the control of others; or else he is necessarily a slave. (*Enchiridion* §14)

By placing responsibility for one's happiness squarely on one's own shoulders, Stoicism might be compared to existentialism, or to Hindu and Buddhist ideas about attachment as the source of human suffering.

A prominent Stoic metaphysical teaching is that the world is an organic whole: unified, inter-connected, and one. When Epictetus speaks of lost things as 'given back', it is to this organic whole they are given. This wholeness is mainly a matter of all things having the same nature, that is, the same inner order and constitution: 'There is one universe out of all things, one god pervading all things, one substance, one law, one common reason [*logos*] in all intelligent beings...' (*Meditations* 7.9) This is a recognizably pantheist idea: indeed pantheism, as a philosophical theme, arguably begins with the Stoics. And although this idea was sometimes pursued by Stoics for its own sake, it also served as a support for Stoic moral teachings:

> Whether atoms or a natural order, the first premise must be that I am part of the Whole which is governed by nature; the second, that I have some close relationship with other kindred parts. With these premises in mind, in so far as I am a part I shall not resent anything assigned by the Whole. Nothing which benefits the Whole can be harmful to the part, and the Whole contains nothing which is not to its benefit... So remembering that I am part of a Whole so constituted will leave me happy with all that happens to me. (*Meditations* 10.6)

The Stoics may have inherited Heraclitus' idea of *logos* here, for it often appears in discussions of the one-ness of the world. 'The substance of the Whole is passive and malleable, and the reason [*logos*] directing this substance has no cause in itself to do wrong, as there is nothing wrong in it; nothing it creates is wrongly made, nothing harmed by it.' (*Meditations* 6.1) And this *logos* can certainly be trusted, because it 'knows' itself: 'The governing reason [*logos*] knows its own disposition, what it creates, and what is the material for its creation.' (*Meditations* 6.5) The idea here, so it seems to me, is not only to make a point about the nature of the world. It is also to give people confidence. It is a way of saying that in the grand scheme of things, or 'under a certain aspect of eternity' (as Spinoza would say), all is well, and all things are working themselves out for the best. And therefore one's unhappy times are actually not so hard; and you can bear them with Stoic (!) endurance. Actually the argument as Marcus Aurelius presents it, in that quotation and others, is a case of the fallacy of division. But the point is clear: it is that as each of us is part of a whole, which is working itself out for the best, so we can remain at peace within ourselves, as part of that whole, even while enduring turns of ill fortune.

The Stoics had a word for this confidence: *apatheia*, which could be translated as 'without passion', in the sense of being without worry, fear, or distress.

In the mind of one who is chastened and cleansed [i.e. one who has achieved apatheia] you will find no suppuration, no simmering ulcer, no sore festering under the skin. Fate does not catch him with his life unfulfilled, as one might speak of an actor leaving the stage before his part is finished... (*Meditations* 3.8)

This might look rather cold and dispassionate. But apatheia does not require us to purge or suppress our emotions. Rather it requires us to 'live each day as if it were your last, without frenzy, without apathy, without pretence.' (*Meditations* §7.69), or as we might say today, to 'live in the moment'. Thus apatheia can be seen as a kind of enlightenment; certainly the Stoics of the ancient world would have seen it as a kind of freedom. Similarly, Epictetus said we should 'keep before your eyes day by day death and exile, and everything that seems terrible... and then you will never have any abject thought, nor will you yearn for anything beyond measure.' (*Enchiridion* §21) And this way of living, grim as it may sound because of its invocation of death, can leave one feeling surprisingly cheerful. Released from concern for – dare I say attachment to – that which is beyond your control anyway, what remains is your own self, your own powers, and the actual moment in which you find yourself. The

Stoic promise is that if you can do this, you will find the world opening up to you, and you will be better able to appreciate and enjoy your life as it truly is.

§ 16. The Epicureans

Perhaps the best known of the three branches of Classical thought, Epicureanism began in Greece, with a philosopher named Epicurus (341-270 BCE). Like Stoicism, its main concern is the nature of the good and happy life. But it starts with a few slightly different premises.

One of the main ways in which Epicureans differed from Stoics is that Epicureans were more likely to be atheists, or agnostics, while the Stoics tended to be more like deists and pantheists. Epicurus himself seems to have believed that the gods existed, but his deism made almost no contribution to his tradition. So you could be an Epicurean without it. In fact, early Epicureans (as well as the Skeptic philosopher Sextus Empiricus), are credited with the first formulation of 'the problem of evil'. To explain: it's rational to suppose that if the gods are all-powerful and all-loving, as most people believe they are, then they would have got rid of evil by now. Since this has not happened, it follows that either the gods are unable to get rid of evil, or that they do not want to. In either case something is seriously wrong with the usual idea of the nature of the gods. It is even possible the gods do not exist at all.

Indeed most Epicureans of ancient times were materialists. Their metaphysics followed the theory of a Pre-Socratic philosopher named Democritus who claimed that everything in the universe is composed of tiny, indivisible pieces called atoms. (That's where modern scientists got the word.) Thoughts, feelings, and even souls, are made of atoms, according to this theory: and when we die these atoms simply disperse in the world. So there is no such thing as immortality, according to this way of thinking; and therefore, no point in hanging one's hopes for happiness on the afterlife. As Epicurus wrote in a letter to his friend Menoeceus:

> Become accustomed to the belief that death is nothing to us. For all good and evil consists in sensation, but death is deprivation of sensation. And therefore a right understanding that death is nothing to us makes the mortality of life enjoyable... because it takes away the craving for immortality. (Epicurus, *Letter to Menoeceus*, cited in Johnson, *Ethics*, pg. 85)

In short: without a god to take care of you, and without an immortal soul to survive your death, and with no rewards for a good life waiting for you in the Otherworld, the only place where you can find lasting happiness is here in the embodied mortal world. Actually, this is a different way of making the same broad point we've already seen in the Stoics and the Pelagians: that we are all responsible for our own happiness, here and now.

Thus arises the famous association between Epicureanism and hedonism, the love of physical pleasure. But let us have a close look at what Epicurus had in mind. Hedonism means the love of pleasure, but it did not mean indulgence and debauchery, as it is sometimes thought to mean today. 'Pleasure is the first good and [is] natural to us... yet not every pleasure is to be chosen: even as every pain is also an evil, yet not all are ways of a nature to be avoided.' (Epicurus, *ibid*, pg. 86-7) Thus we see that Epicurus believed that some desires are good for us, and some are bad for us, and some painful things may actually be useful and necessary. The happy life involves intelligently discerning which is which, and pursuing what does in fact bring you pleasure, and avoiding what doesn't. As you can see, it's very practical advice. But it may surprise you to read that according to Epicurus, the very greatest kind of pleasure is nothing more than the absence of pain:

When, therefore, we maintain that pleasure is the end, we do not mean the pleasures of profligates and those that consist in sensuality, as is supposed by some who are either ignorant or disagree with us or do not understand, but freedom from pain in the body and from trouble in the mind. For it is not continuous drinkings and revellings, nor the satisfaction of lusts, nor the enjoyment of fish and other luxuries of the wealthy table, which produce a pleasant life, but sober reasoning, searching out the motives for all choice and avoidance, and banishing mere opinions, to which are due the greatest disturbance of the spirit. (Epicurus, *ibid*, pg. 87)

So the Epicurean view is that the best kind of pleasure is the kind that remains when we have got rid of everything that's troubling and painful. (An associate of mine once called the Epicureans the 'Star Trek Vulcans' of the ancient world.) And they had a word for this pleasure: *ataraxia*, a word which the Stoics often used as well, and which meant something like 'tranquility'.

Incidentally, this notion provided a kind of solution to the aforementioned problem of evil. The gods, if they exist, do not interfere with mortal affairs because they live in a perpetual state of ataraxia. To involve themselves in human lives, even to prevent natural disasters or to punish evil-doers, would disturb their tranquility. So they keep to themselves. On the basis of this argument, as well as their atomist materialism and their use of the Problem of Evil in the first place, Epicureans were often accused of being atheists: a dangerous accusation at any time before, say, the nineteenth century. It was, after all, one of the charges raised against Socrates, for which he was convicted and executed. But the logic seemed sound to them, and their commitment to reasoning about these matters is a large part of what made them philosophers.

§ 17. The Neo-Platonists

Of the three major branches of Roman thought, Neo-Platonism was the most mystical. The proposition that identifies it more than any other, is the proposition that the world we know with our physical senses is not the whole of the world. Some may go so far as to say that the world as we know it with the senses is not the *real* world. This proposition is strongly derived from the works of Plato, especially his Theory of Forms, and probably would have been balked at by Stoics and Epicureans alike. But where Plato himself emphasized that the theory was mostly about education, by contrast the Neo-Platonists thought the theory had to do with reality. Now the difference here is perhaps only a matter of emphasis, and not a matter of a principled disagreement. Certainly, most Neo-Platonists would have simply called themselves 'philosophers in the tradition of Plato'. The term 'Neo-Platonism' did not arise to describe them until the Renaissance, hundreds of years later. But this shift of emphasis defines the Neo-Platonic tradition at its very heart. Furthermore, the Neo-Platonists introduced a theological component into Plato's thinking. For 'behind' the visible world, according to the Neo-Platonists, there's something divine at work, and the existence and creative work of this divinity is somehow responsible for the existence of the visible world. It could be said that Neo-Platonism spells out a kind of creation story. But if so, it is not at all similar to the creation story of the Biblical book of Genesis, for no Neo-Platonist philosopher makes any claim about creation having happened at a definite historical moment in the past (say, in the year 4004 BC). Instead, God's responsibility for the creation of the world is a matter of logical, not temporal, priority: it's something that God is always doing. So creation still happening, and is always happening. It had no historical beginning, and will have no temporal end. Neo-Platonism is a philosophical vision of eternity.

Neo-Platonism has that much in common with Gnosticism, a

philosophical movement that flourished around the same time, which also treated creation stories as allegories for an ongoing, never-ending process. And like Neo-Platonism, Gnosticism also regarded human beings as 'imprisoned, asleep, drunken, fallen, ignorant' until such time as they learn to do philosophy, and so discover the truth. (Barnstone & Meyer, *The Gnostic Bible*, pg. 3) But Gnosticism treated the created world as the work of a different supernatural being, other than God: it was created by one 'who is at best incompetent and at worst malevolent.' (*ibid* pp. 31-2)

In the Platonic tradition, and in the Christian, God and the embodied visible world are strictly separate. But the Platonic tradition makes no statement about the fallen-ness or the corruption of the embodied world. For the world is *dependent* on God and the Forms. But in the Christian tradition the world is *opposed* to God. As observed by historian E.R. Dodds,

...no Stoic or Aristotelian, and no orthodox Platonist, could condemn the cosmos as a whole. Where we meet such condemnation we must suspect that it derives ultimately from a source farther east, a dualism more radical than Plato's. The visible world as a whole [including the stars, etc.] could only be called evil in contrast with some invisible Good Place or Good Person outside and beyond the cosmos: radical dualism implies transcendence. Stoicism recognized no such place or person: it was a one-storey system. Platonism of course did; but for orthodox Platonism the relations of the visible cosmos to the world of forms was one of dependence, not of opposition. (Dodds, *Pagan and Christian in an Age of Anxiety*, pg. 13)

We'll see more of the Neo-Platonist school when we get to Plotinus. But first, let's look at a Roman writer who, in various ways, embodied all three of these schools at once.

§ 18. Marcus Tullius Cicero (106-43 BCE)

Anyone who studies Roman philosophy eventually studies Cicero: he was perhaps the most multi-faceted, prolific, and diverse thinker in the entire history of ancient Rome. Although specializing in political thought, he wrote about almost everything: nature, the gods, fate and destiny, magic (mostly divination), and also cosmology. But in some ways he wasn't an especially original thinker; most of his best ideas could already be found in Greek literature. Cicero's claim to greatness is that he brought Greek ideas to Rome, and applied them to the political problems of his day, and so almost single-handedly initiated Roman philosophy. Thus when Greek and Roman philosophy was re-discovered during the Renaissance some fifteen hundred years after his death, it was Cicero's books that led the way. And if the works of Plato and Aristotle were also admired, still people usually discovered them in the first place when they read Cicero.

But I do not wish to give the impression that he was only a cheerleader for the Greeks. He was also a startlingly original thinker, especially in the field of humanism. Other philosophers, including Socrates himself, criticized things people believed about the gods: Cicero brazenly questioned whether the gods existed at all. Now Cicero himself might not have used the term 'humanist': it was coined in 1856 by German philologist Georg Voigt, who inclined it to mean the study of classical Greco-Roman philosophers (including Cicero) as the basis of a secular political education. But even if Cicero did not coin the term, still the theme that there's something special about being human stands out in his work. Cicero's humanism seems to rest on the proposition that every human being possesses a portion of the divinity which pervades the whole universe.

That animal which we call man, endowed with foresight and quick intelligence, complex, keen, possessing memory, full of reason and prudence, has been given a certain distinguished status by the supreme God who created him; for he is the only one among so many different kinds and varieties of living beings who has a share in reason and thought, while all the rest are deprived of it. But what is more divine, I will not say in man only, but in all heaven and earth, than reason? And reason, when it is full grown and perfected, is rightly called wisdom. Therefore, since there is nothing better than reason, and since it exists both in man and God, the first common possession of man and God is reason. (Cicero, *On Laws*, I.7.22)

Let's look briefly at Cicero's use of the word 'reason'. The word being translated here is the Latin word *ratio*. In a tradition that begins with Heraclitus and his discussion of *logos*, but is carried forward by the Stoics and especially by Neo-Platonists, *ratio* is not just an intellectual process by which people come to understand things. It's also a force of nature. It's a kind of universal plan in terms of which all things come into being, persist and transform over time, and then fade away. Thus there's some overlap with the ancient idea of nature as the body of laws that make things what they are. Human reason is that which enables us to discern this plan. Yet human reason is also in some sense part of the plan: we're able to discern the plan precisely because it is at work in our minds and souls, as much as it is at work elsewhere in the world. So when Cicero and his associates speak of reason, they're often speaking of a spiritual quality. But observe a distinction here: they are not speaking of a mystical quality. Knowledge of the divine does not come from unknown sources beyond understanding. It comes from your own patient hard-slogging work of figuring it out for yourself.

Cicero certainly followed this view of the importance of reason: he also closely associated the exercise of reason with moral goodness and with happiness. In his *Discussions at Tusculum* he wrote: 'Once, therefore, this human soul has received the appropriate training, once its vision has been seen to

– so as to make sure it is blinded by no errors – the result will be perfect mind, flawless reason: which is the same thing as perfect moral goodness.' (Cicero, cited in *On the Good Life*, pg. 73)

Because of statements like that one, Cicero is regarded as one of the earliest supporters of individualism and individual rights. Yet this 'distinguished status', this 'spark of the divine' as Cicero refers to reason, imparts to every human being not only a special moral standing, but also a special social responsibility. For the divine rationality which we all carry in common also creates a strong bond of spiritual unity between all people, and this bond calls upon us to treat each other with respect.

Some people today may think this is an impossible pairing. We are either individuals, possessing rights that protect us from interference from others, or else we are members of some kind of collective, which can make moral demands upon us for service to others. And the teaching of the modern world view, aside from some very special exceptions, is that the individual always takes precedence over any groups that the individual may be part of. But Cicero's view was more balanced: for instance he thought that the worship of the gods was a patriotic duty. Anyway, arguing in favor of individualism, even in a limited way, was probably radical enough in his time.

Historically, however, Cicero is best praised for how he almost personally kickstarted Roman philosophy, and how hard he worked to apply philosophical ideas to political life. And he was perhaps the most vigorous activist for the Republican cause as Rome transitioned from Republic to Monarchy and then to Empire. But it was a losing battle for him, in the end. When in 43 BCE Marc Antony and two others formed the Second Triumvirate, effectively ending the Roman Republic, Cicero was declared an enemy of the state, and murdered.

§ 19. Plotinus (205-270 CE)

The man widely regarded as the greatest Neo-Platonist

philosopher also happens to be widely regarded as the last of the great pagan philosophers. He was born in Lycopolis, a Romanized city in the Nile Delta of Egypt. Not much is known about his early life, although anecdotal evidence suggests he grew up in a fairly prosperous and politically well-connected family. At the age of twenty-seven it seems he 'got philosophy', in a way similar to how some people 'get religion', and he traveled to the great Library of Alexandria in search of a teacher. There he met Ammonius Saccas, a very mysterious figure, with whom he studied for eleven years. Plotinus may have acquired a secret philosophical teaching from Ammonius, for as his biographer Porphyry wrote: 'Errenius, Origen, and Plotinus had made a compact not to disclose any of the doctrines which Ammonius had revealed to them. Plotinus kept faith, and in all his intercourse with his associates divulged nothing of Ammonius' system.' (Porphyry, *On the Life of Plotinus and his Work*, as cited in Plotinus, *The Enneads*, pg. civ.) This, by the way, is one of the great detective stories of the history of philosophy: who was Ammonius Saccas, and what was his secret teaching? But I digress.

After studying with Ammonius, Plotinus became interested in the ideas of the Persian Magi and the Hindu Brahmin, so to study them he joined the army of Emperor Gordion III and marched east to Persia. It must have been a very exciting time for him: traveling to exotic places, encountering people with strange and inspiring new ideas in religion, politics, art, and culture, and of course fighting battles and experiencing the terrors and glories of war. But in 244 CE, while still on his campaign, the Emperor was murdered, and it's reported that Plotinus had some difficulty escaping back to Rome. This suggests either that he was involved in the murder, or just too close to the Emperor for his own good. I think the latter is the more likely. At any rate he returned to Rome, and a few years later he tried to persuade another Emperor, Gallienus, to create a 'City of Philosophers' where people would live by the teachings of Plato. Gallienus gave him his blessing, but not his money, so the city didn't happen. When Plotinus learned that Ammonias Saccas died, he went into seclusion for the rest of his life. It was said that at the moment he died, a snake was seen crawling out from under his bed and then out of the house through a hole in the wall. It might have been his spirit departing.

Throughout his life Plotinus wrote a huge collection of notes and letters that his student and friend Porphyry later compiled into six books, which together are called *The Enneads*. Philosophically, Plotinus inherits from Plato the Theory of Forms. But he considers more carefully how the Forms might be responsible for the existence of things in the world, and what the process or the mechanism might be. In a way, Plotinus is continuing not only Plato's philosophy, but also the work of the Pre-Socratic thinkers, in their search for a single, unifying, and non-mythological explanation for the existence of the world. Plotinus' method is to intellectually 'reverse-engineer' the world, starting with the visible realm of the material world of nature, where we observe the most complexity and diversity, and from there proceeding to simpler and more immaterial forms. His working hypothesis was that 'the complex cannot beget the simple', or to put it another way, complex things are always created by something simpler, which stands above or behind it, and whose presence moves it along. Thus he moves from nature, to the souls of various things, to the World Soul, to the 'Intellectual Principle' or 'Divine Mind' (the word being translated here is *'nous'*, which has lots of possible translations, all having to do with intelligence or the mind) and then finally to The One-And-All.

> For the Universe is not a Principle and Source: it springs from a source, and that source cannot be the All or anything belonging to the All since it is to generate the All, and must be

not a plurality but the Source of plurality since universally a begetting power is less complex than the begotten. Thus the Being that has engendered the Intellectual-Principle must be more simplex than the Intellectual-Principle. We may be told that this engendering Principle is the One-And-All. (*Enneads* III.8.10)

The One-And-All is not a god as such, nor has it any intelligence (as made clear at III.8.11 and other places), but rather it is a kind of impersonal power. Think of The Force, from the Star Wars series of films. At its centre, Goodness and Beauty and Reason come together into a single metaphysical presence. (cf. V.8.9) And The One 'radiates' or 'emanates' its presence outward, filling and in-forming the world, in a manner which Plotinus compares to water wells or tree growth:

Imagine a spring that has no source outside itself; it gives itself to all the rivers, yet is never exhausted by what they take, but remains always integrally as it was; the tides that proceed from it are at one within it before they run their several ways, yet all, in some sense, know beforehand down what channels they will pour their streams. Or, think of the Life coursing throughout some mighty tree while yet it is the stationary Principle of the whole, in no sense scattered over all that extent but, as it were, vested in the root: it is the giver of the entire and manifold life of the tree, as it were, but remains unmoved itself... (*Enneads*, III.8.10)

In other places, Plotinus compares the work of The One-And-All to the light of the sun (a very Platonic metaphor) which shines on things and allows them to be seen, while losing none of its own energy or force. Plotinus even offers us a guided meditation with which to help us understand his idea! He invites us to:

...make a mental picture of our universe: each member shall remain what it is, distinctly apart, yet all is to form, as far as possible, a complete unity so that whatever comes into view, say the outer orb of the heavens, shall bring immediately with it the vision, on the one plane, of the sun and all the stars with earth and sea and all living things as if exhibited upon a transparent globe. Bring this vision actually before your sight, so that there shall be in your mind the gleaming representation of a sphere, a picture holding all the things of the universe moving or in repose or (as in reality) some at rest, some in motion. Keep this sphere before you, and from it imagine another, a sphere stripped of magnitude and of spacial differences; cast out your inborn sense of Matter, taking care not merely to attenuate it: call on God, maker of the sphere whose image you now hold, and pray Him to enter. And may He come bringing His own Universe, with all the gods that dwell in it... (Plotinus, *Ennead*, V.8.9)

It's worth noting that for Plotinus, this vision of cosmic unity was not merely to be contemplated, but that it was something which, through contemplation, could be experienced, in a kind of mystical vision. Porphyry wrote that he witnessed Plotinus achieve enlightenment with this meditation four times in his life. But he didn't say anything about what that enlightened state was like. I suspect the secret teaching Plotinus inherited from Ammonias Saccas had something to do with it, but I don't know that.

Despite all this heavy monotheism, why do we still call Plotinus a pagan and not a Christian? Because Plotinus' God was Father Zeus, and not Christ. In some parts of his text he explains the creative process of the world using the lineage of the gods as his model: 'This is the meaning hidden in the Mysteries, and in the Myths of the gods: Kronos, as the wisest, exists before Zeus, he must absorb his offspring that, full within himself, he may be also an Intellectual-Principle manifest in some product of his plenty.' (*Enneads* V.1.7) It may also interest some to know that Plotinus' basic idea, that 'the complex cannot beget the simple', was picked up in later centuries by Augustine, and other Christian philosophers, who used it to build the Argument of the First Cause, one of several great 'Proofs' of the existence of God. Thus Christians cannot claim that this argument is an original Christian idea. It's actually a pagan idea. Bet you didn't expect that!

But there are important differences between the Christian version of the argument and the Neo-Platonic version. The Christian version, while it accords to God the same logical rather than temporal priority in the process of creation, nonetheless assumes that God created the world at a definite moment in the historical past. (And that moment, if you believe Bishop James Ussher of Armagh, was the night before Sunday, 23rd October, 4004 BCE.) The Neo-Platonic version has no such historical side. It assumes that as God is eternal, therefore so is God's creation. The world was not created at any particular time, and in the future it shall have no end. And so creation is ongoing, and still in progress, at every moment. Even right now, as you read this book.

§ 20. Hypatia of Alexandria (370-415 CE)

With the greatest respect I include Hypatia of Alexandria, who might not have wanted to be included here, but who has become something of an icon for modern pagans and for feminists. Hypatia was a professor of philosophy at the Great Library of Alexandria, in northern Egypt, during the delicate time when Christianity gained its standing as the official religion of the Roman Empire. She may not have been a pagan in the sense of a person who believes in pagan gods and who gives them offerings or consults them to gain knowledge. Yet the Christian writer Bishop John of Nikiu claimed that 'she was devoted at all times to magic, astrolabes, and instruments of music, and she beguiled many people through Satanic wiles.' (John, Bishop of Nikiu, *Chronicle*, 84:87) Now the accusation that one practices magic might be nothing more than slander, so it isn't good evidence that someone is a pagan. And a bigoted man of the time could probably not conceive a woman influencing others using reason and intellectual persuasion, and so would have to explain it as 'Satanic wiles'. Those are the typical accusations of paganism, and they haven't changed much in seventeen hundred years. But Hypatia certainly was no Christian, and her devotion to music and astrolabes, if true, is perfectly consistent with the Neo-Platonic tradition of philosophy she inherited from her father. So well respected was she as a thinker and teacher, that one of her chroniclers said she 'used to put on her philosopher's cloak and walk through the middle of town and publicly interpret Plato, Aristotle, or the works of any other philosopher to those who wished to hear her. In addition to her expertise in teaching she rose to the pinnacle of civic virtue.' (*The Suda* (Byzantine encyclopedia) cited in Hecht, J. *Doubt: A History* pg. 207) This is no small thing, given the normal situation of women in fourth-century Roman Egypt, where bigotry, misogyny, and xenophobia were considered quite acceptable. It's also known that she wrote several books on mathematics and geometry, and that she may even have been the head of the Great Library for a while.

Alas Hypatia is best known not for her thoughts, but instead for the manner of her death. The local patriarch, St. Cyril, whose job description included inciting riots against non-Christians (especially Jews), was passing by Hypatia's house where he saw a large group of people waiting by her door. When he enquired what they were waiting for, he was told that Hypatia was about to emerge, and that she typically gave free philosophy lectures and debates on the street side. Cyril was apparently so full of jealousy that he secretly ordered his followers to lynch her. As the historian Gibbon wrote, she was 'torn from her chariot, stripped naked, dragged to the church, and inhumanely butchered by the hands of Peter the Reader and a troop of savage and merciless fanatics: her flesh was scraped from her bones with sharp oyster-shells and her quivering limbs were delivered to the flames. The just progress of inquiry and punishment was stopped by seasonal gifts.' (cited in Russell, *History of Western Philosophy*, pg. 365; see also Dzielska, *ibid.*, pg. 19) The words 'seasonal gifts', by the way, really mean 'bribes'. Thus ended the career of one of philosophy's great martyrs. In the contemporary pagan community, the 15th of March is celebrated as her birthday, and as a day to generally celebrate the achievements of women in the arts, humanities, and sciences.

§ 21. Philosophical Riddles in the Dark

Constantine the 1st, 'the Great', was the first Roman Emperor to convert to Christianity. In 313CE, he issued the Edict of Milan which provided for the equality and tolerance of all religions. Emperor Julian the Philosopher, who reigned from 361-363, and whom Christians prefer to call the Apostate, attempted to restore Neo-Platonism to its previously-held prominence, and attempted to restore Roman pagan religious rituals too. He commissioned his friend Sallustius, with whom he shared the office of Consul, to write a kind of pagan reference handbook, for use in religious education: that book was called *On the Gods and the Cosmos*. But these efforts turned out to be too little, too late. Julian's immediate successor, Emperor Jovian, immediately re-established Christianity as the official religion, and made the practice of magic a punishable crime.

But the decline of Roman paganism perhaps has less to do with official political pronouncements, and more to do with the way the economic and political order of the Empire was declining into disorder. In that situation, people began to think that it didn't make much sense to look for spiritual revelations in the embodied world, as the pagan pantheists used to do. Nor did it make much sense to delight in the arts and in culture, as the pagan humanists used to do. And praying to the gods didn't seem to help much anymore. Here are the words of Saint Cyprian, a second century bishop:

> The world today speaks for itself: by the evidence of its decay it announces its dissolution. The farmers are vanishing from the countryside, commerce from the sea, soldiers from the camps, all honesty in business, all justice from the courts, all solidarity in friendship, all skill in the arts, all standards in morals – all are disappearing. (Cited in Dodds, *ibid*, pg. 12)

Cyprian might be exaggerating a little bit, but his sentiment was surely based on observable evidence. And what in Cyprian's time might have been only a small decline in the quality of civilization, by the time of Marcus Aurelius two centuries later it had become a pronounced slide into postmodern malaise. Human aspirations, conflicts, and endeavors began to appear pointless and even unreal, and no more meaningful than 'the empty pomp of a procession, plays on the stage, flocks and herds, jousting shows, a bone thrown to puppies, tit-bits [bread-crumbs] into the fishponds, ants toiling and carrying, the scurries of frightened mice, puppets dancing on their strings,' as wrote the Emperor in his *Meditations* (7.3). 'In all this murk and dirt, in all this flux of being, time, movement, things moved, I cannot begin to see what on earth there is to value or even to aim for.' (5.10) And so, as historian E.R. Dodds observed, 'To identify oneself with such a world, to take it seriously as a place to live and labor in, must have demanded more courage than the average man possessed: better to treat it as an illusion or a bad joke, and avoid heartbreak.' (Dodds, *ibid*, pg. 12)

Marcus Aurelius' solution was to say one should withdraw into one's own mind, and also identify oneself with the whole of nature, at which level everything works out for the best. But even this model of enlightenment, high-minded and inspirational as it was, eventually lost its appeal. People began to think that there was something wrong with human nature itself, and something wrong with the world. Christianity, which taught that salvation could come only from a God who stood outside the world and beyond human nature, appeared more attractive. In the year 410 CE the Visigoths, a Germanic tribe from north of the Alps, sacked and occupied Rome. To most Romans, the very idea that their great city, the centre of universal civilization, could fall to a tribe of unlettered 'barbarians', was impossible to comprehend. It was as if the universe itself had lost its centre. Saint Augustine, the Christian Bishop of Hippo, in North Africa (modern day Tunisia), had the job of providing spiritual consolation to refugees arriving in his town. In part, he explained the fall of Rome as God's punishment for the continued worship of the Roman pagan gods. But, more originally, he blamed it on a fault in human nature, a predisposition to sin against God and to harm our neighbor, which we inherited from Adam and Eve. This predisposition he named The Doctrine of Original Sin. And he offered the people an alternative civilization, a 'City of God' which we all carry in our hearts, to replace the rapidly disintegrating City of Men, embodied by the slowly falling Empire of Rome.

In 590 CE, Emperor Justinian 1st ordered the closure of all the philosophy schools, because he thought they were an intellectual threat to Christian teachings. At this point, the investigative side of this study of the history of pagan philosophy truly begins. For it is at this moment in history that pagan philosophy loses the support of institutions like schools, libraries, businesses, and the sponsorship of wealthy individuals and of governments. Did pagan ideas flourish as the bearers of a developing critical tradition without that support?

Here's what happened. Within the next few decades after the closure of the philosophy schools, all remaining distinctively pagan ways of thinking were absorbed and incorporated into

Christianity, or they were suppressed, or they simply went the way of all good things. After this point in history, it is simply not possible to discuss a pagan philosophy, or pagan theology, except in terms of *determinatio est negatio* beside the religion which had become the dominant social, ideological, and political force in Europe – Christianity. And the situation for pagan philosophy remains that way for more than a thousand years. But during this long dark age there are occasional glimmers of it, like the light of a distant campfire in the woods at night. Here's one of them.

§ 22. John Scottus Eriugena (815-877)

Eriugena was a ninth century Irish Neo-Platonist philosopher who was among the first to re-introduce Neo-Platonism and to some extent pantheism into European thought. We see this in the following passage from his theological masterwork, The *Periphyseon*, which characterizes nature as a theophany, that is, a manifestation of the presence of God:

> For both the creature, by subsisting, is in God; and God, by manifesting Himself, in a marvellous and ineffable manner *creates Himself in the creature*... So it is from Himself that God takes the occasions of His theophanies, that is, of the divine apparitions, since all things are from Him and through Him and in Him and for Him. And therefore even that matter from which it is read that He made the world is from Him and in Him, and He is in it in so far as it is understood to have being. (Eriugena, pg. 163, emphasis added.)

The idea here is that all things are absolutely dependent on God for their existence: by itself, this proposition would not have troubled any of his peers. But he is also expressing the idea that God depends on his creatures too. That is what follows logically, according to him, from the proposition that God dwells in and with the world, and that everything is somehow contained within God and part of God. Look at the statement that God 'creates himself in the creature': together with the first proposition, it is a bit like saying that God's act of creating the creature is at the same time an act of creating *himself*. We find this idea confirmed in various places in his text, for instance in statements like this one: 'Every visible and invisible creature can be called a theophany, that is, a divine apparition.' (*ibid*. pg. 167) and 'God is the maker of all things and is made in all things.' (*ibid* pg. 171) Eriugena described this process as follows:

> ...then He proceeds through the manifold form of the effects to the lower order of the whole of nature, in which bodies are contained; and thus going forth into all things in order He makes all things and is made in all things, and returns into Himself, calling all things back to Himself, and while He is made in all things He does not cease to be above all things and thus makes all things from nothing. (*ibid*. pg. 173)

Notice the fountain-like imagery, and the very Neo-Platonic idea of a God whose creation proceeds from a divine source and then returns back to that source. And that is where the controversy lay for him. Eriugena wrote of his fear that his argument would be considered dangerously blasphemous 'even by those who are regarded as wise'. (*ibid*. pg. 99) Thus he may have added the statement 'He does not cease to be above all things' as a kind of disclaimer, to signal to his peers that he was still part of the same team. (As it turned out, he is now regarded as not dangerously unorthodox at all, but actually as the very best European philosopher of his time.) But it's also the case that nothing in his argument leads to the conclusion that the things God creates share in his divine nature: an essential conclusion for any pantheist. And therefore, it is probably wrong to claim that Eriugena was truly a pantheist. But we could plausibly claim that he is a 'panentheist', a term coined by German scholar Karl Krause, which names the view that God is present in nature and reveals himself through nature, but is nonetheless distinct and separate from it. And that is a step in the direction of pantheism, but that was probably about as far in that direction which he could possibly go. And we can't condemn him for that, after all.

§ 23. Al Ghazali (1058-1111)

I mention this important Islamic philosopher not as someone whose teachings preserved kernels of pre-Muslim paganism. Rather he is the Muslim thinker who did the most to purge those kernels out of Islamic thought. From its beginning, most Islamic philosophy was rooted in the work of Plato and Aristotle, just like the philosophy of the early Christian community. Al Ghazali did the most to change that. In a short but enormously influential text called *The Incoherence of the Philosophers*, Al Ghazali identified twenty 'beliefs' of the philosophers of his time that he felt were contrary to the teachings of Islam. His main complaints about the philosophers were that they were atheists (cf. pp. 1-3), and that they had little consensus among themselves: 'there is nothing fixed or constant' about their views (pg. 4). Indeed he claims that all the good material that one finds in philosophical work already appears in the holy books, and thus the works of the philosophers were redundant. Al Ghazali's approach is typically described as mystical rather than systematically rational, although I suppose it is more accurate to say his philosophy places mystical experience and rational argumentation on an equal footing. The philosophers of his time, especially the Gnostics and the Neo-Platonists, had their own idea of what a mystical experience was, and occasionally incorporated statements derived from mystical knowledge alongside statements derived from rational argumentation. So this mystical-rational method was perhaps considered acceptable, even if not especially common. (Of course, this is not to say that all mystics share the same vision.)

Criticisms and counter-arguments against Al Ghazali came from various directions, notably from other Muslim philosophers such as Averroes. Nonetheless, after Al Ghazali, the Muslim world became far more critical of atheism and polytheism than it had ever been before. And it was much better able to pursue its own way.

§ 24. The Renaissance, Or, The Pagans Strike Back

Around a thousand years after Justinian closed the philosophy schools of the late Roman period, northern Italy had a revival of Neo-Platonism and pagan humanism. Books and documents from the Greek and Roman world, lost for a thousand years, were rediscovered in Irish monasteries and Arabic libraries. Writers like Petrarch, Marsilio Ficino, and Pico della Mirandola, cited classical pagan writers in their works right alongside Christian writers, treating them both as equally authoritative. Today we call this revival of Greek and Roman humanism 'The Renaissance'. But this revival of interest in pre-Christian ideas frequently landed Renaissance humanists in trouble with the authorities, both religious and secular. For regularly quoting Cicero, Petrarch had to apologize, and to reassure his peers that he was still batting for the same team as them, and so was Cicero if only they understood him:

Cicero, read with a pious and modest attitude... was profitable to everybody, so far as eloquence is concerned, to many others as regards living. This was especially true in [Saint] Augustine's case... I confess, I admire Cicero as much or even more than all whoever wrote a line in any nation... If to admire Cicero means to be a Ciceronian, I am a Ciceronean. I admire him so much that I wonder at people who do not admire him... However, when we come to think or speak of religion, that is, of supreme truth and true happiness, and of eternal salvation, then I am certainly not a Ciceronian, or a Platonist, but a Christian. I even feel sure that Cicero himself would have been a Christian if he had been able to see Christ and to comprehend His doctrine. (Petrarch. 'On His Own Ignorance and That of Many Others', *The Renaissance Philosophy of Man*, pp. 114-115)

Classical Greek and Roman pagan philosophy returns to respectability during the Renaissance, although with caveats like the one uttered by Plutarch above. Humanist thinking, mainly in the style of Cicero, is re-asserted with seriousness by writers like Giovanni Pico della Mirandola, and Niccolo Machiavelli. Here's what Mirandola said was God's true message to humankind, in a short humanist manifesto called *Oration on the Dignity of Man*:

The nature of all other creatures is defined and restricted within laws which We have laid down; you, by contrast, impeded by no such restrictions, may, by your own free will, to whose custody We have assigned you, trace for yourself the linaments of your own nature. We have made you a creature neither of heaven nor of earth, neither mortal nor immortal, in order that you may, as the free and proud shaper of your own being, fashion yourself in the form you may prefer. It will be in your power to descend to the lower, brutish forms of life; you will be able, through your own decision, to rise again to the superior orders whose life is divine. (*Oration* pg. 7-8)

But it's mainly in the arts where pagan culture makes a huge Renaissance comeback. Wealthy Italians hired architects to install follies of Greek temples in their back yards. Some even staged parades and public festivals ostensibly in honor of Greco-Roman deities, complete with actors playing the parts of gods and mythical creatures! Painters were producing major works depicting events and characters from Greek, Roman, and sometimes Teutonic mythology, as well as allegories of pagan virtues. The most famous such works are veritably iconic today: Botticelli's *The Birth of Venus*, Mantegna's *Primavera* and *Parnassus*, and Da Vinci's *Leda and the Swan*. Historian Jocelyn Godwin offered what I think is one of the best reasons why there was such a resurgence of interest in classical pagan arts and culture.

> I do not suppose that anyone in the fifteenth or sixteenth centuries was a pagan, in the sense of rejecting Christianity and adopting a pre-Christian religion... What I do suggest is that some people during this period 'dreamed' of being pagans. In their waking life they accepted the absurdities acknowledged as the essence and *credenda* of Christianity, all the while nurturing a longing for the world of antiquity and a secret affinity for the divinities of that world. (Godwin, *The Pagan Dream of the Renaissance*, pg. 2)

To put it simply, people got tired of the austerities of Christian discipline and the misanthropy of the Doctrine of Original Sin. They maintained the appearance of being committed Christians, of course: all the artists I mentioned also produced magnificent portraits of characters and scenes from Biblical mythology. But in their spare time they dramatized for themselves a world that never knew Original Sin, and so still existed in a state of original blessing. In that imagined world it was no sin to 'dance, sing, feast, make music, and love'. And it was no sin to pursue human excellence, or even decadence, in artistic works; and it was no sin to take pride in political, commercial, or military success. That dramatization of an imagined pagan world re-opened Pandora's box. And despite the heroic efforts of puritanical counter-Renaissance activists like Savonarola, the box would never be shut again.

The history of the Renaissance, and of its art, has been told before, and much of it is a little beyond the scope of this book. So

I'd like to move on to a period of pagan intellectual history that almost never gets told. And that leads me to Pantheism in the Age of Reason.

Third Movement: Pantheism in the Age of Reason

In the transition decades between the late mediaeval and the early modern periods, the dominant paradigm in science (using Thomas Kuhn's definition of 'paradigm') was called Scholasticism, and its supporters were called the Schoolmen. This paradigm, derived from the works of Aristotle, held that to study nature scientifically meant to study the properties of things, of which there are two types: accidental, and essential. The accidental qualities are those which, if changed, would not change the definitive nature of what it is; essential qualities, by contrast, have to do with the deep truth of the thing, without which it would not be what it is. Think of it this way: the fact that you are a thinking human creature is essential to who you are; but the fact that your hair is red or blonde or black is only an accident, and you are no more or less human than the next person for it. Further, the scholastic philosophy held that these natural properties, essential and accidental, have their own formal existence (as in the Platonic philosophy of Forms). And moreover, they may even possess inherent quasi-rational intentions, or dispositions, such as the disposition to always do what is best, or to 'abhor a vacuum' – a line the Schoolmen attributed to Aristotle. A related paradigm, derived from the work of alchemists like Flamel, Paracelsus, and Agrippa, involved the workings of the four classical elements, as well as three formative substances named for chemical materials: salt, sulphur, and mercury. The four elements and the three alchemical substances functioned a lot like Aristotelian qualities, in that they were said to possess a formal reality and various quasi-rational dispositions. The appeal of these paradigms is that they allowed a generous overlapping of theology and empirical science, and thus they offered a world view which appeared both consistent and elegant. The alchemical side of the paradigm was open-minded to the practice of magic, too, so it also offered mystical knowledge and worldly power. Apparently its principles were so well known that in the year 1610 Elizabethan playwright Ben Jonson could include them in a popular comedy called *The Alchemist*. (Which is loads of fun, so if it's playing in a theatre near you, go see it.)

§ 25. Robert Boyle Versus the Pantheists

Robert Boyle (1627-1691) thought that all this talk of alchemical principles and elemental qualities was nothing but pagan pantheism in fancy dress. To counter it, he conducted a series of experiments involving vacuum tubes. The surface-level purpose of the experiment was to demonstrate that the movement of the liquids in his tubes could be explained completely and entirely in mechanical terms, such as pressure, and weight. But Boyle's deeper-level purpose was to undermine the Scholastic idea that nature has intentions and dispositions. Near the beginning of his book, *A Free Enquiry into the Vulgarly Received Notion of Nature* (1686), Boyle wrote that his purpose was 'to keep the glory of the divine author of things from being usurped or entrenched upon by his creatures.' (Cited in Jacob, *Boyle's Atomism*, pg. 215) In other words, his purpose was to put a stop to idolatry. As explained by philosopher J.R. Jacob, here's why the naturalist teachings of the Schoolmen troubled him:

> If water is endowed with the ability to avoid a vacuum, then in some sense it is possessed of a kind of rationality and thus exists on a par with man. In turn if man is fundamentally no different from the rest of creation, why should he think of God as treating him differently: why should he be subject to God's judgment, why should he be saved or damned in the afterlife, why indeed should his soul, alone among created things (apart from angels) be immortal? And most serious of

all, why then should he be concerned to live according to the rules of established religion here on earth? (Jacob, *ibid*, pg. 213)

The uncomfortable answers to these questions can lead to what Jacob called 'pagan naturalism', that is, the idea that matter possesses an innate rational-spiritual intentionality. This idea, he says, is pagan because it comes close to pantheism, which itself comes 'dangerously close to confusing Creator and creature, to worshipping nature, the sin of idolatry.' (Jacob, *ibid*, pg. 215) And furthermore, this idea was fixed in the heart of seventeenth-century Catholic and deist teachings, at least as seen from the point of view of Anglican Protestants. Anti-Catholic propaganda from the period claimed that Catholics '...adore God in Pictures and Images, as he was adored by the Heathens in the Sun, Moon, and other less noble Creatures...' (*ibid.*) And since Scholasticism was the intellectual world view favored by Catholics at the time, so undermining Scholastic science meant undermining Catholic theology too. Boyle may have thought this an urgent cause, since James II, a Catholic, had just become King of England. Against the deists, Boyle wrote:

> ...there is lately sprung up a sect of men, as well professing Christianity, as pretending to philosophy, who (if I be not mis-informed of their doctrine) do very much symbolize with the ancient Heathens, and talk much indeed of God, but mean such a one, as is not really distinct from the animated and intelligent universe; but is, on that account, very differing from the true God, that we Christians believe and worship. (Boyle, *A Free Enquiry*, cited in Jacob, *ibid*, pg. 216)

Those deists, he surmised, were probably secretly pagans, and so their science had to be undermined as well. Boyle's scientific publications, as you can see, thus serve as Protestant polemics.

In the place of this pagan naturalism Boyle asserted what he called 'the corpuscular philosophy'. Superficially similar to the atomism of Democritus, the theory holds that all material phenomenon can be understood as the workings of little particles, which he called corpuscles, which have no spiritual properties and which act only in accord with nonspiritual, mechanical laws. As explained by Thomas Duddy, Boyle's text 'warns against the tendency of some natural philosophers or 'physiologers' to give an excessive veneration to nature, to see nature as itself intelligent and god-like. Such a view causes philosophers to deny God. But the mechanical philosophy, precisely because of its emphasis on mechanism, finds no evidence of intelligence in nature itself...' (Duddy, *A History of Irish Thought*, pg. 59) And therefore the idea of a separate, transcendent God is safe and secure. And nature is no longer worth worshipping in its own right, nor even venerating or respecting in the pantheistic manner. But if something like an intelligent design can be discerned in nature, Boyle's paradigm holds that it is the intelligence of a separate creator God, who dwells at a distance from the creation. And this, so he hoped, would assure the success of Protestantism.

About those deists that Boyle worried about: they were just getting started as an intellectual force in the early 1600s, and they would eventually spawn an intellectual revolution that we now call the Age of Enlightenment. Deism is the view that God exists, and that God created the world, set in motion the laws of physics and chemistry, gave everything a little push to get it started (cf. the Argument of First Causes) and them mostly left the world to its own devices. The deists rejected all scriptures and all institutional religious authorities. They even rejected miracles and supernatural events as evidence for God's existence. They wanted a religion based entirely on reason, and on what reason could discern about God from the study of nature.

John Toland, writing in a manifesto of deism called

Christianity Not Mysterious (1696), said that anyone who wanted to reveal some truth to you, whether that person is your next door neighbor or your God, must offer that truth using clear and easy-to-understand sentences, and not using paradoxes or obscurities. Otherwise, the revelation isn't worth your time. To those who objected that requiring God to speak like that limits or constrains him, or that God should be permitted to speak in riddles and tongues if he wants to, Toland replies: 'How dare we blasphemously attribute to the most perfect Being, what is an acknowledg'd Defect in one of our selves?' (Toland, *Christianity Not Mysterious*, pg 42) That insistence upon clear intelligible discourse is part of what makes Toland a philosopher. And it's an insistence that can apply to any religious text, not just to the Gospels.

For a few hot and heady decades, deism was a very strong rival to mainstream Christianity, both Catholic and Protestant. Its appeal was in the way it let people be religious in almost whatever way they wanted, but without the problems of sectarianism and the horrible violence which sectarianism tends to inspire. Remember, from 1618 to 1648 Catholics and Protestants were killing each other in battlefields all over Europe, during what we now call the Thirty Years' War. Thoughtful people were looking for a way to be religious without threatening anyone. Deism rejected scriptural and doctrinal authority, and claimed to reduce religion down to the simplest elements, so that anyone could find it agreeable. So it looked like it fit the purpose. Deist principles thus appeared in the United States Declaration of Independence (1776) and France's Declaration of the Rights of Man and the Citizen (1793).

Deism bears some similarities with pagan Neo-Platonism. The early deists certainly knew their classical philosophy, and the god they sought was something comparable to the *logos* of Heraclitus, the *demiurge* of Plato, the One-And-All of Plotinus. Deists of the period thought that the problems with religion came not from religion itself, but from the churches and the priests, who manipulated or corrupted God's original teachings for political gain. Here's an example of that view from Matthew Tindal, author of the deist handbook *Christianity as Old as the Creation* (1730):

> It can't be imputed to any defect in the light of nature that the pagan world ran into idolatry, but to their being entirely governed by priests, who pretended communication with their gods, and to have thence their revelations, which they imposed on the credulous as divine oracles. Whereas the business of the Christian dispensation was to destroy all those traditional revelations, and restore, free from all idolatry, the true primitive and natural religion implanted in mankind from the creation. (Tindal, *Christianity as Old as the Creation* (1730), cited in Waring, *Deism and Natural Religion*, p. 163)

If you put the word 'Wiccan' or 'Neo-Druidic' or almost any other neo-pagan category in the place where Tindal has put the word 'Christian', and put the words 'scriptures and dogmas' in the place of 'traditional revelations', and correct the gendered noun 'mankind' to 'humankind', you would have something almost identical to thousands of modern pagan 'coming-out' stories.

The vigorous demand for an understanding of God without doctrines, scriptures, and organized institutions, can make deism look like paganism. And some of deism's critics and opponents were happy to portray it that way. The political aspirations of the deists, if not their religious views, were more obviously pagan: they were based on classical Roman republicanism. And this is still acknowledged today, for instance by American political journalist Robert Kaplan who wrote: 'The Founders [of the United States] adhered to the idea of pagan virtue. Recognizing that faction and struggle are basic to the human condition, they substituted the arenas of party politics and the marketplace for actual battlefields.' (Kaplan, *Warrior Politics*, pg. 87) But at the end of the day, it's probably wrong to class the deists as card-carrying pagans. For one thing: the deists were not really looking to give up Christianity altogether. They were looking for new ways to describe the moral and spiritual teachings of Christianity. For instance Toland's *Christianity Not Mysterious* was an attempt to show that absolutely everything in the Gospels could be understood by means of reason, and that there is nothing in it which one should accept on blind faith.

And for another: when the deists looked at 'the true primitive and natural religion' of humanity historically instead of theoretically, they did *not* discover that ancient people were serenely enlightened proto-Christian deists. In 1651 Thomas Hobbes described how ancient people, ignorant of the true causes of things, ended up inventing religions based on fear, '...when there is nothing to be seen, there is nothing to accuse, either of their good, or evil fortune, but some power, or agent invisible, in which sense perhaps it was, that some of the old poets said, that the gods were at first created by human fear...' (Hobbes, *Leviathan*, 1.XII.6) So, ancient people didn't worship God out of rationality and wonder after all. What is more, a few decades later, David Hume observed that ancient people probably were not even monotheists:

> If we consider the improvement of human society, from rude beginnings to a state of greater perfection, polytheism or idolatry was, and necessarily must have been, the first and most ancient religion of mankind... As far as writing or history reaches, mankind, in ancient times, appear universally to have been polytheists. (Hume, *The Natural History of Religions*, section 1, pg. 2)

And by the way, Hume also argued that polytheism was tolerant and accepting of differences in cultures and individuals, and monotheism was not. 'Polytheism or idolatrous worship... is attended with this evident advantage, that, by limiting the powers and functions of its deities, it naturally admits the Gods of other sects and nations to a share of divinity, and renders all the various deities, as well as rites, ceremonies, or traditions, compatible with each other.' (Hume, *ibid*, section 10, pg. 38) Again this was evidence to the contrary of the universal peace-making hopes of the deists.

In this way deism, as simple and as straightforward as it appeared at first, turned out to be more complex and problematic after all. Indeed it turned out to have almost none of the intellectual support which its first adherents claimed for it. But this can lead to one of the more enlightening propositions that can be learned from the study of the history of ideas. Every time someone hits upon an idea that they believe to be an eternal and universal truth, a generation later the idea is unmasked as merely an expression of the prejudices of its time and place.

Thus for various reasons, starting in the early 1800s, the influence of deism declined. Aporias in the theory's own logic, like those just described, certainly played a part. But the growing influence of scientific materialism and atheism probably hastened the decline, as did rival world views such as universalism. But the great project of deism, the search for a 'true' and 'pure' spirituality, unencumbered by scripture and superstition and dogmatism, would continue in other ways, as we shall see.

§ 26. Baruch Spinoza (1632-1677)

Notwithstanding the defeat Boyle handed to the scientific pantheists, the idea of pantheism reappeared several times in the decades and centuries to come. It just didn't appear as a theory of science. Instead, it would appear as a theory of something else.

Baruch Spinoza, 'Prince of Philosophers', argued that nature and spirit are the same substance – an argument which earned him accusations of pantheism. Spinoza's argument was that all things in the world are made of one infinite and indivisible substance, and this substance has two main attributes: 'thought' and 'extension'; the latter attribute meaning physical material. He also wrote that the substance of the world is 'modified' in various ways, thus producing different materials like stone and metal and wood. This much is perhaps a re-statement of the ancient wisdom that the universe is a single organic whole; Spinoza's unique contribution was to express that wisdom using the language of geometry. But he also argued that this universal substance, the same for the whole world, is also God (Spinoza, *Ethics*, 1.13) 'Extended substance is one of the infinite attributes of God' (*Ethics* 1.15), and 'the human mind is a part of the infinite intellect of God' (*Ethics* 2.11) So, all things are part of God, and everywhere we look we see something of God. Think of the character Delenn, from the Sci-Fi television series *Babylon 5* (1993-98), saying 'We are the universe, made manifest, trying to figure itself out!'

But Spinoza's God, as an infinite substance from which all things are made, is profoundly impersonal: he has no free will (*Ethics* 1.32.c1); and he has no passions. He feels neither joy nor sorrow, and neither loves nor hates anyone. (5.17) Therefore 'he who loves God cannot strive that God should love him in return.' (5.19) The most we can strive for is a contemplative, intellectual love of a very abstract God, and not the emotional love of a personal God. But that contemplative love should be satisfying enough, because it is 'the very love with which He loves Himself.' (5.35)

Although this line of thinking, which I have sketched out in painfully sparse detail, was attacked in its time for being too much like pantheism, I think Spinoza's view is closer to panentheism. He describes God as an immanent God, which is a pantheist idea. Yet there's evidence in his works which suggest that God had more attributes than just thought and extension, which in turn suggests that God is more than just that which is revealed in the natural world. Although a strong defense of pantheism was not Spinoza's purpose, the contemporary understanding of pantheism more or less emerged through the various ways people accused him of it. This had already begun with Robert Boyle, as we saw. But where Boyle thought pantheism would lead to paganism, Spinoza's opponents thought pantheism would lead to atheism, an even worse kind of heresy. Actually, Aristotle had already written about God in that impersonal way, as did a lot of the Neo-Platonists, especially Plotinus. Spinoza's accusers really should have known better. But nonetheless, when Spinoza was only 23 years old, he was excommunicated from the Jewish community of Amsterdam, in which he was born. Normally, expelled Jews were expected to make various acts of contrition, to earn re-admittance to the community. But Spinoza didn't bother. It seems he thought that if they didn't want him, then he wouldn't have them either. He worked the rest of his life as a private scholar and as a maker of glass lenses for microscopes and telescopes, although the latter occupation eventually claimed his life. Glass dust in the air of his workshop gave him a lung disease, probably silicosis, and he died in The Hague at the young age of 44.

§ 27. John Toland (1670-1722)

The first philosopher of the modern era to deliberately embrace a recognizably 'pagan' way of thinking is John Toland. He was born on the Inishowen Peninsula of county Donegal, Ireland, to a Catholic family, and educated at Protestant schools. He seems to have been a well-read, well-traveled, and well-connected young man, and also ambitious, flamboyant, argumentative, and radical. He made new friends quickly, and they grew tired of him quickly. Despite his religious upbringing and education, he eventually rejected any kind of mainstream religion and became a freethinker, a word which, at the time, was almost synonymous with deist. It meant a person who refused to join an organized church and who preferred to make up his own mind about religious questions, like the meaning of scripture. It did not necessarily make him an atheist.

I've already mentioned Toland's *Christianity Not Mysterious*. But his best work is one called *Pantheisticon* (1720), a work of theology, partially Neo-Platonic in character, but also strongly pantheist. In fact the word 'pantheism' was probably invented by Toland. And it's for this reason, mainly, that I've included him in this history of pagan philosophy. It's a surprising and bold text, and difficult to read, and in some ways it breaks Toland's own rule about requiring revelations to be phrased in simple sentences. However, as described by philosopher Thomas Duddy: 'What looks like an uneasy, almost bewildering conflation of ideas from disparate sources... can be read as a kind of stylistic reflection or rehearsal of the esoteric version of pantheism that is argued for in the course of the text.' And while this eclectic fusion of ideas without deference to conventions or authorities can make the text look 'scarcely serious' (as one critic of the time put it), Duddy says, 'It is also possible to see the use of that format as playfully celebratory rather than irreverent, as part and parcel of the upbeat pantheistic 'fusion' that is taking place in the form as well as in the argument of the text.' (Duddy, *A History of Irish Thought*, pg. 95)

Toland describes God as 'the Mind, if you please, and Soul of the universe' and while that statement can look like a transcendentalist separation of the material world from God, he also tells us in the same sentence that God is 'not separated from the Universe itself, but by a Distinction of Reason alone.' (Toland, *Pantheisticon*, pg. 17-18) This caveat suggests that for Toland, the distinction between God and the material world is only a matter of words, and not a matter of reality. Or perhaps it is better to say: this material world is all that there is, and this material world is divine. In an early section of the book he offers an imaginative vision of the earth as a living organic being in its own right:

> If one should say, that in Plants there are certain Figures of a Trunk, Branches, Leaves, Blossoms, Fruit, Seeds, so also in these [minerals and metals] all this may be found, either analogous, or in a different Manner: And as Plants themselves shrub not after the same way, why then should we admire, if Things propagated under the Earth, meet with a different kind of Life? The Man who at any time observed innumerable Gems, beautifully distinguished by various Figures, to grow in certain places, there's no reason he should believe they were less actuated with Life, than the Teeth and Bones of Animals... Who (say they) can believe that the vast bulks of Stones and Metals are nourished like Bones, and increase by Vegetation? (*Pantheisticon*, pp. 30-31)

The argument here is a kind of analogy. Just as everything in a living animal or plant body grows, so too does everything in the earth grow, including inorganic materials like gems, metals, and stones, which Toland compares to the teeth and bones of animals. And although we today have better scientific knowledge of how minerals grow in the earth, still the analogy is compelling. Indeed it appears that Toland invented the idea of the Gaia Hypothesis some two-hundred and fifty years before James Lovelock and Lynn Margulis, who were prompted to begin their scientific explorations by exactly the same analogy.

Actually, the exact same argument-by-analogy appears for the first time in literature in the Icelandic text *The Prose Edda*, the collection of stories of the Norse gods assembled by Snorri Sturlson around the year 1220. Sturlson describes the analogy and then concludes: 'Thus they understand that the earth is alive and has a life of its own... It gives birth to all living things and claims ownership over all that dies. For this reason, they gave it a name and traced their origins to it.' (Sturlson, *The Prose Edda*, pg. 4) It also appears in the Homeric Hymns, in the sixth century BCE, and the writings of the philosopher Lucretius, in the first century BCE, among other places. And that is to cite only the European examples. Worldwide, the symbol of Mother Earth is one of the most widespread and universal images of humanity's religious life. So there might be something elemental about this idea. That is to say, it might be the kind of idea that naturally recurs when people observe and contemplate the world in a certain way. But I shall consider this prospect later.

Toland's argument finishes with a statement of pantheist identity which a present-day environmentalist could recognize instantly:

> In a Word, every Thing in the Earth is organic, and there is no equivocal Generation, or without its own Seed, of any Thing in Nature. Wherefore it is not without Reason, that the Earth should receive the Appellation of Mother Panspermia, to whom the Sun Pammestor is a never dying Husband; and this justifies my Answer to a German Inn-keeper, who impertinently importuned me to tell him, what countryman I was? *The sun is my Father, the Earth my Mother, the World's my Country, and all Men are my Relations.* (pg. 33, emphasis his)

The idea that the earth is a living being doesn't really 'justify' the conclusion that all the world is one's only country and the whole human race is one's family. The inference, as presented, is a case of the fallacy of missing middle premise. But the sentiment is at least consistent, and the expression of that sentiment is undeniably poetic. And at any rate, the missing premises in the logic would eventually be filled in by others, notably by various twentieth century naturalists such as Aldo Leopold, and Arne Naess.

Praised by his successors as 'the father of modern Irish

philosophy', Toland also holds an interesting place in the history of the modern pagan movement. According to Ross Nichols, in *The Book of Druidry* (1975/1990), Toland was the very first Chosen Chief of the Order of Bards, Ovates and Druids, which was founded by him and a few of his associates in the year 1717. In fact Nichols claims that the Order was founded on 28th November of that year, in the Apple Tree Tavern (an auspiciously Druidic name for a tavern!), in Covent Garden, London. (Nichols, *The Book of Druidry*, pg. 99) Today, the Order is the oldest and still the largest neo-Druidic organization in the world. Yet while Toland wrote a mountain of books and pamphlets, there's surprisingly few kind words for Druids in them. In fact, as historian Ronald Hutton has pointed out, there's actually no documented evidence at all to substantiate Nichols' claim that Toland was a Druid, or that he was the founder of a Druidic society. (Hutton, 'The Origins of Modern Druidry', in *The Mount Haemus Lectures* Vol 1, pg. 6) However, as Duddy observes, Toland's *Pantheisticon* was also written with a quasi-political flavor: 'It contains the makings of a materialistic, naturalistic pantheism in keeping with the claims of the new science, but it also lays out a programme for the establishment of a secret 'Socratic' society – a kind of philosopher's Masonic lodge. More implicitly, in the references in its 'liturgical' sections to Roman republicans like Cato and Cicero... it gives expression to the republican philosophy.' (Duddy, pg. 96) Especially in the last sections of the text, it's clear that Toland thought that a republican government (meaning a society organized as a republic, instead of as a theocracy or a hereditary monarchy) was the only kind of social order compatible with pantheism. More than that, it seems he thought that such a social order was in some way prompted or demanded by the logic of pantheism itself. Thus Toland's hidden purpose in writing the *Pantheisticon* might have been to provide the theology for some kind of quasi-secret society, in which like-minded philosophical people could discuss, develop, and perfect the idea of pantheism, and also co-ordinate their efforts to steer the body politic of England in more naturalistic, republican, and anti-clerical (I do not say anti-religious) direction. Certainly, the subtitle of the book itself suggests that very purpose: 'The Form of Celebrating the Socratic Society'; as do the opening pages, which describe the necessity and the natural-ness of human community in a manner reminiscent of certain chapters of Aristotle's *Politics*.

In a very telling passage near the end, Toland says that '...philosophy is divided by the pantheists, as well as other ancient sages, into External, or popular and depraved, and Internal, or pure and genuine' branches. He was probably thinking of the two schools of Pythagorean thought, one of which was open and public, the other of which was a secret society. Toland's use of this distinction suggests that he had in mind a mostly-secret, invitation-only community in which the members would practice a contemplative kind of religion, as opposed to the more ritualistic and mythological kind practiced by ordinary people. In Toland's words, the members of this society would 'talk with the People, and think with the Philosophers'. (Toland, *Pantheisticon*, pg. 57) Now by today's standards, this statement is painfully elitist. But it was written in a time and place where people who openly discussed democracy and republicanism, or who called for abolishing organized churches, hereditary nobility, and hereditary monarchy, or those who had any critical words for Christianity, ran a serious risk of being arrested or killed. So the statement was perhaps a necessary safety precaution. At any rate, it is followed by a revolutionary invitation to the reader to abandon oppressive religious organi-zations and to join more enlightened ones:

> But should the Religion derived from one's Father, or enforced by the Laws, be wholly, or in some respects, wicked, villainous, obscene, tyrannical, or depriving Men of their

Liberty, in such Case the Brethren may, with all the Legality in the World, betake themselves immediately to one more mild, more pure, and more free. They [the pantheists] not only steadfastly assert and hold to a Liberty of Thought, but also of Action, detesting, at the same time, all Licentiousness, and are sworn Enemies of all Tyrants, whether despotic Monarchs, or domineering Nobles, or factious Mob-leaders. (pg. 57)

Might the Order of Bards, Ovates, and Druids have been that enlightened society that Toland was inviting people to join? Ross Nichols implies as much in *The Book of Druidry*. But, as far as documented evidence is concerned, we will never know for sure, because there isn't any. And at any rate, Toland died only two years after publishing the *Pantheisticon*, and five years after the Order was supposedly founded. We know he was preparing a book about the Druids, but he couldn't find a patron to pay the cost of printing it, and the incomplete work was published posthumously. So if he did create the Order for that ambitious purpose, he never had the chance to be part of it.

§ 28. Edward Williams, a.k.a. Iolo Morganwyg (1747-1826)

In his lifetime, Edward Williams was widely respected as a poet and a collector and translator of ancient Welsh Druidic manuscripts. Not long after his death, when people enquired about his sources and found that none existed, he became widely known as a forger and a con man. But for all that, he was among the first people in the modern era to promote a philosophy while wearing the mantle of an ancient pagan holy man, a Druid. In 1792 he founded a Bardic society called the Gorsedd, which still exists to this day, and which promotes Welsh and Celtic poetry, music, and literary works.

In 1862, thirty-six years after his death, many of his works were collected in a single publication, called *The Barddas*.

Leaving aside the impossible pedigree that Williams attributed to it, this text is probably the best presentation of his own thoughts. Supposing we read it as a work of original philosophy. There's a dreamy, romantic, and mystical element to it, perhaps inspired by the Welsh Celtic myths which he had been reading. Or, perhaps inspired by all the laudanum he had been taking. He may have thought that the combination of textual study and psycho-spiritual vision was a useful way to find and to recover an ancient Celtic wisdom. (Weirder things have been known to happen.) The overall character of his philosophy is monotheist, but more in the manner of pantheism and Neo-Platonism, rather than Christianity. Consider the very first lines of *The Barddas*, which take the form of a question-and-answer session between a student and a teacher.

Question: What is God?
Answer: What cannot be otherwise.
(Morgannwg, *The Barddas*, cited in Matthews, *The Druid Source Book*, pg. 207)

It's such a simple exchange: in only three words he poses one of the highest problems in metaphysics, and in four words he answers it with surprising subtlety and force. To understand this, think of the chair you are sitting on right now. The wood or the metal in its frame could have been used to build a table, or a house. The fibers and fabric in its upholstery could have been used to make clothing or curtains. The tree outside your window could have grown shorter or taller, if the weather and soil had been different; or perhaps its place on earth could have been taken by a rosebush, or a lamp post. Everything that you can see, hear, touch, smell, and taste, *could have been otherwise*. Williams is saying that whatever God may be, God can only be God. There's something *absolute* and *necessary* to his existence. Even the words we use to describe God, like the male pronoun, could have been otherwise – so God is beyond words, too!

Next, Williams lists 'the living and dead; good and evil; God and Cythraul, and darkness in darkness, and powerless inability' as 'two things existing of necessity', and therefore of the nature of God. (Morgannwg, *ibid*, pg. 208) I think this misses the point of his own opening move. But in the moves which follow, the Neo-Platonism begins to shine through, although with his own unique variation on the theme. Here is how he handles the Neo-Platonic creation story:

> God mercifully, out of love and pity, uniting himself with the lifeless, that is, the evil, with the intention of subduing it unto life, imparted the existence of vitality to animated and living beings, and thus did life lay hold of the dead, whence intellectual animations and vitality first sprang. And intellectual existences and animations began in the depths of Annwn, for there is the lowest and least grade... Thus may be seen that there is to every intellectual existence a necessary gradation, which necessarily begins at the lowest grade, professing from thence incessantly along every addition, intervention, increase, growth and age, and completion, unto conclusion and extremity, where it rests for ever from pure necessity, for there can not be any thing further or higher or better in respect of gradation and Abred. (Morgannwg, *ibid*, pg. 208)

This discourse asserts that Being emerges from lower orders of existence, rather than emanates from higher orders, as Plotinus claimed. But it still holds that an immaterial, eternal and intellectual being, here named God, is responsible for the existence of the world. The main difference is that in *The Barddas*, God starts at the bottom, rather than at the top. Williams also asserts, like Plotinus, that the highest and most perfect grade of existence is purely intellectual. He also asserts that the material world and the lower orders of existence are impure and imperfect. And he holds that God dwells in a purely disembodied, spiritual realm, called *Abred*, the contemplation of which brings enlightenment.

§ 29. Jean Jacques Rousseau (1712-1778)

I shall write only a few brief words about Rousseau, one of my favorite philosophers of all time. Most of his philosophical interests lie outside this book's realm of concern. But pertinent to the present purpose, Rousseau completely transformed how everybody thought about nature: not only human nature, but also the natural world beyond the walls of cities and civilization. After Rousseau, nature was not just a principle of order that you can reason about: it also became a place you can visit.

When he was a teenager, the young Rousseau was in the habit of hiking by himself in the hills and forests surrounding Geneva, his home town. Twice he returned home after the guards had closed the gates, and twice his father had to vouch for him so he could be re-admitted. And twice his father beat him as punishment for it. So the third time that happened, he decided to keep on walking: south to Annecy, a distance of about forty kilometers, where he eventually found employment as a music tutor. But the experience granted him a life-long love of nature. He is the first person in modern literary history to use the word 'nature' to refer to landscapes and the nonhuman environment. 'Seeking refuge in mother nature,' he wrote in his journals, 'I sought in her arms to escape the attacks of her children. I have become solitary, or, as they say, unsociable and misanthropic, because to me the most desolate solitude seems preferable to the society of wicked men which is nourished only in betrayals and hatred.' (Rousseau, *Reveries of a Solitary Walker*, pg. 95) Similarly, in hallmark Romantic fashion, he wrote in his autobiography (a literary genre he invented) that he had a certain preference for rough and dramatic landscapes:

It is already clear what I mean by fine country. Never does a plain, however beautiful it may be, seem so in my eyes. I need torrents, rocks, firs, dark woods, mountains, steep roads to climb or descend, abysses beside me to make me afraid. (Rousseau, *The Confessions*, pg. 167)

I count Rousseau not as a pagan philosopher, but as a philosopher who sometimes had pagan thoughts. It's his love of the natural world, so strongly expressed in his more personal writings, which leads me to count him so. But soon we shall see other philosophers who, with Rousseau's strong shoulders to stand on, made the love of nature the central preoccupations of their life and thought.

§ 30. Thomas Taylor (1758-1835)

Taylor was first person to translate the works of Plato and Aristotle into English, as well as the works of most of the important Neo-Platonist thinkers, the fragments of the Pythagoreans, and the Hymns of Orpheus. For publicly committing himself to live by Plato's teachings, and for being an outspoken opponent of corruption in various Christian churches, he earned for himself the nickname 'Thomas the Pagan'.

It's difficult to pin down exactly what Taylor's own philo-sophical ideas were, since the majority of his work involved translating and interpreting the works of ancient Greek texts. A decent guess can be made, however, by looking for consistent themes in his commentaries. The main thesis of Taylor's flagship text, *The Eleusinian and Bacchic Mysteries* (1790) is that the whole point of the rituals and initiations of these ancient Greek secret societies was to teach a certain secret doctrine. He also asserts that Pythagoras and Plato and their followers knew what that teaching was, and that they described it in their books, although using a secret code. Taylor asserted that only Plotinus reported the secret teaching in plain language, without using any metaphors or concealed meanings. (By contrast, you may recall,

Porphyry said that Plotinus was the only one to keep the secret safe!) And what was that secret teaching? Its first proposition, as Taylor describes it, runs as follows:

> The dramatic spectacles of the Lesser Mysteries were designed by the ancient theologists, their founders, to signify occultly the condition of the unpurified soul invested with an earthly body, and enveloped in a material or physical nature; or, in other words, to signify that such a soul in the present life might be said to die, as far as it is possible for a soul to die... (Taylor, *Eleusinian and Bacchic Mysteries*, pg. 5)

In other words, when a person is born, a soul unites with a body – but then the soul 'dies' and 'is buried in the body as in a sepulchur'. (Taylor, pg. 7) Other authorities cited by Taylor say that the soul is not dead but 'asleep', and therefore all that we see in this world is actually a kind of dream. The study of philosophy, especially Platonic philosophy, could help the soul awaken, which leads to the second secret teaching.

The second teaching involved a claim about what the soul could expect in the afterlife. There was a kind of public teaching, or 'outer' doctrine, among the ancient Greek thinkers, which claimed that the gods punished or rewarded people based on the way they conducted themselves in life. But there was also a secret, or 'inner' teaching, which asserted that '...the soul's punishment and existence hereafter are nothing more than a continuation of its state at present, and a transmigration, as it were, from sleep to sleep, and from dream to dream.' (Taylor, *ibid*, pg. 6) So the soul, which 'died' or 'fell asleep' when it joined with a material body, might remain asleep when the body dies, if the person didn't do anything in life to arouse it. But if the person led the right kind of life, and purified itself in various ways, and studied philosophy (as you might expect), then the soul would awaken, and proceed to the next world where it could become enlightened.

There are two implications of this view that I would like to emphasize. The first is that the afterlife that awaits the soul is something that a person *creates for herself*, or draws upon herself. It is not a punishment or a reward given or imposed by a god, or the fates, or some other force beyond the self. Rather, you must be your own liberator, or else remain your own jailor. Second, Taylor's account describes what the person has to do to awaken the soul. Obviously (to him, anyway), attendance at the Orphic mystery rituals is helpful, because that's where the postulant learns the basic teachings. The rituals were also said to have a purifying effect in their own right. Thereafter the postulant must awaken himself with 'philosophy', which in a footnote Taylor says means 'the discipline of the life', that is, an ethical life. Elsewhere he suggests that philosophy also means caring for reality, truth, and 'divine things' (Plato's eternal Forms, for instance), and not caring very much about material wealth or worldly fame. In this way, Taylor claimed to have achieved the same experience of enlightenment previously achieved by his predecessor Plotinus.

Now it is possible that Taylor didn't want the Orphic mysteries to seem too threatening to Christian sensibilities. Taylor's Orpheism is at least superficially similar to certain brands of Neo-Platonic Christianity which were popular in his time, especially in its misercorpism (i.e. the denial of the spiritual significance of the body, and of the material world generally.) Friedrich Nietzsche, as we will soon see, made a very different interpretation of the Dionysian tradition, and would probably have dismissed Taylor's interpretation for being excessively anti-life. Nietzsche also didn't care who he offended. But Taylor invokes a small army of classical writers in support of his thesis, and it's hard to dismiss them so easily.

Taylor's influence is much larger than is normally acknowledged. For instance, Taylor knew most of the important English romantic poets of the time, including Byron, Shelley, and Wordsworth. William Blake was reading Taylor's translation of Plato, and it seems that book was a major influence on Blake's views about the importance of humanity's artistic and creative powers. (cf. Damon, *ibid*, pg. 33) And some evidence suggests that Taylor's family was landlord to the Wollestonecraft family, including Mary Wollestonecraft, who would eventually publish *A Vindication of the Rights of Women* (1792), and whose daughter Mary Shelley would eventually publish *Frankenstein* (1818). And remember the list of Greek books that Frankenstein's creature used to teach himself to read? All translated by Thomas Taylor. Philosophy appears in the most surprising places!

§ 31. Ralph Waldo Emerson (1803-1882)

I include this eminent American essayist and poet in this collection, not only for his poetry, but mainly for his plaintive call for a transformation in the religious and spiritual life of America.

> The foregoing generations beheld God and nature face to face; we, through their eyes. Why should not we also enjoy an original relation to the universe? Why should not we have a poetry and philosophy of insight and not of tradition, and a religion by revelation to us, and not the history of theirs? Embosomed for a season in nature, whose floods of life stream around and through us, and invite us by the powers they supply, to action proportioned to nature, why should we grope among the dry bones of the past, or put the living generation into masquerade out of its faded wardrobe? The sun shines to-day also. (Emerson, *Nature*, pg. 5)

Notice the literary allusion to Plato's Parable of the Sun. This is Emerson's way of saying we should look at the light of the sun ourselves, and not just listen to the words of those who looked on it hundreds of years ago. I write this with some irony, since this is a book about a history of ideas, after all. But surely you get the idea.

Emerson named his new philosophy Transcendentalism. But it's easy to get confused by this term. It refers not to a belief in a transcendental God, as one might expect from an analytic definition of the word. Rather, Emerson's Transcendentalism refers to a short-lived but interesting American intellectual movement, more or less founded by Emerson and his associates, which taught that individuals must overcome ('transcend') organized religion and formal political parties, in order to have an 'original relation to the universe'. Emerson's associate William Henry Channing defined it as follows:

> Transcendentalism was the assertion of the inalienable integrity of man, of the immanence of Divinity in instinct. In part, it was a reaction against Puritan Orthodoxy; in part, an effort of renewed study of the ancients, or Oriental pantheists, or Plato and the Alexandrians, of Plutarch's Morals, Seneca and Epictetus... Transcendentalism, as viewed by its disciples, was a pilgrimage from the idolatrous world of creeds and rituals into the temple of the Living God in the soul. It was a putting to silence of tradition and formulas, that the Sacred Oracle might be heard through intuitions of the single-eyed and pure-hearted. (Miller, *The American Transcendentalists*, pg. 36-7)

Thus it's a political and moral point being made here, not just a metaphysical one: and it's the social world, not the material world, which Emerson wanted to transcend. In this sense his Transcendentalism is curiously similar to the deism of figures like Tindal and Toland. Interestingly, Emerson began his argument with a complaint against corrupt politicians and priests, as did Toland a century and a half before him – and just as interestingly, he hit upon a very similar solution. It's almost as if something was in the water.

Emerson's 1836 essay 'Nature' was Transcendentalism's founding manifesto. To my ears, however, its argument sounds a lot like pantheism. Actually, Emerson doesn't really specify whether God and nature are one, which would be true pantheism. Nor does he indicate whether God is separate from the natural world but reveals himself through it, which would be correctly called panentheism. Evidence for both kinds of thinking appear in the text. Here's an example:

> In the woods too, a man casts off his years, as the snake his slough, and at what period so ever of life, is always a child. In the woods, is perpetual youth. Within these plantations of God, a decorum and sanctity reign, a perennial festival is dressed, and the guest sees not how he should tire of them in a thousand years. In the woods, we return to reason and faith. There I feel that nothing can befall me in life, no disgrace, no calamity, (leaving me my eyes,) which nature cannot repair. Standing on the bare ground, my head bathed by the blithe air, and uplifted into infinite space, all mean egotism vanishes. I become a transparent eye-ball. I am nothing. I see all. The currents of the Universal Being circulate through me; I am part or particle of God. (Emerson, *Nature*, pp. 12-3)

It's also important to note that Emerson does not simply proclaim the healing and enlightening power of nature, like a kind of prophet: he also reasons about it. He wants to figure out how it works, and what else it might involve. For instance he supposes that nature's healing power comes not from nature itself, but from the right combination of natural experiences and the human will: 'the power to produce this delight, does not reside in nature, but in man, or in a harmony of both.' (Emerson, *Nature*, pg. 14) And he supposes that God is somehow involved too:

The presence of a higher, namely, of the spiritual element is essential to its [nature's] perfection. The high and divine beauty which can be loved without effeminacy, is that which is found in combination with the human will, and never separate. Beauty is the mark God sets upon virtue. (Emerson, *Nature*, pp. 24-5)

Emerson's choice of the word 'without effeminacy' to describe the way one can love divine beauty, can be read in several ways. He's calling for a love which is calm, rational, and dispassionate; he's also expressing the unconscious misogyny of his time. It's an unfortunate combination, to say the least. But I think the point Emerson was trying to reach was a point similar to that raised already by Spinoza, and to some extent Aristotle: that the right way to approach God is through contemplation, rather than through worship. But even that is perhaps saying too much, because Emerson's manifesto doesn't actually say much about God at all. However, that lacuna is perhaps consistent: for if you truly believed God and Nature are one, you wouldn't have to say much about God anyway. You'd assume that everything you wanted to say about God was already covered when you spoke of Nature.

Emerson's call for an original relationship to the universe would meet with broad appeal, for a while. Several of America's best nature writers would count themselves Emerson's followers, as we shall now see.

§ 32. Henry David Thoreau (1817-1862)

Widely praised as the best American nature writer, Thoreau's whole philosophy could be almost completely contained in this sentence:

I wish to speak a word for Nature, for absolute freedom and wildness, as contrasted with a freedom and culture merely civil – to regard man as an inhabitant, or a part and parcel of Nature, rather than a member of society. (Thoreau, *Walking*, cited in Botzler & Armstrong, pg. 99)

And this word spoken for Nature was a twofold proposition. The first, as is plain, was a word in praise of the landscapes and elements and wild things. The second, as is implicit, was a word of protest against the growing industrial-mechanical takeover of the earth. Jean Jacques Rousseau had already uttered such a word about a hundred years earlier. But Thoreau brought it to America. Now, this industrial takeover of the land was still only beginning in Thoreau's time: he could still claim that 'there are square miles in my vicinity which have no inhabitant' and 'in one half hour I can walk off to some portion of the earth's surface where a man does not stand from one year's end to another...' (Thoreau, *ibid* pg. 101) But Thoreau could see how this was soon to change. In an essay called 'Wild Apples' (*The Atlantic Monthly*, November 1862) he wrote: 'I fear that he who walks over these fields a century hence will not know the pleasure of knocking off wild apples. Ah, poor man, there are many pleasures which he will not know.'

In the year 1852 Thoreau left his hometown of Concord Massachusetts, and built a wooden hut near the shore of Lake Walden, and lived there for over two years. His reason for doing so appears in one of the most quoted paragraphs in the book he wrote about the experience:

I went to the woods because I wished to live deliberately, to front only the essential facts of life, and see if I could not learn what it had to teach, and not, when I came to die, discover that I had not lived. I did not wish to live what was not life, living is so dear; nor did I wish to practice resignation, unless it was quite necessary. I wanted to live deep and suck out all the marrow of life, to live so sturdily and Spartan-like as to put to rout all that was not life, to cut a broad swath and shave close, to drive life into a corner, and reduce it to its lowest terms, and, if it proved to be mean, why then to get the whole and genuine meanness of it, and publish its meanness to the world; or if it were sublime, to know it by experience, and be able to give a true account of it in my next excursion. (Thoreau, *Walden*, pg. 98)

Thoreau's desire to 'live deliberately' and 'front the essential facts of life' is an echo of Ralph Waldo Emerson's call for 'an original relation to the universe'. And this desire is expressed in gentle, smooth, and loving prose. His arguments are few, and his propositions many, but he's no less philosophical for all that. The proof of his propositions is in the great wealth of literary knowledge and environmental awareness he brings to his text. In the aforementioned essay 'Wild Apples', for instance, he lists over a dozen ancient books which describe apple trees in poetic terms: from the usual herd of Greeks and Romans, to the Bible, and *The Prose Edda*. He also brings to his works an extraordinary depth of self-awareness, which many might claim to attain, but few do. In my ears, his style falls half way between philosophy and poetry. It's as if he's sitting just behind you, talking away, letting his thoughts guide his words as a friendly wind might guide a boat across his lake. Of course, this sometimes leads him around topics that may seem unrelated to each other. On one page he might praise the inherent goodness of the simple life; on the next he might lament that so few people can read Plato and Homer in the original Greek. Yet the careful reader hears the full force of his argument so powerfully that you cannot help but see things exactly as he does, for a while.

Thoreau's general argument, as expressed in *Walden* and other texts, is that the ability to live simply and mostly self-sufficiently, in terms of material and intellectual needs, in natural environments, and especially in wild environments, is absolutely necessary for the spiritual life. And the ability to appreciate the beauty of such places as a solitary walker, is similarly necessary. Therefore such wild and natural places deserve protection, as do such lifestyles that involve entering, exploring, writing about, thinking about, and dwelling in such places. There's a subtlety to Thoreau's spirituality. When he discusses God he generally does so as a deist, that is, one who believes God exists but who subscribes to no particular religious institution. In his day he would have been labeled a 'Transcendentalist', following in the footsteps of his mentor Emerson. So when Thoreau discusses God, he usually sounds like this:

> Men esteem truth remote, in the outskirts of the system, behind the farthest star, before Adam and after the last man. In eternity there is indeed something true and sublime. But all these times and places and occasions are now and here. God himself culminates in the present moment, and will never be more divine in the lapse of all the ages. (*Walden*, pg. 105)

This idea owes more to Vedic Hinduism than to Christianity, and Thoreau nearly says as much (cf. pg. 318-9). But such passages appear rarely, and almost as digressions, in his prose. It's as if God just isn't Thoreau's main concern. But he is a spiritual man nonetheless. This next passage is a better example of the way he talks about the spiritual life most of the time:

> Every morning was a cheerful invitation to make my life of equal simplicity, and I may say innocence, with Nature herself. I have been as sincere a worshipper of Aurora as the Greeks. I got up early and bathed in the pond; that was a religious exercise, and one of the best things which I did. (*Walden*, pg. 96)

A ritual like this should be recognizable to any neo-pagan alive today. Consider next how he characterizes the life of those who do not see in their hearts what he sees in his, as the natural world has awakened it: 'The millions are awake enough for physical labor; but only one in a million is awake enough for effective intellectual exertion, only one in a hundred millions to a poetic or divine life. To be awake is to be alive.' (*ibid*, pp. 97-8) And in the light of that proposition, notice how he plays upon the meaning of the word 'sleeper' in this passage about the railroad:

> We do not ride on the railroad; it rides upon us. Did you ever think what those sleepers are that underlie the railroad? Each one is a man, an Irishman, or a Yankee man. The rails are laid on them, and they are covered with sand, and the cars run smoothly over them. They are sound sleepers, I assure you. And every few years a new lot is laid down and run over; so that, if some have the pleasure of riding on a rail, others have the misfortune to be ridden upon. (*ibid*, pg. 100)

Those are fighting words. They condemn the soullessness of the new industrial era, still in its infancy in his day. As an aside, it always seemed significant to me that *Walden* was published the same year that Karl Marx published *The Communist Manifesto*. Both books, although in different ways, were responding to the same problem: industrialization, as a danger to the life of the working class, for Marx; and for Thoreau, as a danger to landscapes and to the spiritual life. Therefore in an essay called 'Walking' (which is really about thinking), Thoreau warned:

> But possibly the day will come when [the land] will be parti-tioned off into so-called pleasure-grounds, in which a few will take a narrow and exclusive pleasure only – when fences shall be multiplied, and man-traps and other engines invented to confine men to the *public* road, and walking over the surface of God's earth shall be construed to mean

trespassing on some gentleman's grounds. To enjoy a thing exclusively is commonly to exclude yourself from the true enjoyment of it. Let us improve our opportunities, then, before the evil days come. (*Walking*, pg. 101)

Before continuing on, take a moment to think about whether Thoreau's warning has come true.

§ 33. John Muir (1838-1914)

Another important American nature writer in the tradition of Emerson and Thoreau is John Muir. Although born in Scotland, his most important works were written during the many years he walked the length and breadth of America, literally, from Wisconsin to the Gulf of Mexico, entirely by himself. He had an important role in creating America's system of national parks, and especially Yosemite National Park; he was also the founder of the Sierra Club, probably the most important conservationist organization in America.

Muir's main philosophical position was that wildernesses and landscapes deserve protection from industrial and urban takeover because they are beautiful – demonstrably, wonderfully, and irreplaceably beautiful. And much of his writings describe that beauty in rich poetic and scientific terms. Muir wrote numerous books as well as travelogue articles for magazines, so that people who lived in the urban east coast of America could experience a bit of that beauty through his eyes. Here's a sample from 'The Mountains of California', first published 1894.

Before I had gone a mile from camp, I came to the foot of a white cascade that beats its way down a rugged gorge in the canyon wall, from a height of about nine hundred feet, and pours its throbbing waters into the Tuolumne. I was acquainted with its fountains, which, fortunately, lay in my course. What a fine traveling companion it proved to be, what songs it sang, and how passionately it told the mountain's joy! Gladly I climbed along its dashing border, absorbing its divine music, and bathing from time to time in waftings of irised spray. Climbing higher, higher, new beauty came streaming on the sight: painted meadows, late-blooming gardens, peaks of rare architecture, lakes here and there, shining like silver, and glimpses of the forested middle region and the yellow lowlands far in the west... In so wild and beautiful a region was spent my first day, every sight and sound inspiring, leading one far out of himself, yet feeding and building up his individuality. (Muir, *The Eight Wilderness Discovery Books*, pg. 317)

For the most part, Muir's argumentative strategy, if it can be called that, is to describe the world as he saw it, and describe how seeing the world made him feel, as if such descriptions were argument enough. If I was a tougher-minded logician, I'd have to say description alone is not a fully-fledged philosophy. But I recognize the literary and inspirational power of his writings nonetheless. His style of writing mixes philosophical, scientific, and religious thoughts into a single narrative; sometimes he mixes these modes of thought in the same sentence. For instance he might describe the beauty of a mountain valley with invitingly poetic words, and also report that his position was 10,000 feet above sea level. Discerning the philosophical content of his work is not difficult, although it takes time. Muir writes from an age when people thought about things in paragraphs, not in talking-points or sound-bytes. Yet his work is also abundantly quotable, and one could use them to build a collection of propositions from which emerge a generally consistent world view, thematically unified by the importance of the beauty of the earth for human physical and spiritual health.

In this he can be distinguished somewhat from his predecessor Thoreau, with whom he otherwise has much in common.

For Thoreau, the important thing was the moral character which a nature-bound lifestyle fostered. For Muir, by contrast, what mattered most was the aesthetic effect of the sights and sounds and other impressions upon the mind and spirit. We find that emphasis in propositions like this one: 'Everybody needs beauty as well as bread, places to play in and pray in, where nature may heal and give strength to body and soul alike.' (Muir. *The Yosemite*, pg. 256) Muir also says more than Thoreau does about the inter-connectedness of living things on earth: one of his most often quoted statements says: 'When we try to pick out anything by itself, we find it hitched to everything else in the Universe.' (Muir, *My First Summer in the Sierra*, pg. 110) But I do not wish to give the impression that the two men's thoughts were miles apart. As I see it, they start from different premises but reach approximately the same broad conclusion.

Muir's work is spiritual without being dogmatic, in the sense that his spirituality belongs to no particular religious creed or church. His occasional references to 'the Lord' are, of course, borne from the dominant Christian world view in which he lived, and yet it is clear that the mountains and forests are the only places where anything spiritual ever revealed itself to him. And the same natural revelation also included an introspective turn: for as he wrote in his private journals, 'I only went out for a walk, and finally concluded to stay out till sundown, for going out, I found, was really going in.' (Marsch Wolfe, ed. *John of the Mountains*, pg. 439) And when he looked within, this is what he discovered:

We all flow from one fountain Soul. All are expressions of one Love. God does not appear, and flow out, only from narrow chinks and round bored wells here and there in favored races and places, but He flows in grand undivided currents, shoreless and boundless over creeds and forms and all kinds of civilizations and peoples and beasts, saturating all and fountainizing all. (Bade, *Life and Letters of John Muir*)

I shall make no claim about whether Muir's understanding of God was pantheist, panentheist, or transcendent; such distinctions did not seem important to him, although his words seem strongly pantheist to me. When he bothered to speak of God at all, it was usually within the framing language of monotheism. Yet in at least one fragment he spoke of Creation as an on-going event, in a manner that resembles the best pantheist and Neo-Platonic insights:

> I used to envy the father of our race [i.e. biblical Adam], dwelling as he did in contact with the new-made fields and plants of Eden; but I do so no more, because I have discovered that I also live in 'creation's dawn.' The morning stars still sing together, and the world, not yet half made, becomes more beautiful every day. ('Explorations in the Great Tuolumne Cañon', *Overland Monthly*, August, 1873)

And I shall make no claim about whether John Muir was a pagan – but that last passage, like many others quoted here, expresses a very pagan point of view.

§ 34. Walt Whitman (1819-1892)

The last of the American writers in Emerson's 'Transcendentalist' tradition is Walt Whitman. The two men certainly knew each other: they shared a postal correspondence, some of which was eventually published in local newspapers. Emerson had particular love for Whitman's collection of poetry, *Leaves of Grass*, which Whitman had published at his own expense in 1855: indeed Emerson's letter of praise for the book, which Whitman published in The New York Tribune, probably made Whitman's career. The lead poem in the collection, 'Song of Myself', is an American literary masterpiece. I include it here as an instance of what I've called the third branch of pagan thinking: humanism. For Whitman's humanism is religious. Although he identifies himself by name right inside the poem (line 497), at the same time the 'self' that he sings of is a higher, universal self, whose presence expands beyond the individual person, and which reaches toward the immensities of life and death: '*I pass death with the dying and birth with the new-wash'd babe, and am not contain'd between my hat and boots / And peruse manifold objects, no two alike and every one good...*' (133-4) Thus the 'self' which speaks in the poem is present everywhere in the world. As I read it I'm strongly reminded of the Hindu concept of the Atman: perhaps this 'Song of Myself' is what the Upanishads might have been like if they were written by an American. This Self is 'not an earth nor an adjunct of an earth' (136), so it's not really a pantheist self. Nor is it the same as God, although it is somehow close to God: '*And I know that the hand of God is the promise of my own / And I know that the spirit of God is the brother of my own...*' (92-93) Rather, it appears that Whitman is describing the experience of being human as an inherently spiritual thing:

> *Seeing, hearing, feeling, are miracles, and each part and tag of me is a miracle.*
> *Divine am I inside and out, and I make holy whatever I touch or am touch'd from,*
> *The scent of these arm-pits aroma finer than prayer,*
> *This head more than churches, bibles, and all the creeds.*
> *If I worship one thing more than another it shall be the spread of my own body, or any part of it...* (523-527)

Further, this spiritual experience enables Whitman to feel kinship with all other people everywhere:

> *I am of old and young, of the foolish as much as the wise...*
> *Maternal as well as paternal, a child as well as a man...*
> *Of every hue and caste am I, of every rank and religion,*
> *A farmer, mechanic, artist, gentleman, sailor, quaker,*

Prisoner, fancy-man, rowdy, lawyer, physician, priest. (330-348)

And Whitman also includes numerous types of socially marginalized people in his litany, such as prostitutes, runaway slaves, drunkards, people with mental illnesses, and people of mixed racial parentage. The spiritual heights from which he views his humanity enables him to see the beauty in everyone, no matter who they are, and to share a kind of kinship with them. Incidentally, this radical inclusiveness got him in trouble: various critics in his time accused him of promoting obscenities. On at least one occasion, when his employer found out about the poem, Whitman lost his job.

The speaker of the poem affirms that this experience of expanded selfhood is available to everyone. We find this in the very first lines of the poem, and he gently reminds the reader of it several times again in the poem's body, such as with this short run of philosophical questions: *'What is a man anyhow? what am I? what are you? / All I mark as my own you shall offset it with your own, / Else it were time lost listening to me...'* (391-393) And finally, in lines famously quoted by Lord Summerisle, the speaker of the poem declares that this sense of spiritual kinship with others extends to animals as well.

> *I think I could turn and live with animals, they are so placid and*
>   *self-contain'd,*
> *I stand and look at them long and long.*
> *They do not sweat and whine about their condition,*
> *They do not lie awake in the dark and weep for their sins,*
> *They do not make me sick discussing their duty to God,*
> *Not one is dissatisfied, not one is demented with the mania of*
>   *owning things,*
> *Not one kneels to another, nor to his kind that lived thousands of*
>   *years ago,*
> *Not one is respectable or unhappy over the whole earth.*

So they show their relations to me and I accept them,
They bring me tokens of myself, they evince them plainly in their
possession. (684-693)

As mentioned in our brief look at 'The Wanderer', poems are often full of philosophical questions and propositions, but tend to be short on arguments. And the propositions found in poetry are often expressed in symbols and in emotionally-charged phrases, rather than in precise analytic statements. In a very strict sense of the term, then, a poem is not a philosophical text. But this isn't a criticism. Poetry is a different genre of writing than prose nonfiction, and so it can use different techniques, and aim for different purposes, and perhaps reach different accomplishments. But if poems are not philosophical texts in the strict sense of the word, still they often contain the building-blocks of such texts, and certainly can inspire philosophical thought and discussion among the readers. Whitman's 'Song of Myself' is like an extended, multi-tiered, artistic expression of the proposition that the human soul is a divinity which encompasses all people and all life on earth into a unified personal experience, and which delights in that experience. No arguments or logical proofs that this proposition is true appear in the poem. But we do find two things that are almost as good: the author's personal testament of the experience, an invitation to seek that experience for ourselves.

§ 35. Pantheism and Science, Again

As we saw, Boyle and the first wave of modern scientists ensured that God could no longer serve as a hypothesis of science. Instead, God would remain a separate, transcendent creator. This would remain the dominant attitude toward God at least until the late twentieth century when the mathematics of self-organizing systems was discovered, and scientists no longer needed to postulate a role for God at all. However, pantheism would make a few re-appearances in the centuries to come. Nineteenth century Irish scientist John Tyndall (1820-1893), whose career mainly involved arguing for a very strict separation between religion and science, occasionally expressed pantheist views. (c.f. Duddy, *A History of Irish Thought*, pg. 256) In a speech he gave to the British Association for the Advancement of Science, 1874, he asserted: 'All religious theories, schemes and systems, which embrace notions of cosmogony, or which otherwise reach into the domain of science, must, *in so far as they do this*, submit to the control of science, and relinquish all thought of controlling it.' (Tyndall, *Address Delivered Before the British Association*, pg. 61) But in the same speech he also asserted that:

Nature in her productions does not imitate the technic of man. Her process is one of unravelling and unfolding. The infinity of forms under which matter appears were not imposed upon it by an external artificer; by its own intrinsic force and virtue it brings these forms forth. Matter is not the mere naked, empty *capacity* which philosophers have pictured her to be, but the universal mother who brings forth all things as the fruit of her own womb. (*ibid.* pp. 19-20)

Although he does not specify in this speech whether this process of 'unravelling' is self-organized, or guided by immanent (not externally-imposed) supernatural forces, still this is a strongly pantheist way of talking. Furthermore, in a letter to his friend Thomas Archer Hirst, Tyndall wrote:

The leading idea of Emerson's and indeed of almost all philo-sophic minds is the unity of the universe... I think the universe is best illustrated by a human body.
All are but parts of one stupendous whole,
Whose body nature is, and God the soul.
The universe is a body with life within it, and through it,

permeating its every fibre. Man is one form of that life, vegetables are another... Everything in nature is in the act of becoming another thing... The universe is life, rendered, so to speak, concrete... Man is an offshoot from this eternal stock, his spirit is the spirit of the universe. (Cited in Ruth Barton, 'John Tyndall, Pantheist: A Rereading of the Belfast Address' *Osiris*, 2nd Series, Vol. 3, (1987), pg. 127)

Notice the quotation from a poem by Alexander Pope in the midst of the letter. How could Tyndall be a materialist scientist and a pantheist at the same time? In his view, science was the realm of intellectual inquiry, whereas religion was reserved for feelings. So long as each remained within its proper place, there need be no conflict between them. But this distinction did not satisfy him forever. Near the end of his life he leaned closer to the materialist side of his thinking, and declared that the concept of the soul is only 'a poetic rendering of a phenomenon which refuses the yoke of ordinary physical laws.' (Cited in Barton, *ibid*, pg. 133)

Another scientist worth noting for his pantheist views is William Graham (1839-1911). In a book called *The Creed of Science* (1881) he wrote: 'There is a mighty living and universal Power which, though not itself individual, is for ever bursting forth into endless individual life... a Power which, though not personal, yet lives and moves in the innermost being and essence of all persons...' (Graham, *The Creed of Science*, London: Kegan Paul, Trench & Co., 1884, pg. 347-8) What makes Graham a true pantheist is the claim that when people talk of God, they are really talking of Nature, although they are talking of an uplifted and glorified Nature:

...there are certain emotions which the contemplation of Nature calls up within us, which, taken singly or in blended composition, may be the very identical intuitions supposed to be specially related to a personal conscious Deity. There is before us mighty and infinite Nature herself, the benignant and beautiful mother, known but unknown, all-producing, all-absorbing, full of mystery and awe and terror, as well as of grace and bounty and beauty; the all-sustainer, the all-destroyer; who produces us for a moment and then swallows us up; who has passed already through unimaginable and eternal years, but who is still more fresh and beautiful than in her earliest youth. Her infinity and grandeur... as well as the reverse side of her face, her seeming cruelty and indifference... are all calculated to arouse those mingled emotions of awe and reverence... which are the abiding essence of all religious feeling; emotion really aroused by Nature, but which men have habitually referred to personified powers or to a single personality behind her. The emotions begotten by the contemplation of Nature are well calculated to beget the sense of a perpetual, mighty, and universal Presence and Power. But the presence and the power which exists is that of great Nature herself, who is, as Schelling conceived her, divine and identical with the divine in us... (Graham, *The Creed of Science*, pg. 363-4)

What is a pantheist statement like that doing in what is otherwise a textbook about science? It seems that Graham was impressed by the work of philosophers like Spinoza and Hegel, but especially by poets like Goethe, Shelley, and Wordsworth. He wanted to find a place for their quasi-spiritual feelings in the scientific world view. And he wanted that place to be somehow compatible with the mechanistic paradigm of nature which the new science was now presupposing. Nature is impersonal and mechanistic, but it somehow still induces in people religious feelings; those feelings are the true location of our spirituality, and yet nature is somehow responsible for prompting or inducing them.

But Robert Boyle's mechanistic paradigm of nature won the day in the end. It's the paradigm that simply produces more and better scientific knowledge and technological applications. The idea of inherent intentionality within matter, as a scientific (not religious) hypothesis, was now for the most part dead in the water. There it remained until 1988 when French scientist Jacques Benveniste proposed the theory of water memory. That theory was killed almost as soon as it was born, because Benveniste's lab results could not be independently reproduced. Also, in 1999 Japanese writer Masara Emoto published *Messages from Water*, which claimed that samples of water exposed to music, prayer, and positive 'words of intent' produce more beautiful crystals after they have been frozen. I'm inclined to think these theories are cases of error, rather than fraud. But a generation of New-Age seekers took up these theories in earnest as the basis of various natural health products, apparently oblivious to basic scientific principles such as double-blind testing, placebo effect, and observer bias. But a theory can fail the test of science and yet still pass the test of capitalism. For these theories helped a lot of people get very rich.

§ 36. Arthur Schopenhauer (1788-1860)

I shall mention the German Schopenhauer and his masterwork, *The World as Will and Representation* (1818) only briefly. He deserves a place here because, like Spinoza, he was accused of being a pantheist. He also initiated a stream of thought that would turn out to influence the contemporary pagan movement quite profoundly, although only indirectly.

Like many philosophers before him, going back to the Pre-Socratics of Greece, Schopenhauer sought for a principle of primordial unity which will explain the world in non-mythological terms. And here's what he found. In nature, it seems, everything is in motion: everything is striving, reaching, growing, grasping, seeking, consuming, and indeed dying. Every living organism in earth, and human beings no less, are engaged in a kind of perpetual striving for something. The name Schopenhauer gives for all this striving is *the Will*. It's a will to life, mostly: it is observed in the way organisms eat, breathe, drink, reproduce, compete for resources, and grow.

> The act of will and the action of the body are not two different states objectively known... but are one and the same thing, though given in two entirely different ways, first quite directly, and then in perception for the understanding. The action of the body is nothing but the act of will objectified... Only in reflection are willing and acting different; in reality they are one. Every true, genuine, immediate act of will is also at once and directly a manifest act of the body. (Schopenhauer, pg. 100-101)

Schopenhauer carefully distinguishes human will from the will of nature: the two are not *qualitatively* the same. The will as we find it in people can know itself as well as express itself, whereas the will as we find it in nature only expresses itself. But this qualitative difference does not imply that there are two wills: in fact there is only one, immanent and common to all things, acting in two ways. This was enough for his critics to accuse him of pantheism.

The object of the will isn't what concerns him: rather, Schopenhauer is more concerned with *the activity of willing*. It is something you can see in the behavior of organisms, but it's also something you know by your own inner experience: 'The concept of will is of all possible concepts the only one that has its origin not in the phenomenon, not in the mere representation of perception, but which *comes from within*, and proceeds from the most immediate consciousness of everyone.' And as it is an impulse that everyone and everything shares, so it is the same will for everyone and everything: and thus a principle of (pantheist) primordial unity. 'It is free from all plurality, although its phenomena in time and space are innumerable. It is itself one, yet not as an object is one, for the unity of an object is known only in contrast to possible plurality... it is one as that which lies outside time and space... outside the possibility of plurality.' And it is only an illusion of perception – here he borrows ideas from Vedic Hinduism such as the 'Veil of Maya' – which leads people to think that their own will is different from that of other beings.

But the Will, as a principle of primordial unity, is not a source of enlightenment. Rather, according to Schopenhauer, it is a source of suffering. And why is this so? Because the Will, in its constant striving, *can never have what it strives for*. As soon as it grasps the object of its striving, it immediately strives for the next thing. And after it gets that, it strives for the next thing. And then it strives for the next thing. And so on. Forever!

And if we recognized the primordial unity of the will, by which one's own will is the same as everyone else's, we would experience this frustration on a much larger scale.

If that veil of Maya, the *principium individuationis* [principle of the separateness of beings], is lifted from the eyes of a man to such an extent that he no longer makes the egoistical distinction between himself and the person of others, but takes as much interest in the suffering of other individuals as in his own... then it follows automatically that such a man, recognising in all beings his own true and innermost self, must also regard the endless sufferings of all that lives as his own, and thus take upon himself the pain of the whole world. (Schopenhauer, pg. 378)

Schopenhauer isn't much studied anymore, except as a kind of hiccup in the history of philosophy, probably because his pantheism leads to such an unhappy conclusion. Leave it to his main successor, Friedrich Nietzsche, to argue that the Will is actually a source of celebration and joy – but Nietzsche's will, as we shall see, comes with problems of its own.

§ 37. Friedrich Nietzsche (1844-1900)

Why include Nietzsche in a book about pagan philosophy? Not because he was a religious person; in fact he is probably the first philosopher to tackle honestly the contradictions and errors of religious thinking. He's the one who first provocatively declared that 'God is dead'. (*Zarathustra* I.2 and *The Gay Science* §125) Nor was he interested in magic, mysticism, or anything supernatural, even if impersonal, which one can conceivably 'believe in' without necessarily being religious. He had nothing but contempt for the grand mystical visions of the Neo-Platonists, and for anyone who thought that the 'true' world was hidden from the physical senses but grasped only by the mind, or by psychic vision: 'Mystical explanations are considered deep. The truth is they are not even superficial.' (*The Gay Science* §126) As far as he was concerned, such grand mystical visions represented a deep and logically mistaken distrust of one's own eyes and other senses. Similarly, Nietzsche had contempt for institution-alized religion, and contempt for religious morals which gave others more rights than the self, or which taught 'practical sympathy for the botched and the weak – Christianity.' (*The Antichrist* §2) Yet there is much that is spiritual, or perhaps religious, in Nietzsche's work, although such a statement stretches the meaning of the word 'religious' almost to the breaking point. Erich Heller referred to him as 'one of the most radically religious natures that the nineteenth century brought forth.' (Heller, *The Importance of Nietzsche*, pg. 11) Nietzsche's religion, for lack of a better word, is a kind of humanism, for his god is human – indeed, alas, all too human. And it's a religion of strength, of adventure, of striving and struggle, of impossible hope and tragic defeat. It is a religion that affirms all that is involved in life and in being alive: including, perhaps absurdly, perhaps stubbornly, its suffering, its misery, even its foolishness.

> Have you ever said Yes to a single joy? O my friends, then you have said Yes to *all* woe. All things are entangled, ensnared, enamored; if ever you wanted one thing twice, if ever you said 'You please me, happiness! Abide, moment!' then you wanted *all* back. All anew, all eternally, all entangled, ensnared, enamored – oh, then you *loved* the world. (*Zarathustra* 4.1.10)

Nietzsche's various bursts of enthusiasm for ancient Greek heroic society is where this spirit appears most visibly. In his first major work, *The Birth of Tragedy* (1872), he says of the Greek spirit:

> Anyone who approaches these Olympians with a different religion in his heart, seeking elevated morals, even sanctity, ethereal spirituality, charity and mercy, will quickly be forced to turn his back upon them, discouraged and disappointed. Nothing here suggests asceticism, spirituality or duty – everything speaks of a rich and triumphant existence, in which everything is deified, whether it be good or evil. And thus the onlooker may be disquieted by this fantastic exuberance of life, wondering what magic potion these boisterous men must have drunk to enjoy life so much that, whichever way they look, Helen, 'floating in sweet sensuality', the ideal image of their own existence, smiles back at them. (*Birth of Tragedy*, §3)

Similarly, in *The Twilight of the Idols*, he tells the readers: 'The tragic artist is no pessimist: he is precisely the one who says Yes to everything questionable, even to the terrible – he is *Dionysian*.' (*Twilight* §3.6, emphasis his.) And in *Beyond Good and Evil* he says: 'What is amazing about the religiosity of the ancient Greeks is the enormous abundance of gratitude it exudes: it is a very noble type of man that confronts nature and life in *this* way.' (*Beyond Good and Evil* §49, pg. 64) To those who would criticize him for putting suffering on as high a pedestal as art and beauty, he says: 'The discipline of suffering, of *great* suffering – do you not know that only *this* discipline has created all enhancements of man so far?' (*Beyond Good and Evil* § 225) And to those who would criticize him for 'going back' to those ancient sources for his inspiration, he says: 'Yes, but you understand him badly when you complain. He is going back like anybody who wants to attempt a big jump.' (*Beyond Good and Evil* §279, pg. 224)

And the target of his jump is a new model of a spiritual human being, the *Ubermensch*, the person who can affirm life in the extraordinary way Nietzsche says is necessary. Having discovered that God is dead, and having discovered that 'we have killed him', then we are forced to ask: 'Is not the greatness of this deed too great for us? Must we ourselves not become gods simply to appear worthy of it?' (*The Gay Science* § 3.125) That line is perhaps one of the most important statements in all of Nietzsche's corpus. It is the basis of his grandest philosophical projects: 'the trans-valuation of all values' and 'the elevation of the type Man'.

It is not the works, it is the *faith* that is decisive here, that determines the order of rank – to take up again an ancient religious formula in a new and more profound sense: some fundamental certainty that a noble soul has about itself, something that cannot be sought, nor found, nor perhaps lost. *The noble soul has reverence for itself.* (*Beyond Good and Evil* §287, pg. 228, emphasis his.)

Such is the spiritual motto which, as Nietzsche says, allows the Ubermensch to live a meaningful and worthwhile life even in the face of nihilism and the absence of God.

Another of Nietzsche's pagan leanings is his enthusiasm for polytheism, as a mode of life. But we should be clear about his use of the term. He is not calling for a return of the old gods *as gods* for us to worship. That, in his view, would replace one empty fiction for another. Rather, Nietzsche is calling for a return of what those gods represented, namely, a plurality of moral and philosophical values, a diversity of modes of life. This is why his spirituality is humanist not religious. Monotheism, to continue the thought, is the doctrine that there is one set of moral and philosophical values, one mode of life, for everyone. Here are his words:

> The wonderful art and gift of creating gods – polytheism – was the medium through which this impulse could discharge, purify, perfect, and ennoble itself; for originally it was a very undistinguished impulse, related to stubbornness, disobedience, and envy. Hostility against this impulse to have an ideal of one's own was formerly the central law of morality. There was only one norm, man; and every people thought that it possessed this one ultimate norm. But above and outside, in some distant overworld, one was permitted to behold a plurality of norms; one god was not considered a denial of another god, nor blasphemy against him. It was here that the luxury of individuals was first permitted; it was here that one first honored the rights of individuals... the freedom that one conceded to a god in his relation to other gods – one eventually also granted to oneself in relation to laws, customs, and neighbors. Monotheism, on the other hand, this rigid consequence of the doctrine of one normal human type – the faith in one normal god beside whom there are only pseudo-gods – was perhaps the greatest danger that has yet confronted humanity. (*The Gay Science* §3.143)

Monotheism, understood this way, means conformity. In *Twilight of the Idols* he called it 'monotono-theism'. (*Twilight*, 3.2) It prevents the movement, the experimentation, and the constant changing-up of things by which life discharges its energies and flourishes. But 'in polytheism the free-spiriting and many-spiriting of man attained its first preliminary form – the strength to create for ourselves our own new eyes – and ever again new eyes that are even more our own...' (*The Gay Science* §3.143)

This great project of self-creation, though I agree it is a spiritual project, requires the exercise of a *will to power*. The idea of the Will is partially borrowed from Schopenhauer, whom Nietzsche admired for a time; but Nietzsche adapted and refined the idea for his own purposes. In particular, where Schopenhauer thought that the Will is a natural part of everyone, Nietzsche says that only *some* people are capable of willing to power. Those who are not capable of willing to power must live in terms of 'slave morality', that is, the morality imposed on them by stronger-willed others. Not only that. The 'suffering' referred to earlier does not only refer to the suffering of the individual who struggles to create himself. It is also the suffering *imposed on other people* as an effect, or sometimes as an irreducible requirement, of the project of self-creation. In a notorious chapter of *Beyond Good and Evil* he leaves no room for ambiguity:

But as soon as this principle [of practical sympathy for the suffering of others] is extended, and possibly even accepted as the *fundamental principle of society*, it immediately proves to be what it really is – a will to the *denial* of life, a principle of disintegration and decay. Here we must beware of superficiality and get to the bottom of the matter, resisting all sentimental weakness: life itself is essentially appropriation, injury, overpowering of what is alien and weaker; suppression, hardness, imposition of one's own forms, incorporation and at least, at its mildest, exploitation...' (*Beyond Good and Evil* §259, emphasis his.)

Therefore, the Ubermensch has to accept that others may suffer so that his spirit may thrive. The will of the Ubermensch '...will have to be an incarnate will to power, it will strive to grow, spread, seize, become predominant – not from any morality or immorality but because it is *living* and because life simply *is* will to power.' (*ibid.* §259) Nietzsche occasionally turns to Germanic heroes for his mythological precedent for this point. As he believed they embodied the virtue of *hardness*, which allows the Ubermensch to resist the demands and influences of others, so that his creation of himself will be truly original. "A hard heart Wotan put into my breast,' says an old Scandanavian saga: a fitting poetic expression, seeing that it comes from the soul of a proud Viking. Such a type of man is actually proud of the fact that he is *not* made for pity...' (*Beyond Good and Evil* § 260)

And as everyone now knows, the practical consequence of applying this idea to the real world was the gas chambers of Auschwitz and Treblenka, and more than 1,200 other camps like them, set up by the Nazis during the Second World War. Nietzsche himself was no supporter of militant racism, and much less of German nationalism, but it's not as if he did not give his blessing to acts of cruelty and barbarism when committed in the name of freedom. In a send-up of the Christian message, he wrote: 'Jesus said to his Jews: 'The law was made for servants – love God as I love him, as his son! What are morals to us sons of God!" (*Beyond Good and Evil* §164, pg. 91) It's a consistent message, even a pagan message, to be sure. But someone who takes himself to be a god in this sense could do no wrong: even as hundreds or maybe millions of people die painfully at his command.

Oh, and one more thing: I have to use the male pronoun when I speak of the Ubermensch, not just because of the 'male-ness' of the idea of the Ubermensch and his project, but also to be consistent with Nietzsche, who thought women were incapable of it. For another part of the dangerousness of his idea is the misogynist streak, which excludes half of humanity from his project. A woman can delight in her husband's or lover's will, but not her own will.

Nietzsche's work is important because he brought to a crashing end, once and for all, everything in European religious and philosophical thinking that was contradictory, groundless, plainly stupid, or otherwise logically doomed to failure. After Nietzsche, there's no going back, no ignoring what he did, and no pretending that reality is other than it is. But as with some of the other philosophies we have studied in this survey, Nietzsche's ideas are not safe. Playing with them is playing with fire. The temple to the Ubermensch that he built for us is both glorious and sublime, and yet he built it on the backs of slaves. Nietzsche gave us a way to be pagan and to be spiritual, without putting one's faith in something beyond oneself and beyond the mortal world. But this temple is full of both light and darkness. For better or worse, there it is.

Fourth Movement: Resurgence, Reinvention, Rebirth

Lots of people over the years have tried to show that the teachings of all the world's great religions are basically the same. This way of thinking about religion is called 'syncreticism'. The early Gnostics are among the world's oldest syncreticists for which we have documented evidence. As Barnstone and Meyer wrote, 'Gnostics sought knowledge and wisdom from many different sources, and they accepted insight wherever it could be found... In addition to Jewish sacred literature, Christian documents, and Greco-Roman religious and philosophical texts, gnostics studied religious works of the Egyptians, Mesoptamians, Zoroastrians, Muslims, and Buddhists.' (Barnstone & Meyer, *The Gnostic Bible* pg. 2) There is also lots of precedent for syncreticism in the ancient pagan world. Polytheism is part of that precedent: for if it is acknowledged that there's more than one god, there is no point in claiming that one of them is more worthy of devotion than another. As a fourth century pagan Roman prefect wrote: 'What does it matter by which wisdom each of us arrives at truth? It is not possible that only one road leads to so sublime a mystery.' (Cited in Chuvin, *A Chronicle of the Last Pagans*, pg. 58) Similarly, the Greek and Roman gods, while they were often capable of human vices like petty jealousy and irrational anger, never demanded absolute and exclusive loyalty from human beings. They never punished anyone for worshipping another god, and never made the worship of another god into a crime punishable by death. We have seen how Nietzsche wrote that in a polytheist world view, the worship of one god need not be a denial of another god. And as Plato himself wrote, the gods are not jealous of each other:

So then, many and blessed are the sights and pathways within the heavens, along which the race of happy gods passes to and fro, each one of them doing his own thing; and he who on each occasion is willing and able, follows: for envy stands outside the divine chorus. (*Phaedrus* 247a)

Aside from the seventeenth century deists, the modern world's first serious syncreticist was probably the nineteenth century Islamic prophet Baha'u'llah, founder of the Bah'ai faith. The core of his teaching had to do with the unity of God, religion, and humankind. Also in the nineteenth century a Hindu Renaissance emerged in India, which was partly a nationalist movement and partly a religious reformation. Its various proponents, including Swami Vivekananda and Sri Aurobindo, taught that all the world's religions are only different paths up the same mountain. There were also a few English-speaking religious syncreticists, but they came much later: for instance, Aldous Huxley's anthology of world religious texts, *The Perennial Philosophy*, was published in 1945.

Probably the most recent and best known syncreticist is the American psychologist Joseph Campbell (1904-1987). Identifying what he called 'the monomyth', or 'the hero's journey', he wrote that the basic narrative structure of all the world's mythologies is as follows: 'A hero ventures forth from the world of common day into a region of supernatural wonder: fabulous forces are there encountered and a decisive victory is won: the hero comes back from this mysterious adventure with the power to bestow boons on his fellow man.' (Campbell, *The Hero with a Thousand Faces*, pg. 23) In the text Campbell compares the careers of Buddha, Moses, Jesus, and Hercules, and numerous others, to make his point. Not only that: Campbell links the myths of the world together by treating the characters and events of mythological storytelling, including the monomyth, as representative of psychological forces in the mind and physiological workings of the body, especially those which play out at certain important passages in human life such as birth, maturity, marriage, old age, and death. Mythology, he wrote, is 'the song of the imagination, inspired by the energies of the body. (*The Power of Myth*, pg. 27) On being asked by a journalist to respond to the objection that the study of mythology is all well and good for scholars but isn't relevant to the lives ordinary people, Campbell replied, 'You bet it is... If the person insists on a certain program, and doesn't listen to the demands of his own heart, he's going to risk a schizophrenic crackup. Such a person has put himself off centre. He has aligned himself with a program for life, and it's not the one the body's interested in at all.' (*ibid* pg. 181) Campbell is now widely regarded as one of the great spiritual teachers of his time. His studies of mythology exercised a powerful, if sometimes unacknowledged, influence on the pagan movement: for instance, it was he who first coined the popular spiritual motto 'Follow your bliss'. (*ibid* pg. 147) I think he is also more responsible than most for popularizing the study of mythology, and indeed for treating mythology as a source of universal, pedagogical, and therapeutic wisdom. Alas, most of his fame was posthumous: most people (including myself) were introduced to his thought through an interview which broadcast on television the year after his death, under the name *The Power of Myth*, in which he famously applied the monomyth to the Star Wars films!

I'm introducing syncreticism here because many, perhaps most, of the pagan philosophers to be discussed in this section followed syncreticism as a method. They gathered information about rituals, myths and legends, goddesses and gods, languages, ideas, and so on, from hundreds of cultures around the world. Then they looked for common patterns in the dataset, from which to draw general conclusions. To my knowledge, no other philosophical or theological stream of thought placed eclecticism in the very core of its intellectual method. Even my own philosophy, if I could include it in this history, has a syncretic flair, as evidenced by the wildly different individuals whose work I've chosen to include in this book. This isn't true of all contemporary and late modern pagan writers, but it's certainly true of many of them. And those who were not themselves syncreticists often relied on other authors who were. And with that said, let's look at a few of them.

§ 38. Helena Blavatsky (1831-1891)

While Friedrich Nietzsche was attempting to dismantle every religion in the world, Helena Blavatsky was attempting to unite them all under one big tent. She made what is probably the most ambitious and best marketed attempt to create a syncretic world religion. Indeed I can think of few in her time who were as well-read and well-traveled as she was; and few whose imagination was more cosmic and far-seeing. I suspect her motivations may have been similar to that of the seventeenth century deists. She perhaps wanted to identify religious ideas that could cross doctrinal barriers and unite people. But it also appears that she made a spiritual discovery which she found inherently fascinating, and felt compelled to bring to the world. Her core ideas were published in her first book, *Isis Unveiled* (1877), and again in another ten-volume work, *The Secret Doctrine* (1888), as well as in hundreds of journal articles and shorter publications.

Although Blavatsky claimed to have discovered the Mother of All Spiritual Teachings, it remains surprisingly difficult to express that teaching in a few short sentences. Reading *Isis Unveiled* is a bit like watching television while changing the channel every twenty seconds. An almost bewildering array of influences leap forward, and every page brings a new confirmation of one of her theories from an unexpected source. But it also seems her most important source of influence was Theravada Buddhism, which she helped introduce to the Western world. The name she gave to her syncretic world view was Theosophy, from the Greek words for the love of God; she also founded an organization called The Theosophical Society to help spread and further develop this world view. By the way, in *The Key to Theosophy* (1889) she claimed that the name 'Theosophy' came from Ammonius Saccas, the mysterious figure who taught Plotinus. Remember him?

The general idea of Theosophy, if I understand it right, seems to go like this. The universe is at every moment created and sustained by a divine principle called variously 'The Absolute', the 'One Reality', etc., which originates on *Adi*, the highest (the seventh) plane of existence. This principle is perhaps comparable to the One-And-All of Neo-Platonism. This principle communicates its presence, its laws, and its energies, to the visible world, but these pass on its way through a sequence of stations resembling the ten Sephiroth of the Cabbalistic Tree of Life, and also resembling the seven Chakras of Hindu mysticism. Thus upon reaching the visible world, the communication is incomplete and corrupted. And all things are striving to return to the highest level of development again. Thus do civilizations rise and fall. From Hesiod's *Theogony* and the various Hindu texts which describe the *yugas*, or Great Years, Blavatsky got the idea that the rise and fall of civilizations occurs in accord with a pattern of definite and measurable cycles. Also from the Hindu sources she got the idea that the present age of humanity, the *Kali Yuga*, was nearing its end and that the cycle was about to embark on the next age. From Darwinian thinking she got the idea that this pattern of cycles is ultimately leading, or 'evolving', towards a higher state of spiritual perfection. From Christianity and from Eastern mysticism she acquired the idea that when the *Kali Yuga* ends, a great World Teacher will emerge to inaugurate the next age and to carry us all to enlightenment. This teacher, associated with the second coming of Christ but also with Maitreya the Future Buddha, and with Kalki the Tenth Avatar of Vishnu, will initiate the next age – 'the new age' – of knowledge and peace.

Blavatsky believed Theosophy was a science, not a religion. I think what made her believe it scientific was the way in which it sought patterns and common themes in a huge variety of mythological, religious, and philosophical sources, from around the world. In that sense it's fair to say Blavatsky invented the study of comparative religion. Indeed, without intending disrespect, I dare say she invented eclecticism too. Here's a selection from *Isis Unveiled*, which expresses her teaching concerning cycles, and which gives an idea of what her eclectic writing style was like.

The 'coats of skin,' mentioned in the third chapter of *Genesis* as given to Adam and Eve, are explained by certain ancient philosophers to mean the fleshy bodies with which, in the progress of the cycles, the progenitors of the race became clothed. They maintained that the god-like physical form became grosser and grosser, until the bottom of what may be termed the last spiritual cycle was reached, and mankind entered upon the ascending arc of the first human cycle. Then began an uninterrupted series of cycles or *yugas*; the precise number of years of which each of them consisted remaining an inviolable mystery within the precincts of the sanctuaries and disclosed only to the initiates. As soon as humanity entered upon a new one, the stone age, with which the preceding cycle had closed, began to gradually merge into the following and next higher age. With each successive age, or epoch, men grew more refined, until the acme of perfection possible in that particular cycle had been reached. Then the receding wave of time carried back with it the vestiges of human, social, and intellectual progress. Cycle succeeded cycle, by imperceptible transitions; highly-civilized flourishing nations, waxed in power, attained the climax of development, waned, and became extinct; and mankind, when the end of the lower cyclic arc was reached, was replunged into barbarism as at the start... How analogous this theory is to the law of planetary motion, which causes the individual orbs to rotate on their axes; the several systems to move around their respective suns; and the whole stellar host to follow a common path around a common centre! Life and death, light and darkness, day and night on the planet, as it turns about its axis and traverses the zodiacal circle representing the lesser and the greater cycles. Remember the Hermetic axiom: — 'As above, so below; as in heaven, so on earth.' (Blavatsky, *Isis Unveiled*, Vol.1, ch.IX, pg. 293-4)

The reader will have noted at the end of this selection the appearance of the Law of Correspondence, one of the so-called Laws of Magic. The notions of psychic energy, cycles, laws of the universe, laws of magic, spiritual evolution and development, ascended masters, avatars, higher and lower planes, and even the term 'New Age' itself, comes from her. Indeed the contemporary new-age practitioner has inherited almost all her vocabulary from Blavatsky.

As mentioned, Blavatsky and her associates would have insisted that Theosophy is a science, and not a religion, and that its principles are founded upon reason and not upon mysticism. But I'm sorry to say I have my doubts on that last point. Blavatsky often sought corroboration for her theories not only in far-flung mythologies, but also in psychic phenomenon and in dreams. She treated the content of mystical visions as equally authoritative as the written works of ancient sages. For instance, in the chapter that follows the one I've just quoted above, she cites an anthropologist whose study of stone-age humans supposedly proves that human beings evolve spiritually, not just physically. Then she springs this piece of non-science on the reader: 'Let us see how far they are corroborated by clairvoyant psychometry.' (pg. 295) And with that she presents an account of an anthropologist's wife discerning the face of a Neanderthal by psychically reading a fragment of bone. Blavatsky probably thought that psychic experiences from different people, if those experiences were consistent with each other, could serve as further confirmations of the conclusions she was reaching in her study of world religious literature. Actually her use of clairvoyant evidence made her theory vulnerable to charges of observer bias, and accusations of con-artistry. And for all her insistence that Theosophy is a science, she occasionally expresses anti-scientific sentiments. For example, in the very last chapter of *Isis Unveiled*, Blavatsky presents her general conclusions in the form of ten principles of magic. The last of them reads: 'There are occult properties in many other minerals, equally strange with that in the lodestone, which all practitioners of magic *must* know, and of which so-called exact science is wholly ignorant.' (*ibid.* pg. 589) And I shake my head. Maybe it's true that some people have magical powers like clairvoyance, and maybe it's not. Maybe it's true that some materials like crystals have magical properties, and maybe it's not. But whether those propositions are true or false, they belong to mysticism, not science. And while mysticism and philosophy can sometimes go together, it has to be possible to examine the methods and the revelations of mysticism using systematic critical reason. Otherwise, the relationship won't work. As I see it, there's just too much stuff in Theosophy that has to be taken on faith.

Theosophy eventually got too weird for its own good. Various splinter groups broke away and formed their own organizations, most notably the Anthroposophical Society, founded in 1912 by Rudolph Steiner (1861-1925). But what's more interesting than the splinter groups is the way the weirdness was curiously dispelled from within. One of the great projects which the Theosophical Society undertook was the search for the World Teacher for the next age. C. W. Leadbeater, a leading Theosophist from England who claimed clairvoyant powers, eventually discovered the World Teacher in the person of Jiddu Krishnamurti (1895-1986), although at the time Krishnamurti was only a child, playing games on the shore of the Adyar River in India, with his brother. The Theosophical Society arranged for the young Krishnamurti's education, and created an organization called The Order of the Star in the East to help promote his eventual career. During this time, by the way, he met Joseph Campbell, and the meeting inspired in Campbell an appreciation for the syncretic study of world religion, especially Hinduism and Buddhism, which would inform most of the rest of Campbell's career. But by 1929 Krishnamurti thought the whole Great Teacher project foolish. 'I maintain that truth is a pathless land, and you cannot approach it by any path whatsoever, by any religion, by any sect,' he famously told his supporters in a radio address. Leadbeater was standing nearby at the time, and I'm sure he felt betrayed. Krishnamurti disbanded the organization and became a Buddhist philosopher, although he also denied belonging to any particular religion. To me, that seems like a happy ending.

§ 39. James George Frazer (1854-1941)

The Scottish social anthropologist James Frazer seems to me to stand somewhere between Blavatsky and Nietzsche. Where the former was building a new religion up, and the latter tearing religion down, Frazer seems to have been doing both at the same time. That wasn't his original intention: as he says in the first lines of the preface, he started out with the modest purpose of describing the strange ritual followed by the priesthood of Diana at a place in Italy called Lake Nemi. And here's his description of that ritual:

> Within the sanctuary at Nemi grew a certain tree of which no branch might be broken. Only a runaway slave was allowed to break off, if he could, one of its boughs. Success in the attempt entitled him to fight the priest in single combat, and if he slew him he reigned in his stead with the title King of the Wood. (Frazer, *The Golden Bough*, pg. 3)

But as often happens when researching something curious and peculiar, new questions emerge, and new unexplored lands reveal themselves. Frazer thought he discovered that the ritual succession at Nemi was one instance of a world-wide pattern, to be found in cultures, mythologies, and religious practices all over the world. And so he began documenting them and considering their meanings, and in 1890 he published his discoveries in an extraordinary work called *The Golden Bough*. The name of the book he drew from the aforementioned tree branch which the runaway slave had to steal, and which represented 'the Golden Bough which, at the Sibyl's bidding, Aeneas plucked before he essayed the perilous journey to the world of the dead.' Similarly the slave himself represented Orestes, and the fight to the death with the priest was 'a reminiscence of the human sacrifices once observed down to imperial times...' (pg. 3) So the ritual at Nemi was a re-enactment of Roman mythology. Indeed one of the great contributions Frazer made to the study of religion was his discovery of the important connection between mythology and ritual. But Frazer also wanted to know why the ritual killing of the priest, with the grandiose title King of the Wood, was seen as necessary at all. His research led him to the conclusion that in the ancient world, kings could be priests and priests could be kings, at the same time. 'Kings were revered, in many cases not merely as priests, that is, as intercessors between man and god, *but as themselves gods*, able to bestow upon their subjects and worshippers those blessings which are commonly supposed to be beyond the reach of mortals...' (pg. 11, emphasis added.) This he asserted to be the case on the basis of evidence that 'magicians appear to have often developed into chiefs and kings' (pg. 96) an idea he develops at great length. He also asserted this principle on the basis of various laws of magic which underlie the mythological world view. There's a law of sympathy, which states that 'like affects like', and a law of contagion, which states that things which were once in contact with each other continue to act upon each other at a distance. There's a lot of detail here that I've omitted for the sake of simplicity. But the conclusion Frazer reaches is that the world view of mythology asserts an important relationship between a community's leaders and the land in which the community dwells. The ritual killing of the king, then, is an enactment of that relationship, as follows:

...the king's life or spirit is so sympathetically bound up with the prosperity of the whole country, that if he fell ill or grew senile the cattle would sicken and cease to multiply, the crops would rot in the fields, and men would perish of widespread disease. Hence, in their opinion, the only way of averting these calamities is to put the king to death while he is still hale and hearty, in order that the divine spirit which he has inherited from his predecessors may be transmitted in turn by him to his successor while it is still in full vigour and has not yet been impaired by the weakness of disease and old age. (pg. 313)

Frazer named this principle 'The Sacred King', and he claimed to have discovered it, or variations of it, in religious traditions all over the world. The text would go on to become one of the top ten most influential books of the twentieth century. It is perhaps the first serious work of modern anthropology ever written. And it would re-invigorate a public interest in magic which we still find in literature and the cinema even today.

Now at this point it may appear as if Frazer's position is similar to that of Blavatsky and the Theosophical Society. I think their methods were in some way similar: they both sought common patterns in a very large and eclectic dataset of religious practices from around the world. (By the way, instead of traveling the world personally, as Blavatsky did, Frazer employed people to send him field reports.) The notion of the sacred king itself, as a ritual which embodies a cycle of a sort, may also appear superficially similar to Blavatsky's ideas about the cycles of civilizations and great ages. But Frazer and Blavatsky had profoundly different purposes. For while Blavatsky believed she had discovered a great truth, Frazer believed he had discovered a great falsehood. 'Magic,' he said, 'is a spurious system of natural law as well as a fallacious guide of conduct; it is a false science as well as an abortive art.' (pg. 13) The mistake of magic involves what Frazer calls a misapplication of the association of ideas. It's not that the magic-worker is wrong to think the world operates in accord with laws. Actually Frazer asserts that the part of the magical world view which is concerned with natural laws is quite correct. But the error lies in a wrong understanding of what those laws are, and how they work.

> The principles of association are excellent in themselves, and indeed absolutely essential to the working of the human mind. Legitimately applied they yield science; illegitimately applied they yield magic, the bastard sister of science. It is therefore a truism, almost a tautology, to say that all magic is necessarily false and barren; for were it ever to become true and fruitful, it would no longer be magic but science. From earliest times man has been engaged in a search for general rules whereby to turn the order of natural phenomena to his own advantage, and in the long search he has scraped together a great hoard of such maxims, some of them golden and some of them mere dross. The true or golden rules constitute the body of applied science which we call the arts; the false are magic. (pg. 57)

But Frazer's target is not the idea of magic in general. European Protestants had been working hard for centuries to strip the magic out of religion, in accord with their interpretation of the first and second of the ten commandments. Actually Frazer places the belief in magic in a kind of historical sequence which leads eventually to modern science. For although he described the people who practiced magic as 'primitives', 'savages', 'heathens', and 'low people' (his choice of words, not mine), still at the same time he wrote that their mistakes were forgivable, because '...their errors were not willful extravagances or the ravings of insanity, but simply hypothesis, justifiable as such at the time when they were propounded, but which a fuller experience has proved to be inadequate.' (pg. 307) Thus a strong notion of intellectual progress pervades the text; a progress 'from magic through religion to science' (pg. 824) So magic might be logically mistaken, but it is a useful milestone on the way to modern civilization.

Frazer's real target is Christianity. *The Golden Bough* treats Christian religion as one mythology among many, and Christ as one more Sacred King in a collection of hundreds of Sacred Kings from around the world. It was Frazer who first published the evidence that early Christians had assimilated or usurped earlier pagan holidays, especially Easter and Christmas. And Frazer was the first to show how the major events in the life of Christ, from his miraculous virgin birth, to his public career, his murder at the hands of political rivals, and his subsequent resurrection, were almost identical to major events in the lives of other eastern Mediterranean gods, especially Attis, Mithras, and Osiris. And this similarity was not a coincidence: it was a deliberate policy. As Frazer says:

In point of fact it appears from the testimony of an anonymous Christian, who wrote in the fourth century of our era, that Christians and pagans alike were struck by the remarkable coincidence between the death and resurrection of their respective deities, and that the coincidence formed a theme of bitter controversy between the adherents of the rival religions, the pagans contending that the resurrection of Christ was a spurious imitation of the resurrection of Attis, and the Christians asserting with equal warmth that the resurrection of Attis was a diabolical counterfeit of the resurrection of Christ... Taken altogether, the coincidences of the Christian with the heathen festivals are too close and too numerous to be accidental. They mark the compromise which the Church in the hour of its triumph was compelled to make with its vanquished yet still dangerous rivals. (pg. 419)

Frazer observed that early Christians explained this coincidence by claiming that all those dying and returning pagan gods were planted in history by the devil, in order to distract people from the Christian message. (Since this proposition is not an argument, there can be no counter-argument: the only possible reply is an equally adamant counter-proposition.) Frazer's treatment of early Christianity, classing it as just another case of pagan superstition, turned out to be hugely controversial, as you might expect. When an abridged edition of the book was published in 1922, most of the references to Christianity were excluded, to protect people's Christian sensibilities. (A 1994 reissue published by Oxford University Press restored them.)

Frazer had his critics. Let's briefly consider the way his thesis was examined by one of the greatest philosophical minds of the twentieth century: Ludwig Wittgenstein. In a series of notes that were published posthumously and entitled *Remarks on Frazer's The Golden Bough*, Wittgenstein wrote that, 'Frazer's account of the magical and religious views of mankind is unsatisfactory. It makes these views look like errors.' And, 'No opinion serves as the foundation for a religious symbol. And only an opinion can involve an error.' (*Philosophical Occasions*, pg. 119, 123) Wittgenstein's point is that no one foolishly believes that the sun will not rise if the midwinter ritual is not performed, as Frazer implies ancient people believed. Ritual and magic, according to Wittgenstein, serve different purposes besides that of a mistaken science. 'The same savage who, apparently in order to kill his

173

enemy, sticks his knife through a picture of him, really does build his hut of wood and cuts his arrow with skill and not in effigy.' (*ibid*, pg. 125) So the hunter might perform a ritual to magically ensure a successful hunt, but he still makes professional preparations. What ritual and magic really do, according to Wittgenstein, is social. Wittgenstein looks to Frazer's example of a woman who adopts an orphan by pushing or pulling the child through her legs and her clothes. The woman does not come to believe that she has physically given birth to the child. But she has shown her intention to adopt the child 'as her very own'. The performance of the ritual changes the relationship between woman and child, and also changes some part of the social environment in which they both dwell. It also changes the symbolism which surrounds them all. And in this way, according to Wittgenstein, there is no logical error involved in the ritual. For the ritual makes perfect sense within its own proper realm, namely, the realm of social practices. The error that Wittgenstein attributes to Frazer is the error of presenting religion using the language of physical science, where this business of transforming social relationships and symbols makes no sense. This does not, of course, restore to magic the overall respectability which Frazer took from it; but it does attribute to magic a logical consistency, so long as it remains within its own realm.

Frazer eventually had more critics than just Wittgenstein. Some anthropologists, for instance, were unable to find in their own fieldwork evidence which supported Frazer's claims about the near-universality of rituals like the Great Marriage and the Sacred King. Others did find that evidence, but felt that Frazer's treatment of it was too eclectic, and too reductionist. And now, although the idea is not so influential in anthropology, still I think the book should remain essential reading. For it remains hugely influential in the arts, where it is perhaps no crime to express wistful nostalgia for a time and a place that has never been. The cult-classic film *The Wicker Man* (British Lion, 1973) is based strongly on Frazer's Sacred King, for instance. And the book remains influential in the contemporary neo-pagan movement. Indeed contemporary pagans, working at a time before the book fell into disfavor among anthropologists, treated *The Golden Bough* as a kind of textbook. It provided a basis for a historical critique of Christianity, and a set of instructions for re-inventing a fertility religion. I think this use of the book is quite ironic, given the way Frazer regards magic as logically mistaken. But perhaps this irony should be unsurprising. For even as Frazer disparaged the practice of magic, still he described literally thousands of magical rituals from around the world in exquisite detail. It's as if the whole book is a massive exercise in cultural nostalgia. Perhaps the book became popular so quickly because it induced people to feel that nostalgia. The idea of the Sacred King has everything people want in a really good story: drama, excitement, conflict, interesting characters, surprising plot twists, and happy endings. People love a good story, and sometimes don't care whether the story is true or not. Hence why, I think, Frazer's theory has persisted, even though it's been shown that he misinterpreted his evidence rather wildly. In my own time, with much of the content of the book disputed, ritual dramatizations of the story of the Sacred King remain a regular feature of contemporary pagan camping festivals. I've personally attended many such rituals over the years. They're lots of fun, and for that reason alone, if not for any others, I think they should continue.

§ 40. Robert Graves (1895-1985)

The artist upon whom *The Golden Bough* exercised its greatest influence is probably Robert Graves, the British novelist and poet. For if Frazer gave us the god who dies and is reborn, Robert Graves gave us the goddess who is his ever-changing mistress, mother, and grandmother. That goddess is described in several of Graves' works, but most of all in *The White Goddess* (1948), which is his nonfiction account of what he thinks true poetry should be all about. Graves' idea turned out to be hugely influential on the growing modern pagan movement, as we shall see in subsequent chapters. Curiously, however, there is only one book-length investigation of Graves' work written by a pagan, and from a pagan point of view, in print at this time: *Stalking the Goddess* (2012) by Mark Carter.

Graves' proposition is that poetry is magical; and the magic of poetry has to do with a relationship between the poet and a goddess of inspiration. Here is how he introduces the idea:

> My thesis is that the language of poetic myth anciently current in the Mediterranean and northern Europe was a magical language bound up with popular religious ceremonies in honour of the Moon-goddess, or Muse, some of them dating from the Old Stone Age, and that this remains the language of true poetry – 'true' in the nostalgic modern sense of 'the unimprovable original, not a synthetic substitute'. (Graves, *The White Goddess*, pg. 9-10)

Graves presents his proposition as a historical as well as theological truth. According to his account, ancient Europeans were peaceful and matriarchal. Their economy was based on agriculture instead of manufacturing, and their religion was based on the worship of a goddess, with priests who were at the same time poets. This priesthood used a special magical language to communicate religious ideas. This language had an alphabet based mainly on the names of trees, but that alphabet could also be encoded with the names of birds, land animals, precious stones, months of the year, and so on. The important point was that the language was in some way written on the world, not just on paper. Furthermore, this ancient goddess-centered culture was displaced by a patriarchal culture that had an economy based on warfare and a religion based on a singular male god.

The discovery of the role of men in human reproduction forced this cultural change, as did a series of incursions from warrior-societies migrating into the region; sometimes he says the invaders came from central Asia. The tree language of the poet-priests became corrupted or was lost: in fact Graves coined a new word to describe the process of the degeneration of a language: iconotropy. But this language was preserved best in the Celtic literature of the British Isles. For this reason Graves presents a very intense study of the language and structure of many Irish and Welsh poems and legends. In that way he claimed to have discovered a pattern of poetic storytelling which Graves called The Theme:

> The Theme, briefly, is the antique story, which falls into thirteen chapters and an epilogue, of the birth, life, death, and resurrection of the God of the Waxing Year; the central chapters concern the God's losing battle with the God of the Waning Year for love of the capricious and all-powerful Threefold Goddess, their mother, bride and layer-out. (pg. 24)

Shades of Frazer's Golden Bough should be obvious here. The main difference is that Graves split Frazer's Sacred King into two figures who compete with each other for the Goddess' favor: The Oak King and The Holly King. Although Frazer also discussed the role of a great goddess, it was Graves who contributed the most to the image of a 'triple Goddess' as the first generation of twentieth century pagans would know her. She is a comprehensive goddess with three main faces: 'as Goddess of the Underworld she was concerned with Birth, Procreation and Death. As Goddess of the Earth she was concerned with the three seasons of Spring, Summer and Winter... As Goddess of the Sky she was the Moon... As the New Moon or Spring she was a girl; as the Full Moon or Summer she was woman; as the Old Moon or Winter she was hag.' (pg. 386) This goddess is responsible for agricultural fertility as well as for poetic inspiration; and she is generally peaceful and loving, although for certain purposes she can be frightening and dangerous. Graves also says she often transforms into the shape of various animals, some wild and some tame, and that 'Her names and titles are innumerable.' (pg. 24) Actually Graves had already introduced the idea of a triple goddess in a previous novel of his, *The Golden Fleece* (1944), a retelling of the classical Greek story of Jason and the Argonauts.

To prove that his thesis is true, Graves employs a method similar to that which was followed by Frazer, and by Blavatsky: the seeking of patterns and common themes in a very large dataset of literature, folklore, and mythology. Graves was already an expert in the literature of classical Greek and Roman civilization, and so this method probably came quite easily to him. Before publishing *The White Goddess* he had already published several historical novels, including *I, Claudius* (1934), *Count Belisarius* (1938), as well as the aforementioned *The Golden Fleece*. He also published on contemporary themes, such as a war diary called *Goodbye to All That* (1929), and a social history of interwar Britain called *The Long Week-End* (1941). With an active and inquiring mind, and an excellent memory for fine detail, perhaps no one in his time was better suited to undertake a project like *The White Goddess*.

The idea that there was once in Europe a peaceful pagan matriarchal culture had already been postulated in the mid nineteenth century, most notably by German classicist and archaeologist Eduard Gerhard. But by the time *The White Goddess* reached publication, arguments in support of that postulate were already collapsing. Margaret Murray's *The Witch-Cult in Western Europe* (1921) had been in print twenty-four years when *The White Goddess* came out, and already scholars were pointing out how little real evidence there was for Murray's claims. Academic scrutiny was also already casting large doubts on James Frazer's conclusions in *The Golden Bough*. So why did Graves go ahead with this model of history anyway? In his foreword, he insisted that his conclusions 'are not wanton figments of my imagination but logically deduced from reputable ancient sources.' (pg. 9) But in *The Golden Fleece* he described his research method as 'choosing for my own account whatever version of any incident makes the best sense, and even occasionally in improvising where a gap cannot be bridged by existing materials.' (cited in Hutton, *Triumph of the Moon*, pg. 190) It seems reasonable to suppose that Graves applied the same improvisational method to the materials he relied upon in *The White Goddess*. And in case any historians or literary intellectuals of the academic establishment would call him to task for it, he pre-emptively declares them unfit to understand his work anyway because they are not true poets. As observed by historian Ronald Hutton, Graves 'fully understood that what he was propounding might not actually be true, but in poetic terms that did not matter, for he could declare that 'literal truth is comparatively unimportant, as an artist can tell the truth by a condensation and dramatization of the facts.'' (Hutton, *ibid*, pg. 193) So, perhaps the best way to study this theory of poetry is with the assumption that it is, itself, a work of poetry. That approach is in some way contrary to Graves' own insistence that it is a work of history. We have to turn Graves against himself, in a sense, in order to understand him. Our alternative, it would seem, is to accuse him of concocting a scam, but I think that would be unfair. For Graves genuinely believed he was presenting something original and important to the world. And few, I think, could undertake a project as massive as his, and produce a world view as comprehensive and elegant as his, without being accused of observer bias, or reductionism.

Suppose we left aside the historical claims, given that we now have excellent reasons to believe those claims are either unverifiable, or false. What part of his text remains philosophical, if any at all? What remains, I think, is a highly personal theology. It's not a study of the ritual practices and other behaviors of people who happen to hold certain religious beliefs: that would be anthropology, not theology. Rather, it's a study of the nature of a goddess – a *logos* of the *theos* (thea?) – and it's a study of Graves' own relationship with her. This study is undertaken by means of reason. The search for the language of the goddess in a huge collection of old Celtic poems is part of its rationality, however historically mistaken his conclusions might be, in whole or in part. But it's also rational in the sense that it forms a complicated yet impressively coherent world view. And it's rational in the sense that it is not mystical. In a 1960 postscript to a reprint of the text, he wrote: 'I am no mystic. I avoid participation in witchcraft, spiritualism, yoga, fortune-telling...' (pg. 488) But the same postscript attests an interest in the inspirational power of a goddess, nonetheless. 'Since the source of poetry's creative power is not scientific intelligence, but inspiration – however this may be explained by scientists – one may surely attribute to the Lunar Muse, the oldest and most convenient European term for this source?' (pg. 490) So it's poetic rationality, rather than scientific rationality, which serves him here. One could say he seeks the goddess, not through ineffable mystical experience, but through *knowledge*: poetic knowledge, historical knowledge, and related forms of intellectual investigation. That, too, is a spiritual activity. And while many people today might assume a sharp divide between poetry and rationality, as between science and art, I think that Graves intends no such division. If you can accept that, then you will be able to see the theological merit in the text.

Here's what Graves says the relationship between poet and goddess is like. 'The function of poetry,' he says, 'is religious invocation of the Muse; its use is the experience of mixed exaltation and horror that her presence excites.' (Graves, *The White Goddess*, pg. 14) Referring to A. E. Housman's test of true poetry, that it should make one's hair stand on end, Graves says, 'The test of a poet's vision, one might say, is the accuracy of his portrayal of the White Goddess and of the island over which she rules. The reason why the hairs stand on end... is that a true poem is necessarily an invocation of the White Goddess, or Muse, the Mother of All Living, the ancient power of fright and lust – the female spider or the queen-bee whose embrace is death.' (pg. 24) Graves even ventures a physical description of Her: 'The Goddess is a lovely, slender woman with a hooked nose, deathly pale face, lips red as rowan-berries, startlingly blue eyes and long fair hair...' (pg. 24) As Graves' biographers have observed, this portrait of the Goddess is also a portrait of Laura Riding, one of Graves' first paramours and probably the love of his life. (Carter, *Stalking the Goddess*, pp. 302) To my mind, this physical portrait is a clue to understanding the relationship that he thinks a poet should have with the goddess. In that aforementioned postscript Graves says: 'By ancient tradition, the White Goddess becomes one with her human representative – a priestess, a prophetess, a queen-mother. No Muse-poet grows conscious of the Muse except by experience of a woman in whom the Goddess is to some degree resident...' (pg. 490) And from there he discusses the importance of falling in love with a woman who embodies the Goddess. Thus there's a curious humanism to Graves' theology. The Goddess appears to us not in mystical visions, but in the embodied presence of flesh-and-blood human beings with whom one could have a practical relationship. Graves seems to be saying that to love someone who inspires you artistically, is the same as to love the Goddess.

But Graves' theology also assumes a tragic turn: for the goddess who inspires the poet will eventually kill him. And this is not an optional side track: this is an essential part of the Theme. At the end of Graves' version of *The Golden Fleece*, for instance, the hero Orpheus is rewarded for his service to the goddess by being physically torn apart by the priestesses. 'The Goddess has always rewarded with dismemberment those who love her best, scattering their bloody pieces over the earth to fructify it, but gently taking their astonished souls into her own keeping.' (*Golden Fleece*, 1994, pg. 371) A similar scene appears in Graves' futuristic novel about a Goddess-worshipping matriarchal society, *Seven Days in New Crete* (1949). A young boy is ritually killed in a public spectacle, and his flesh is eaten by the priestesses. But the reader is assured that the boy was a willing participant, and that he brought honor to his family. Here's his explanation of that part of the Theme:

> The true poet who goes to the tavern and pays the silver tribute to Blodeuwedd goes over the river to his death... This paradise lasts only from May Day to St. John's Eve. Then the plot is hatched and the poisoned dart flies; and the poet knows that it must be so. For him there is no other woman but Cerridwen and he desires one thing above all else in the world: her love. As Blodeuwedd, she will gladly give him her love, but at only one price: his life. She will exact payment punctually and bloodily. (pg. 447-8)

These are powerful words. (They certainly make *my* hair stand on end!) Notice the elevation of the terms of reference here to the level of the immensities of life and death. This is a large part of what makes the relationship spiritual. I am strongly reminded here of the relationship between various Celtic heroes such as Cú Chullain, and the goddess of sovereignty, Morrigan, 'The Great Queen'. She gives an heroic life to those whom she loves; but that heroic life must end with an heroic death. Yet this death at the hands of the Muse is the way that the Sacred King attains immortality:

> The Sun-god is born at mid-winter when the Sun is weakest and has attained his most southerly station, therefore his representative, the Sun-king, is killed at the summer solstice when the Sun attains his most northerly station. The relation

between Caer Sidi and Caer Arianrhod seems to be that the burial place of the dead king was a barrow on an island, either in the river or the sea, where his spirit lived under charge of oracular and orgiastic priestesses; but his soul went to the stars and there hopefully awaited rebirth in another king. (pg. 111)

More shades of Frazer's *Golden Bough* are visible here; perhaps also shades of Nietzsche, whose spokesperson Zarathustra declares his love for those who create beyond themselves and thus perish. Researchers such as Ronald Hutton have observed that Graves' ideas about the goddess may have reflected a pattern in his own life. Most of the women he loved also caused him frustration and stress, and eventually left him, including Laura Riding, after whom his portrait of the goddess was probably modeled. Graves also discusses the importance of distinguishing between the goddess and the human woman who is her instrument for a while. For the human woman might leave you, but you might meet the Goddess again as embodied by another woman. This is consistent with his theology perhaps, but there's the smell of sour grapes about it, as if he's trying to talk himself out of a broken heart. There's also a whiff of misogyny, for instance in the places where he issues marching orders to women who want to be poets. Women should 'be a silent Muse' or else 'be the Muse in a complete sense', and write from the position of the goddess herself, rather than the position of a petitioner seeking inspiration from her. (pg. 447) As if women can have no other role! But to be charitable, it is not likely that Graves was being deliberately sexist; it is more likely that he did not fully grasp the implications of his own propositions. (c.f. Carter, *ibid*, pg. 300)

Although I'm including Graves in this informal pantheon of pagan philosophers, Graves' position in *The White Goddess* is in some places anti-philosophical. Indeed he accuses philosophy of contributing to the degradation of the ancient language of the goddess. In the early pages of the text he blames Socrates for rejecting the mytho-poetic teachings of Diotima, and replacing them with a 'new religion of logic'. Under the influence of the philosophers, 'a rational poetic language (now called the Classical) was elaborated in honor of their patron Apollo and imposed on the world as the last word in spiritual illumination...' (*ibid* pg. 10) As an aside, it's worth noting that the distinction between the classical, rational culture of Apollo, and the mytho-poetic culture which preceded it, was first identified by Nietzsche in *The Birth of Tragedy*, although Nietzsche identified the predecessor culture with the god Dionysus, not with a goddess. Nietzsche had also accused Socrates of killing the mytho-poetic spirit of Greek civilization. Now, the rejection of philosophical rationality is, in itself, a philosophical proposition, and so a case of circular fallacy. And this proposition doesn't sit well with his claim that his conclusions were 'logically deduced from reputable ancient sources'. But never mind that for now: let it suffice to say that Graves' anti-philosophical side is part of a general dissatisfaction with modernity, which Graves expresses in various places. Emerson and Thoreau had expressed it before him, as we have seen. Contemporaries of his who had been traumatized by their war experiences, as Graves had been, were also producing works of fiction with anti-modernist messages: people like J.R.R. Tolkien, for example. Think of the scene in *The Two Towers* (1954) in which an army of walking, talking trees destroy Isengard, which had been transformed into a factory for mass producing weapons of war.

There was a feeling in the air, then as now, that scientific rationalism and technological progress had not delivered its promised utopia. Or, the feeling was that the benefits they provided were bought with terrible prices. Mechanized industries destroyed whole landscapes; empire expansions colonized entire nations; huge world wars killed millions of people. There was a loss of confidence in the gains of the Enlightenment culture. In 1984, philosopher Jean-Francois Lyotard gave us a name for that loss of confidence: postmodernism. And that loss of confidence was creating in some writers a kind of nostalgia for an easier, simpler, healthier time in the past, which perhaps never existed as a historical fact, but which could be perceived with an artistic imagination. Graves' theory of poetry is an intellectual perception of precisely that kind. If we fault him for writing bad history, surely we should credit him for writing wonderful poetry.

§ 41. The Book of Shadows

The first people in the twentieth century to deliberately identify themselves as pagans appeared in southern England in the 1940s. The best known among them was a man named Gerald Gardner (1884-1964), a colonial administrator who moved to the New Forest region around that time for his retirement. There he met a number of people associated with an organization called The Rosicrucian Theatre, apparently a front for a half-secretive occult society called The Fellowship of Crotona, whose beliefs were a mixture of Theosophy, Rosicrucianism, and Freemasonry. Gardner already had an interest in esoteric and occult matters, so he got involved. Some of the people at the theatre brought him into their care, and initiated him into a private group called The New Forest Coven. Gardner soon came to believe that these people were inheritors of the Old Religion of witchcraft. He began publishing books, both fiction and nonfiction, which proclaimed to the world the existence of the Old Religion, which he called 'Wicca'. And until the end of his life Gardner worked to develop this religion, by synthesizing his own knowledge of folklore and magic, with the work of Frazer and Graves and Murray, occultists like Aleister Crowley, and universalist druids like Ross Nichols and George Watson MacGregor-Reid.

The full history of Gardner and his associates has been told by others, most comprehensively by Bristol University professor Ronald Hutton in *The Triumph of the Moon* (1999). For my purposes here, I'd like to draw attention to a thing called *The Book of Shadows*, which Gardner wrote and bequeathed to Wicca as one of its central texts. Originally, it was a kind of scrapbook of ritual and spellcraft, which Gardner assembled in various stages over the course of several years. His idea was that each student of Wicca would copy his or her teacher's *Book of Shadows*, then make her own contributions, and then allow her students to copy it and contribute to it in turn.

To me, the most philosophical selection from *The Book of Shadows* is a short text written by Doreen Valiente (1922-1999), who shared with Gardner the leadership of the New Forest Coven. Her literary contribution to Wicca is perhaps more important than Gardner's various publicity efforts. Some of her writings are now among the most important declarations of spiritual identity produced by the first generation of out-and-proud modern pagans. And of her contributions, 'The Charge of the Goddess' is the most important. I have often heard it read out at pagan weddings and funerals, and I often find quotations from it integrated into works of art displayed in pagan homes. Here is the complete text exactly as it appears in Gerald Gardner's *Book of Shadows*, which I was permitted to examine a few years ago. (Except that I added the line numbers here, on the places where Gardner made a line break.)

1. Listen to the words of the Great Mother, who was of Old also called among men, Artemmis, Astarte, Dione, Melusine, Aphrodite, Cerridwen, Dana, Arianrhod, Bride, & by many other names.

2. At mine Altars the youth of Lacedemon in Sparta made due sacrifice.

3. Whenever ye have need of anything, once in the month & better it be when the moon is full, then ye shall assemble

in some secret place and adore the spirit of me who am Queen of all Witcheries.

4. There ye shall assemble, ye who are fain to learn all sorcery, yet who have not won its deepest secrets: to these will I teach things that are yet unknown.

5. And ye shall be free from slavery, and as a sign that ye be really free, ye shall be naked in your rites, and ye shall dance, sing, feast, make music, and love, all in my praise.

6. For mine is the ecstasy of the spirit, and mine also is joy on earth, for my law is Love unto all beings.

7. Keep pure your highest ideal. Strive ever toward it. Let naught stop you or turn you aside: For mine is the secret which opens upon the door of youth: & mine is the cup of the wine of life: and the cauldron of Cerridwen: which is the holy grail of immortality.

8. I am the gracious goddess who gives the gift of joy unto the heart of man: upon earth, I give the knowledge of the spirit eternal: & beyond death I give peace & freedom: & reunion with those who have gone before: Nor do I demand ought in sacrifice: for behold: I am the mother of all living, and my love is poured out upon the earth.

9. Hear ye the words of the Star Goddess, she in the dust of whose feet are the hosts of heaven: whose body encircleth the universe.

10. I who am the beauty of the green Earth: and the white moon amongst the stars: & the mystery of the waters: & the desire of the heart of man: call unto thy soul: arise & come unto me.

11. For I am the soul of nature who giveth life to the universe: from me all things proceed: & unto me all things must return: before my face: beloved of gods & men: thine innermost divine self shall be enfolded in the rapture of the infinite.

12. Let my worship be within the heart that rejoiceth: for

behold: all acts of love & pleasure are my rituals: & therefore let there be beauty and strength: power & compassion: honour & humility, mirth and reverence: within you.

13. And thou who thinkest to seek for me: know that thy seeking & yearning shall avail thee not: unless thou know the mystery: that if that which thou seekest thou findest not within thee: thou wilt never find it without thee.

14. For behold: I have been with thee from the beginning: & I am that which is attained at the end of desire.
   (Source: Gardner's own 1957 *Book of Shadows*, private collection of Richard and Tamara James / Wiccan Church of Canada, Toronto, pp. 15-20)

This isn't a philosophical text because there are no arguments, explanations, or interpretations here. There's only strongly asserted propositions. Hence we are still dealing with the same problem we encountered when trying to read the philosophical content of works of poetry. Indeed the Charge was originally intended for use in magical practice. It is a speech recited by a priestess during a ritual called 'drawing down the moon', in which the priestess invokes the spirit of the goddess in her body and then recites these words. So the Charge is treated as the word of the goddess herself. In that respect, it is possible to think of the Charge as a kind of Wiccan 'revelation' or 'scripture': a work of literature written by a human being but inspired by, or in some way attributable to, a deity. But supposing we ignored that possibility for now, and just looked at what the text actually says, line by line. What do we find?

1. An introductory proclamation which asserts that the goddess is one being, known by many names. Gardner and Valiente probably borrowed this from Universalism and Theosophy, and perhaps also from the works of

occult novelist Dion Fortune (whose proverb 'All gods are one god' remains a standard motto in the movement), and from the revelation of Isis in the second century Roman novel, *The Metamorphosis*, by Apuleius.

2. A factual error: the city of Sparta is in the region of Lacedemon, not the other way around. This line is usually omitted from other published versions of the text.

3. An association between the Goddess and the moon, which reads almost word for word the same as certain lines in Charles Leland's *Aradia: Gospel of the Witches* (1899), a text which claims to report the teachings of a hereditary witch from Tuscany whom Leland had befriended.

4. The Goddess is a teacher and a muse.

5. An association between nudity and freedom. Gardner was an enthusiastic naturist, and at one time the manager of a nudist camp north of London. This line also asserts five 'sacraments', of a sort: five inherently pleasurable activities which the goddess proclaims are the primary activities of Her worship. These sacraments are perhaps comparable to the five Panchamakara of Tantra: bread, meat, wine, fish, and sexual intercourse.

6. A statement of universal brotherly-sisterly love, perhaps comparable to the Biblical command to 'love your neighbour as yourself'. (c.f. Leviticus 9:18, Mark 12:31)

7. An assertion of the importance of the virtues of will and perseverance.

8. Various claims about the generosity of the goddess, including the claim that she does not require sacrifice. This line is clearly borrowed from Crowley's *Book of the Law* (specifically chapter 1 line 58) and is often interpreted to mean that service to the goddess must not be burdensome or strenuous; rather, it should be joyful. (cf. §5 above, and §12 below)

9. Another introductory proclamation, which also asserts the universalism of the goddess, this time elevating her presence to the immensity of the stars.
10. A statement of pantheism, as well as an invitation to enter a relationship with the goddess.
11. Another statement of pantheism, which also asserts that the goddess dwells within the human soul as well as within the natural world.
12. A statement that the goddess is worshipped through activities which are pleasurable and self-rewarding. Also, eight character-virtues, organized into four pairs of co-defined opposites, are asserted here, and the committed goddess-worshipper is asked learn them and live by them.
13. A statement of immanence and perhaps of humanism. Alongside the pantheism of §10 and §12, and the universalism of §9, the goddess asserts that her presence also dwells within the human soul.
14. A concluding statement, which also reasserts the presence of the goddess in the human soul.

So there you have it: The Charge of the Goddess asserts universalism, pantheism, immanence, virtue ethics, neighborly love, intelligent self-interest, a little bit of humanism, and some good old fashioned hedonism. A fitting testament, perhaps, for a self-consciously pagan movement.

Interestingly, almost all of these ideas were in some way represented in the ancient pagan world. Plato and Aristotle taught virtue ethics, although they had a different list of virtues. Aristotle also taught the importance of intelligent self-love. The Epicureans taught a kind of hedonism, and the Stoics taught pantheism and universalism. The one idea which is present in the Charge, but not well represented in ancient pagan sources, is the notion of immanence, although immanence is arguably a quality of pantheism. Finally, and I think very importantly, the text asserts the existence of a god who is female. This is the most visible difference between paganism and Christian scripture. And as we shall see, the pantheism and the femininity of the deity will become extremely important to the next generation of twentieth century pagans.

But before we get that far, we should also observe a moral statement which Valiente and Gardner included in the foundations of Wicca. This moral statement is known as The Wiccan Rede, and here are Valiente's own words to explain it:

Witches in general are inclined to accept the morality of the legendary Good King Pausol, 'Do what you like so long as you harm no one.' This idea has been put into a rhymed couplet called the Wiccan Rede:

Eight words the Wiccan Rede fulfil:
An it harm none, do what ye will...

This quite honestly seems to me to be the only moral code that really makes sense. If everyone lived by it, would not the world be a very different place? If morality were not enforced by fear, by a string of Thou-shalt-nots; but if, instead, people had a positive morality, as an incentive to a happier way of living? It is curious how people seem to accept morality as a system of not doing things, rather than doing them. (Valiente, *Witchcraft for Tomorrow*, pg. 41)

As for the things that we should do, instead of not do, we have the dancing, singing, feasting, music-making, love-making, and other acts of love and pleasure mentioned in the Charge of the Goddess. Yet Valiente and Gardner also attributed a special meaning to the word 'will'. We saw part of that special meaning in Schopenhauer and Nietzsche. But they were also using the word in much the same way that occultist Aleister Crowley used it. Here is how Valiente explained it:

...by 'Do what thou wilt' he [Crowley] did not mean merely 'do as you like', but that people should find out what their true will really is and then do that and nothing else. He said that if everyone did that, there would be no trouble in the world, because people's true wills were in harmony with each other and with the course of nature. The will to crime, for instance, was a false will, born of a dis-ease of the spirit. Because of centuries of repression, people have lost the knowledge of their original nature. Their true will is the essential motion of their being, the orbit of that star which the Book of the Law declares every man and every woman to be... Such a teaching has even acquired for itself a theological name: antinomianism. As Sir John Woodroffe has pointed out in his book *Shakti and Shakta*, it is particularly associated with pantheism, the belief that God is all and all is God. (Valiente, *ibid*, pg. 43-4)

Both Valiente and Gardner were personally acquainted with Crowley, and his influence on the new pagan movement is arguably just as important. We will look at him directly in a moment, but to put him in context we should say a few words about:

§ 42. The Ceremonial Magicians

The practice of magic, whether it be divination, or conjuration, or whatever, is forbidden by the Bible and by the Koran. Yet this has never stopped good Christians and good Muslims from trying to manipulate people and events using psychic powers. Historically, paganism is strongly associated with the practice of magic; and the history of ceremonial magic is long, and admittedly quite fascinating. But practicing magic, by itself, does not make one a pagan. Indeed one can practice magic and continue to subscribe to the Judeo-Christian world view. For example, when the Elizabethan playwright Christopher Marlowe (1564-1593) put a conjuration ritual on the stage in his play *Doctor Faustus*, the ritual works because it is a straight-up inversion of the Christian world view. The demon Mephistopheles appears because, as the character explains, 'when we hear one rack the name of God, abjure the Scriptures and his Saviour Christ, we fly in hope to get his glorious soul... Therefore the shortest cut for conjuring is stoutly to abjure the Trinity and pray devoutly to the prince of hell.' (Marlowe, *Doctor Faustus*, III.52-59)

Ceremonial magic organizations such as the Rosicrucians, and the Hermetic Order of the Golden Dawn, were influenced by Jewish, Christian, and Islamic mysticism, Neo-Platonism, Gnosticism, and the mythologies of various pagan cultures, especially Egypt. It's a very eclectic, very syncretic mix; and much of the intellectual work that trainees in these groups must undergo involves finding the unifying concepts and experiences in this huge array of sources. Probably the most important single influence is Jewish Kabbalah. As Israel Regardie (1907-1985) wrote in *The Complete Golden Dawn System of Magic*, the Kabbalah was 'first taught by God to a select company of angels, who formed a theosophic school in paradise. After the Fall [of Adam and Eve] the angels most graciously communicated this heavenly doctrine to the disobedient children of earth, to furnish the protoplasts with the means of returning to their pristine nobility and felicity. From Adam it passed over to Noah, and then to Abraham, the friend of God, who emigrated with it to Egypt...' (pg. 32-3)

The basic idea of ceremonial magic is that God transmits his presence, laws, knowledge, and love to the universe through a series of ten stages called Sephiroth. These Sephiroth are accessible to a trained magical mind, and can be used to manipulate events on earth by magic, and also to help progress the magician closer to enlightenment. It seems to me that the two most important philosophical propositions inherent in ceremonial magic are monotheism and humanism. For instance, the

Manifesto of Rosicrucianism (2001) states that, 'As for our conception of spirituality, it is based, on the one hand, upon the conviction that God exists as an Absolute Intelligence having created the universe and everything therein; and on the other hand, on the assurance that each human being possesses a soul which emanates from God.' This the authors assert to be a 'spiritualistic humanism.' (pg. 7) Regardie also declared that the practice of magic has a humanist objective:

> Initiation is the preparation for immortality. Man is only potentially immortal. Immortality is acquired when the purely human part of him becomes allied to that spiritual essence which was never created, was never born, and shall never die. It is to effect this spiritual bond with the highest, that the Golden Dawn owes all its rituals and practical magical work. (*The Complete Golden Dawn*, pg. 5)

Notice the strongly Neo-Platonic feeling here, in which the 'spiritual essence' of each human being is effectively eternal, having had no beginning, and heading toward no end.

Aside from Regardie, the most influential occultist writers in the period are MacGregor Mathers (1854-1918), Eliphas Levi (1810-1875), William Westcott (1848-1925), Dion Fortune (1890-1946), Aleister Crowley (1875-1947) and A.E. Waite (1857-1942). The last character in this list is the designer of the first commercially mass-produced Tarot deck: the Rider-Waite deck. Anecdotal accounts of the lives of some of these figures, and also the life of Doreen Valiente herself, suggest they were consulted or employed by British military intelligence. Sometimes it is speculated that there are occult secret society connections in the security service hierarchy. I'm inclined to think this something of a conspiracy. If occultists were ever valuable to governments, it would have been because of their experience handling complex relations of words, languages, symbols, and numbers. This made them excellent natural code breakers. But nowadays the best code breakers are computer nerds.

But enough of context. We were just talking about the 'morality of the will'. So let's look at the work of the most influential and famous, or perhaps infamous, of the ceremonial magicians. It's his notion of the will, more than anyone else's, which is embedded in the Wiccan Rede.

§ 43. Aleister Crowley (1875-1947)

Aleister Crowley, whose own mother in frustration used to call him 'The Beast' when he was a child, and who as an adult called himself the same thing as a badge of honor. Raised into an economically privileged family of conservative Plymouth Brethren Christians, he soon demonstrated an enquiring mind, as well as a penchant for rebellion. He studied philosophy at Cambridge University for a while, and became involved with various occult societies such as the Golden Dawn. He also experimented with polyamory and homosexuality at a time when such acts could still land one in jail, and he also experimented with heroin and other drugs. In effect, he made his lifestyle into an act of rebellion against the puritanical morality of his childhood, although his patrician wealth and status protected him from many of the consequences of his actions. In April of 1904, while visiting Egypt with his wife Rose, and just after exploring the interior of the Great Pyramid with her, he claimed to have heard a disembodied supernatural voice speak to him. The voice identified itself as 'Aiwass the Minister of Hoor-paar-kraat' (that is, the minister of the Egyptian god Horus), and the voice dictated to Crowley a book which he later published as *The Book of the Law*. This book became the central text of several new occult religious communities which Crowley founded, including the Ordo Templi Orientis, the A.·.A.·., the Ecclesia Gnostica Catholicae, and the Order of Thelema. By the way, the word for a person who follows the teachings of Crowley is a Thelemite.

Aside from his literary output on esoteric and occult subjects, which was quite voluminous, Crowley was also an accomplished mountaineer, and a master of the game of chess. And in his life he visited numerous countries in Africa, Asia, and Europe. I suppose it could be said of him that he was, in his time, one of the world's most 'interesting' men.

Crowley's followers generally agree his most important text is *The Book of the Law*. And the most important of Crowley's ideas which appears in *The Book of the Law*, and the idea he spent much of the rest of his life further exploring, is the notion of the True Will. The words 'true will' do not actually appear in that text, but we do find statements of the basic idea there, such as: 'Do what thou wilt shall be the whole of the Law.' (1.40) and 'There is no law beyond Do what thou wilt.' (3.60) It is an idea having to do with ethics, but I say that with qualification: for in one of Crowley's own commentaries on *The Book of the Law, The New Comment* (circa 1921), he wrote that, 'Ethics is balderdash. Each Star must go on its own orbit. To hell with 'moral principle'; there is no such thing.' (*The Law is for All*, II.28) But the True Will is an idea having to do with how people should live, nonetheless. My reading here follows Crowley's own interpretation in an essay entitled 'Duty'. (*Magick*, Book 4, Appendix 1) In general, the True Will is the idea that nobody and nothing should be permitted to interfere with one's freedom to live as one wishes: as it says in *The Book of the Law*: 'The word of Sin is Restriction'. (1.41) And in order to live in accord with one's own will, one must be able to resist interference from other people, and so one must be strong: 'Wisdom says: be strong!... But exceed! exceed!' (2.70-71) There is a minor moral warning against interfering with other people's exercise of True Will: 'Beware lest any force another, King against King! Love one another with burning hearts...' (2.24) And there is also a minor moral note about the potential for spiritual greatness within every person: 'Every man and every woman is a star.' (1.3) From those propositions we might derive every person's entitlement to basic respect. But there is also an endorsement for hardness and for disdaining those who are weak-willed or downtrodden: 'We have nothing with the outcast and the unfit: let them die in their misery. For they feel not. Compassion is the vice of kings: stamp down the wretched & the weak: this is the law of the strong: this is our law and the joy of the world.' (2.21) Indeed there is a suggestion that those who pity the weak or show mercy to others should be attacked with violence: 'Mercy let be off; damn them who pity! Kill and torture; spare not; be upon them!' (3.18) And yet there is also the stuff of romantic tragedy here, for instance in the note that those who exercise their True Will eventually bring about their own undoing, or even their own death: 'Strive ever to more! and if thou art truly mine – and doubt it not, an if thou art ever joyous! – death is the crown of all.' (2.72) But a death which follows as the culmination of a life of True Will is glorious: 'The expiration is sweeter than death, more rapid and laughterful than a caress of Hell's own worm. Oh! thou art overcome: we are upon thee; our delight is all over thee: hail!' (2.63-4) Shades of Graves are audible in that last note.

In sum, the True Will is the idea that people should live in whatever way they wish. Yet as most of Crowley's supporters argue, the True Will is to be distinguished from ordinary practical desires, and distinguished from ordinary selfishness. It is more like the calling of destiny, or the will of God. As observed by occultist and Crowley interpreter Lon Milo DuQuette, a person who lives in accord with True Will has fit themselves into their own proper place in the universe. (DuQuette, *The Magick of Aleister Crowley*, p.12) And that's an interesting and respectable idea. As we have seen, Doreen Valiente understood the idea of the True Will much the same way.

It's interesting stuff; but much of it leaves me unsatisfied. First of all, the trouble with philosophical claims founded in mystical experience is that anyone can make a counter-claim founded in a mystical experience of his or her own. And not all such claims can live in peace and harmony with each other. Groups and communities often split, often angrily, over differing claims about the authority and authenticity of differing mystical visions and the people who have them. In December 1974, for example, a woman from Cincinnati named Nema (a 'magical' name) claimed to have received a new message from Aiwass, and an updated Book of the Law. She also declared that there would be an Age of Maat, which would run concurrently with Crowley's Age of Horus. This produced controversy in her community, as most Thelemites refused to accept that her mystical experience was genuine. (Laubach, Marty (of Marshall University), 'The Epistemology of Esoteric Knowledge', unpublished mss., 2005; also c.f. Nema, 1983, *Cincinnati Journal of Ceremonial Magick* 1(5), pp. 6-9)

The reliability and acceptability of mystical experiences, as foundations for philosophical claims, almost always becomes a matter of social and political negotiation and conflict. And for bargaining chips, people put their own and each other's reputations and loyalties on the line.

Second, we should ask: just who was Aiwass? Commentators and interpreters of Crowley's own work, notably Crowley's own student Israel Regardie, have observed that the text is so close to Crowley's own style that Crowley himself should be considered the sole author. Others have suggested that 'Aiwass' is a manifestation of Crowley's own soul, on a higher plane. In that respect it is possible to read the Book in much the same way I suggested one should read Walt Whitman's *Song of Myself*. Crowley said Aiwass was his personal guardian angel. Personally, I think the name 'Aiwass' is something of a practical joke. It's pronounced exactly the same as the words 'I was': and thus if someone were to ask, 'Who was the author of the book?', Crowley could answer, 'I was!' Crowley's books are veritably drizzled with such practical jokes like that. (And that is not a criticism.) The title of one of his better books of occult teachings, *The Book of Lies* (1913), is another one, because it casts the contents of the entire text into logical paradox. But we should remember Toland's claim that mystical revelations should be cast into ordinary sentences. And at the end of the day mysticism is not philosophy, however much mystics might want to claim the prestige of the word 'philosophy' for themselves. The mere fact that a book might have been dictated by a supernatural being tells us nothing, one way or another, about whether the book is worth reading. Philosophical propositions have to be taken on their own merits.

Philosophically, almost all of Crowley's best ideas had already been presented by other writers. His famous affirmation of the potential for greatness in the human soul, 'Every man and woman is a star', appears in the works of Paracelsus, the mediaeval alchemist and physician. The practical side of the True Will had already been said before, and better, by Friedrich Nietzsche and Arthur Schopenhauer. Valiente observed that the spiritual side of the idea also had a respectable antiquity:

'Do what thou wilt' is by no means new, and was not invented by him. Long ago, Saint Augustine said, 'Love, and do what you will.' The initiate of ancient Egypt declared: 'There is no part of me that is not of the gods.' The pagan Greeks origi- nated the saying: 'To the pure all things are pure.' The impli- cation is that when one has reached a high stage of spiritual development and evolution one has passed beyond the comparatively petty rules of religion and society at some particular time and place, and may indeed do what one wills, because one's true will is then knowable, and must of its own nature be right. The Upanisads or sacred scriptures of ancient India tell us that the known of Brahman is beyond both good and evil. (Valiente, *Witchcraft for Tomorrow*, pg. 44)

This would not be such a big deal if Crowley cited his sources: but instead he claimed to have received these ideas in a personal supernatural revelation. The only part of Crowley's work which seems to me genuinely original is the cloth of occultism and magic in which he dresses everything. Indeed the claim that *The Book of the Law* was transmitted to him by a spiritual being is just such a dressing. He even declared that the name of his god is an affirmation of hedonism: 'Hoor [the Egyptian god Horus] hath a secret fourfold name: Do What Thou Wilt.' (*The Book of Lies*, pg. 14) Ethical hedonism elevated to the level of a cosmic law – that is Crowley.

In a treatise on ceremonial magic he wrote that 'it is by freeing the mind from external influences, whether causal or emotional, that it obtains power to see somewhat of the truth of things.' (*Magick*, pg. 7) If his behavior is taken as a model of that premise, it seems he often counted 'basic human decency' among those external influences. He used to stick his friends with his hotel and restaurant bills, for instance; he also bound and tortured some of his concubines. Valiente, who knew him personally, regarded him as a scoundrel: 'Crowley was a male chauvinist pig of the crudest kind.' (Valiente, *Ibid*, pg. 43) Although to be fair, Valiente also noted that one can admire an idea while at the same time disliking the person who invented the idea. And Crowley also endured a few harmful consequences from his lifestyle. He contracted gonorrhea from a prostitute, for instance; he also spent much of his life addicted to heroin.

Philosophically, some lines of *The Book of the Law* are, at face value, unapologetically anti-philosophical. For instance the text brazenly declares that those 'who doth not understand these runes... shall perish with the dogs of Reason.' (2.27) The text also maligns the asking of the question 'why?' (2.39-31), and also states that 'reason is a lie'. (2.32) Similarly *The Book of Lies* says: 'The slaves of reason call this book Abuse-Of-Language: they are right.' (pg. 58) Remembering the Principle of Charity, I might be persuaded to believe that Crowley's disparagements of reason are actually statements about the importance of mystical experiences which cannot be expressed in words. I agree that we would be wrong to toss all our mystical experiences into the rubbish bin. But I also find that if you cannot put your experiences into words, it is possible to doubt that you fully understand your own experiences. Indeed it is possible to doubt that you are experiencing anything *meaningful* at all. Where language may seem to fail, new words may be coined and new songs sung. For language is an ever-changing thing, and it evolves over time so that human knowledge and human expressive potential may evolve too. What makes a spiritual experience ineffable is not that it is unspeakable: for even the proposition 'the sacred cannot be spoken' *is an attempt to speak of the sacred*. In my view, what makes the spiritual experience ineffable is that however much we may speak of it, there is always more to say. Crowley himself put such experiences into words, as follows:

...this consciousness of the Ego and the non-Ego, the seer and the thing seen, the knower and the thing known, is blotted out. There is usually an intense light, an intense sound, and a feeling of such overwhelming bliss that the resources of language have been exhausted again and again in the attempt to describe it. It is an absolute knock-out blow to the mind. It is so vivid and tremendous that those who experience it are in the gravest danger of losing all sense of proportion. (*Magick*, pg. 9)

Despite his assertion that the experience exhausts the resources of language, he still put the experience into language!

So why is he so popular among modern pagans? In his own lifetime, he was regarded as witty, charismatic, intelligent, and well-spoken, although also egotistical, arrogant, haughty, and abusive. This kind of combination keeps people guessing, and so keeps them interested and attached. And there is always something attractive and compelling about dangerous people.

Crowley cultivated an aura of dangerousness: for instance he filed two of his front teeth to points. Dangerous people seem powerful, and we are often attracted to that power, and want to be part of it. For those who know him only through his writings and his biography, I think the explanation is that Crowley's writings show him to be very knowledgeable and imaginative. There's no doubt that he had a curious and inquisitive mind. His notion of the True Will seems to offer unlimited validation of whatever way of life you might want to live. As he wrote in one of the rituals in *The Book of Lies*, 'There is no grace; there is no guilt; This is the law: DO WHAT THOU WILT!' (§44, capitalization his.) Furthermore, his work also has a hypnotic quality: he expertly balances coherent argument with occult complexity and nonsensical obscurity. This gets the minds of readers thinking and speculating on their own. And while that can be fun, one must remember Nietzsche's warning: 'Those who know they are deep strive for clarity. Those who would like to seem deep to the crowd strive for obscurity. For the crowd takes everything whose ground it cannot see to be deep: it is so timid and so reluctant to go into the water.' (*The Gay Science* §173)

Unwilling to admit we've been hoodwinked by a practical joke, tricked by pareidolia into seeing patterns that are not there, or perhaps under the influence of peer pressure, we carry on praising Crowley's intellect and vision. But at the end of the day, the Master Therion has no clothes. Let us avoid writers who muddy the waters to make those waters appear deep. But I've probably complained too much about the need to reason about the insights which mysticism provides. So let me introduce you to a writer from around the same time who I think did a much better job.

§ 44. George William 'A.E.' Russell (1867-1935)

George Russell was born in Lurgan, county Armagh, Ireland, and led a varied career as public servant, a newspaper editor, the manager of an agriculture co-operative, and (very briefly) a politician. But he saw himself primarily as an artist and a poet. He also claimed to be a clairvoyant, and as such was briefly associated with the Theosophical Society and the Golden Dawn. His magical writings were often published under the pseudonym A.E. This was actually the result of a typo: Russell wanted to use the pseudonym 'Aeon', a word referring to an almost unimaginably long span of time, and representing for Russell the spiritual quest of the soul. But his first publisher didn't know that, and so corrected what he thought was a spelling mistake. (By the way, this occasionally leads readers to confuse Russell with A.E. Waite, who also published using the same initials.) Russell cultivated a close friendship with the other leading lights of the Irish Literary Revival, including Lady Augusta Gregory and William Butler Yeats; and so his name is among those carved on to the famous Autograph Tree in Coole Park.

Listen to these words from the opening page of his masterwork on mysticism and meaning, *The Candle of Vision* (1918):

> After my year in the city I felt like a child who wickedly stays from home through a long day, and who returns frightened and penitent at nightfall, wondering whether it will be received with forgiveness by its mother. Would the Mother of us all receive me again as one of her children? Would the winds with wandering voices be as before the evangelists of her love? Or would I feel like an outcast amid the mountains, the dark valleys and the shining lakes? (*The Candle of Vision*, pg. 1)

In such artistic terms Russell introduced his topic. The chapter is entitled 'Retrospect', and knowing something of his character and of the Irish landscape where he grew up, it is easy to imagine he is describing an actual event from his childhood. Yet in the next sentence he transforms the experience into an allegory of the journey of the soul, wandering the embodied world like an exile, and due to return to God at the end of life. Virtually all of his text is written like this, as if he had one foot on the land and the other in the sea. Yet he is not writing to impress anyone: it's clear in the text he writes as if he is utterly shocked to discover that not everyone in the world experiences life the same way he does. So he tries to share his experience with gentleness, like a friend rather than a master; but at the same time he relates his experiences with certainty and conviction. Here is an account of what his first mystical experience felt like to him:

> The visible world became like a tapestry blown and stirred by winds behind it. If it would but raise for an instant I knew I would be in Paradise. Every form on that tapestry appeared to be the work of gods. Every flower was a word, a thought. The grass was speech; the trees were speech; the waters were speech; the winds were speech. They were the Army of the Voice marching on to conquest and dominion over the spirit; and I listened with my whole being, and then these apparitions would fade away and I would be the mean and miserable boy once more. (pg. 5-6)

Here we find what might be considered the usual insight of Neo-Platonic mysticism, which is that the visible world is in some sense an illusion, and the true world is something behind or above or beneath it. But part of what makes Russell's account interesting is that he reasons about why he was thrown out of the vision at the end:

> ...such is human nature that I still felt vanity as if this vision was mine, and I acted like one who comes across the treasure-house of a king, and spends the treasure as if it were his own.

We may indeed have a personal wisdom, but spiritual vision is not to speak of as ours any more than we can say at the rising of the sun: 'This glory is mine.' By the sudden uprising of such vanities in the midst of vision I was often outcast, and found myself in an instant like those warriors of Irish legend, who had come upon a lordly house and feasted there and slept, and when they woke they were on the barren hillside... (pg. 7)

So the reason that people who seek spiritual visions fail to find them, or having found them unwittingly banish them, is because they wrongfully conceive that the vision is their own. In fact the vision belongs to everyone and to no one. Notice also, by the way, that in the last lines of that paragraph quoted here, Russell employs a literary reference to Celtic mythology, and not to Hermetic or Cabbalistic symbolism as his peers in the ceremonial magic community would have done. Together with W. B. Yeats and a few others, Russell wanted to create a ceremonial magic society that was founded on Celtic mythology instead of those other influences. *The Candle of Vision* was intended to be one of the group's main handbooks. Lady Gregory's two volumes of Irish mythology, *Cuchullain of Muirthemney* (1902) and *Gods and Fighting Men* (1904) were to be the main textbooks on mythology. The latter text, by the way, was one of the first books to be attacked by critics for spreading 'neopaganism'. But very little came of the Celtic ceremonial magic society in the end, partly because there wasn't much interest in such a society outside Ireland at the time, and because Yeats himself, the literary powerhouse of the group, eventually lost interest in occultism altogether. But that story shall have to be told another day.

The notion of the 'possession' of vision, and the 'possession' of the power to call to mind such correspondences as may aid the search for vision, retains its place in Russell's argument. But such possession is not the same kind by which I could claim to possess a handful of coins in my pocket. It is more like the expanded self of the Atman, the Hindu idea that there is only one soul in the universe and we all possess a piece of it, although we erroneously believe we are all separate from each other.

> I knew that all I met was part of myself and that what I could not comprehend was related by affinity to some yet unrealised forces in my being. We have within us the Lamp of the World; and Nature, the genie, is Slave of the Lamp, and must fashion life about us as we fashion it within ourselves... Then does the universe appear to us as it did to the Indian sage who said that to him who was perfect in meditation all rivers were sacred as the Ganges and all speech was holy. (pg. 18)

Russell's 'Atman', if I may call it that, is described in some places in pantheist terms: 'I believe that most of what was said of God was in reality said of that Spirit whose body is Earth.' (pg. 32) Yet his pantheism is mystical rather than naturalistic: to me it reads like a hybrid of pantheist and Neo-Platonic thought. Yet in most of the text, his interest is not on God, but on the Otherworld, which can be perceived by mystical vision, and which he refers to as 'The Many-Coloured Land'. That land, he says, is our true home. And the material earth, and we ourselves insofar as we are embodied animals dwelling on the material earth, are the dream of the Spirit which dwells in that land. Russell also regularly speaks of how we are 'sinking deeper into the Iron Age': this refers to the last of the ages of the world that Blavatsky spoke of. It's an age in which society and individuals take less and less care of their spiritual selves, and as a consequence grow more and more unhappy as individuals, and societies grow more and more unjust. But the Many-Coloured Land is never far away, and all we need do to reach it again is sharpen the will, and perceive, and remember.

In a chapter called 'Analytic', Russell is at his most philosophical. For there he wonders whether all these magnificent visions are no more than fantasies induced by brain-chemical imbalances. 'But what certainty have you that it is not all fancy, and the visions you speak of were not born in the cloudy hollows of your brain, and are not glorified memories of things you have first seen with the sensual eye, and which were afterwards refashioned in memory?' (pp. 38-39) That is the important epistemic question never raised by Blavatsky, nor Crowley, nor even by Plotinus and the first Neo-Platonists. After a discussion of how 'real' his own visions appear to him, indeed as real as any ordinary sensory impression, he gives his answer:

I ask the doubters of my vision to penetrate a little into the mystery of their own thoughts and dreams before they cry out against me, who for many years travelled far and came upon lovely and inhabited regions to which I would also lead them. I know that my brain is a court where many living creatures throng, and I am never alone in it. You, too, can know that if you heighten the imagination and intensify the will. The darkness in you will begin to glow, and you will see clearly, and you will know that what you thought was but a mosaic of memories is rather the froth of a gigantic ocean of life, breaking on the shores of matter, casting up its own flotsam to mingle with the life of the shores it breaks on. (pg. 46)

In short, to those who say, 'But isn't it all in your head?' his reply is, 'Yes, but it's in your head too, if only you look!' I must admit I don't find this explanation completely satisfying. There are people who do look into their own hearts and minds in precisely the manner Russell suggests, and yet they do not see what he sees. It's such an obvious counter-argument that it's surprising Russell missed it. But it is undeniably philosophical to state that one must do one's own searching and one's own thinking. 'The religion which does not cry out: 'I am to-day verifiable as that water wets or that fire burns. Test me that ye can become as gods.' Mistrust it. Its messengers are prophets of the darkness.' (pg. 20) Elsewhere in the text Russell supports the veracity of his visions by invoking syncreticism:

> Whether they are Syrian, Greek, Egyptian or Hindu, the writers of the sacred books seem to me as men who had all gazed upon the same august vision and reported of the same divinity. Even in our own Gaelic wonder tales I often find a vision which is, I think, authentic, and we can, I believe, learn from these voyages to the Heaven-world more of the geography of the spirit... (pg. 149)

This I think opens Russell's argument to some of the same criticisms faced by James Frazer, and which would later be faced by Robert Graves: that his use of the primary sources might be too selective or too reductionist. But, at the end of the day, I think Russell deserves more praise than criticism. Very few people who publish 'travelogues' of the Otherworld are so clear, so artistic, and so personal, about their visions. And very few of them even attempt to analyze and examine their visions by means of reason. (Although I found his attempt somewhat unsatisfying, I'm glad he made the attempt at all – that by itself is more than what most do.) When in a later chapter he offers a 'Celtic Cosmogony', or a Celtic creation story to substitute for that which appears in the book of Genesis or in the Kabbalah, he admits freely that his account is 'a romantic invention' which he has had to 'reconstruct' from various literary and visionary sources. (pg. 152) That kind of direct honesty in a book about clairvoyant visionary experience was very rare in its time. So it is a shame that Russell's mystical works are not much studied anymore. (I suspect the fact that he was Irish may have had something to do with that, but I don't know that for sure.)

For the richness of his literary artistry, and for his abiding honesty, and for the bigness of his heart, I think he deserves much more prominence in the pantheon of mystical writers than he normally receives.

§ 45. The Birth of American Feminist Witchcraft (circa 1970)

Representations of goddesses, alongside male gods or instead of male gods, has a history that goes back to antiquity. There's a scene in the second century Roman novel *The Metamorphosis*, better known as *The Golden Ass,* by Lucius Apuleius, in which the protagonist is accidentally transformed into a donkey by a failed magical spell, but he is saved by the goddess Isis. In a climactic scene, Isis declares: 'I am Nature, the universal Mother, mistress of all the elements, primordial child of time... Though I am worshipped in many aspects, known by countless names and propitiated with all manner of different rites, yet the whole earth venerates me.' (Apuleius, *The Golden Ass,* pg. 183) And then the author includes a long list of the various names by which the goddess is worshipped. It is a fine literary statement of polytheist universalism. But it is the only such statement in all of the ancient Greco-Roman world's literature. (Hutton, *Triumph of the Moon,* pg. 32) It asserts a theological proposition, but it does not argue, examine, nor interpret that proposition. And that is acceptable for art. But it's not enough for philosophy.

The Gnostic traditions had a goddess named Sophia, the personification of the wisdom of the divine. (Barnstone & Meyer, *The Gnostic Bible,* pp. 31-2) But the Gnostics, being a very independently-minded people who rejected the authority of prophets, preachers, and scriptures (even while studying such things very closely), were treated as heretics and their Goddess was cast out of the early Christian pantheon. It should also be noted that the Blessed Virgin Mary, the Mother of Christ, had a relatively minor role in Christianity's pantheon of saints and divine beings, although she was a favorite subject for artists. Mary was not acknowledged in her present exalted position of 'Queen of Heaven' until 1954, when Pope Pius XII issued the encyclical *Ad Caeli Reginam*. For all practical purposes, from the end of the classical pagan period and onward, mainstream Western theology had no goddesses.

To find writers who explore the idea of the goddess more systematically, we have to wait until the twentieth century, when those who advanced full scale critiques of Christianity no longer risked persecution. Thus it was not until 1953 that someone like Simone de Beauvoir could write something like this:

> Man enjoys the great advantage of having a god endorse the code he writes; and since man exercises a sovereign authority over women it is especially fortunate that this authority has been vested in him by the Supreme Being. For the Jew, Mohammedans, and Christians, among others, man is Master by divine right; the fear of God will therefore repress any impulse to revolt in the downtrodden female. (de Beauvoir, *The Second Sex*, pg. 621)

Although de Beauvoir says nothing about the goddess here, she does say a lot about how the idea of a male God is a personification of a patriarchal model of social and political order. Thus de Beauvoir identifies an unjust gender-identity dynamic in the idea of God which hitherto had gone entirely unnoticed in the almost-all-male canon of theologians in the Abrahamic tradition. Some of these theologians deliberately excluded women from their theology: Augustine, for instance, wrote that only men are made in the image of God. Most of them spoke of God as if he was a disembodied mind, and when they bothered to discuss God's gender at all they would typically point to Biblical passages like Galatians 3:28: 'There is neither Jew nor Greek, slave nor free, male nor female, for you are all one in Christ Jesus.' But de

Beauvoir's argument was that even as a disembodied mind, God was still a male mind, and it mattered that he was so, because it left women disempowered. This discovery would be explored deeply by a number of feminist philosophers in the decades to come. Of interest to the topic of this book, however, are the philosophers who began asking, 'What if God is a woman?' And this is not just to ask about whether the God of Abraham has a feminine side. It is to ask whether we have reason to believe that God is, in fact, female, and what that might mean, especially for women. To put it another way: if de Beauvoir's thesis is correct, that the male god is the personification of male social and political power, then might a female goddess be a personification of female power? And what kind of power is that? And what are the consequences for women when that female power is affirmed, and when it is denied?

The most important texts that address these questions include *When God was a Woman* (1976) by Merlin Stone; *The Church and the Second Sex* (1968) and *Beyond God the Father* (1973) both by Mary Daly; *The Spiral Dance* (1979) by Starhawk, *The Holy Book of Women's Mysteries* (1980) by Zsuzsanna Budapest. By the time these works were published the modern pagan movement was well established, and so was the feminist movement, but the two movements had never intersected before. And perhaps that intersection was in some sense inevitable. Abrahamic religion had various female saints, and the Blessed Virgin Mary herself, but no female divinities. On the other hand, the pagan religions did have female divinities – hundreds of them! For pagans, prior to this intersection, it mattered only that one's deities were Greek, or Celtic, or Egyptian, or whatever; afterward, it also mattered that they were male or female. Also, by this time, the feminist movement had evolved into what is now called its second wave. It had expanded its goals from specific legal issues, such as the right to vote, to more comprehensive social issues, such as reproductive rights, violence against women, consciousness-raising (that is, the drawing of public attention to women's experiences), and the overall place of women in society. Second-wave feminists also postulated essential differences between men and women. That is to say, there are irreducible differences in the essence or nature of how women and men think, feel, speak, perceive the world, relate to others, and pursue their lives. (Incidentally, this is why many second-wave feminists, such as Zsuzsanna Budapest, do not accept male-to-female transgendered persons as real women. In the view of second-wave feminists, such persons are still, in essence, men.) Gender essentialism made the idea of a female deity very appealing. To paraphrase Mary Daly, the second-wave feminist thealogians (that's not a spelling error) didn't want to study a God who had undergone a transsexual operation. For 'a trans-sexed patriarchal god is still patriarchal and will function (at least in subliminal or subterranean ways) to serve the interests of the fathers.' (Daly, *Beyond God the Father*, pg. xviii) Rather, the second-wave feminists wanted to study a female Goddess.

Carol Christ, in her essay *Why Women Need the Goddess* (1979), offered what I think is the simplest and most direct explanation of what a Goddess can offer women which a male God cannot. As she explains, the Goddess represents four things. First, 'the acknowledgment of the legitimacy of female power as a benefi-cient and independent power.' The Goddess represents a woman who is the initiator of events in her own life, and is not the subor-dinate of a father, a husband, a king, or a male god. Second, the Goddess offers 'the affirmation of the female body and the life cycle expressed in it.' Christ describes how women's reproductive functions have historically been taken as evidence of their subor-dinate position; the Goddess repositions the reproductive function as 'a direct incarnation of the waxing and waning, life and death, cycles in the universe.' Third, the Goddess represents 'the positive valuation of will in a Goddess centred ritual, especially in Goddess centred ritual magic and spell-casting in womanspirit and feminist witchcraft circles.' This is important because 'women traditionally have been taught to devalue their wills, to believe that they cannot achieve their own will through their own power, and even to suspect that the assertion of [a woman's] will is evil.' Fourth and finally, the Goddess represents 'a revaluation of woman's bonds and heritage', that is, a revaluation of the significance of relationships women have with other women: their sisters, daughters, mothers, grandmothers, and female friends. (Cited in Reid, *Between the Worlds*, pp. 41-55)

Some philosophers in the field, looking to understand the Goddess and what She might mean for women, revived Margaret Murray and Robert Graves' story of the Old Religion. Mary Daly, for her part, also revived the story of the Burning Times, and asserted that around nine million women were killed during that period. And at least one archaeologist, Marija Gimbutas, went looking for physical evidence of the existence of the ancient matriarchal society. She published her discoveries in three books: *The Goddesses and Gods of Old Europe* (1974); *The Language of the Goddess* (1989), and *The Civilization of the Goddess* (1991). The reason for reviving the story of the Old Religion was partly because the story was empowering. If society was once matriarchal, perhaps that might mean there's nothing inevitable, natural, or divinely-ordained about patriarchy. And perhaps society could be matriarchal again some day. The story also gave a sense of urgency to the feminist cause. For it suggested that men had destroyed women's culture in the past – in fact they destroyed it twice, if you count the Burning Times. And they might do so again, if they are unchallenged.

Very quickly, however, Gimbutas was handed criticisms similar to those handed to Murray and to Graves. For instance, it was argued that Gimbutas overlooked evidence of weapons or defensive hill-forts in the Neolithic age, long before the supposed incursions of the war-like, patriarchal Kurgan culture. Evidence was also discovered which showed that the Burning

Times did not kill nine million women, as Daly had asserted. It seems she got that number from nineteenth century writer Matilda Joslyn Gage, who got it from pure conjecture. (c.f. Hutton, *Triumph of the Moon*, pg. 342) The real figure was likely around one-tenth as many, and around one-third of them were men.

It seems to me, however, that the story of the Old Religion could serve a different purpose, not just historical. Whether there once was a goddess-centred matriarchal society, or whether there wasn't, it's surely more important to ask what kind of society *we* want to live in right now. If the story of the Old Religion is rejected as a historical fact, but re-cast as a thought-experiment, then it may help us answer that question. Many male philosophers have produced similar thought-experiments for their own social and political arguments. Thomas Hobbes, John Locke, and Jean-Jacques Rousseau, for example, speculated about life in 'the state of nature', a hypothetical pre-historic time when people had only their human nature, and not governments or laws or institutions, to guide their social interactions. Plato himself designed a theoretical perfect community, the 'Kallipolis', the Beautiful City, in order to explain his ideas about the nature of justice and the origins of injustice. The problem arises when the thought-experiment is assumed to be a historical fact, despite an absence of evidence. This was the problem once faced by the deists of the Enlightenment, as we saw in a previous chapter. It is the problem faced by any feminist today who assumes the story of the Old Religion is a fact of history. The most recent scholarly work to attack the story is *The Myth of Matriarchal Prehistory* (2000) by Cynthia Eller. Her argument was not just that there's no good evidence for such a comprehensive, Europe-wide ancient matriarchy. It was also that attachment to the belief in that ancient matriarchy, as an historical fact, will hurt the cause of feminism. I agree that as a fact of history, the story of the Old Religion as it is normally presented is mostly false. There were a few ancient societies that accorded a lot of political power to women: the Iroquois, for instance, or the Navajo in what is now called the Four Corners area of the American Southwest, or possibly the society of the Greek island of Lesbos during the Bronze Age. The Celts had prominent female chieftains, and their Druids were certainly not an all-male priesthood. But none of these were pure-type cases of what writers like Graves, Daly, and Gimbutas had in mind. But as a thought-experiment about what human society could be like, when grounded in honest observations about human psychology, physiology, language, and so on, I think the story of the Old Religion may be very useful. It could be the feminist and pagan version of Thomas Hobbes' state of nature hypothesis, or John Rawls' original position. Susan Griffin's *Woman and Nature* (1978) treats the story that way. So does Monique Wittig's poetic appeal to women to visualize the Old Religion, and to reclaim it, partially by an act of invention:

> There was a time when you were not a slave, remember that. You walked alone, full of laughter, you bathed bare-bellied. You say you have lost all recollection of it, remember... you say there are no words to describe it, you say it does not exist. But remember. Make an effort to remember. Or, failing that, invent. (cited in Reid, pg. 45)

It's the last sentence in that passage which makes me think of the story of the Old Religion as a thought-experiment. It leaves aside the murky business of claiming a history which might never have existed. In this way, invention might serve as a way to 'remember' that which cannot be remembered because it didn't happen, or because centuries of patriarchal oppression have wiped the memory away. It allows us to invent a story about what life might be like if there was no gender inequality or oppression, or (in accord with the ideas of radical feminism) if women held the highest positions of power, or if women's views

prevailed in matters which affected women. As a thought experiment, the story becomes an act of will and imagination which
allows us to explore possibilities, build arguments, and experiment with practical activist goals.

To me, two things stand out from this discussion of the importance of the goddess. The first is that pagan philosophy from the
dark ages until the middle of the twentieth century had been
about only three things: pantheism, Neo-Platonism, and
Humanism; corresponding to the earth, the gods, and the soul.
Now it could also be about a fourth thing: *power*, especially the
dynamics of male and female power, and the just and unjust
exercise of political power. With the introduction of this fourth
theme, amorphous ideas which hitherto had dominated pagan
thinking about ethics, like the utilitarianism of the Wiccan Rede,
or the quasi-hedonism of Crowley's Law, grew to include specific
moral and political causes which concern the whole of humanity.
It is perhaps not too surprising that power became such a central
concern in pagan thinking. Feminists found that women have
rather little power in society, and often rather little power in their
personal lives. Pagans also found that although they were well
established by the 1970s, they remained in the minority; and at
the time of writing, paganism is still a minority religion.
Questions about the exercise of power are almost always of
supreme importance to those who have little or no power of their
own. Thus the task of feminism has ever been to understand and
to criticize the world views which justify male power, and which
justify men's dominance in political, economic, academic, and
other social spheres. It is also to advance, in theory and in
practice, alternative world views which, at the very least, would
not justify the male monopoly on various forms of power. From
the 1970s onward, pagan philosophy began to take on that task as
another of its own tasks. And now, questions of power and
privilege, oppression and liberation, and their spiritual dimensions, remain major themes in the movement's internal dialogues.

If modern paganism ever acquired serious political and economic power, such as that which is presently enjoyed by groups like the Mormons, Jehovah's Witnesses, or Scientology, I am sure its internal dialogue would be very different.

The second thing which really stands out to me, when I study the intersection between feminism and modern paganism, is that when these two communities adopted each other, pagan philosophy was rescued from the realm of mere propositions. Feminist philosophers systematically observed and questioned reality, built arguments about their discoveries, articulated criticisms of each other's arguments, and improved and expanded the best arguments of their peers. Thus they created a stream of thought that deserves to be called a developing critical tradition. One might object to some of the conclusions of this tradition, such as the gender-essentialism of the second wave. But the point is that those conclusions were arrived at by a systematic process of reasoning, and to object to those conclusions is to participate in the same process. And that is precisely how developing critical traditions begin. After Justinian closed the philosophy schools in the fourth century, pagan philosophy lost its access to institutions, and thus lost its capacity to sustain a developing tradition. But in the 1970s, with the introduction of second-wave feminism, that capacity returned. Some feminists resisted the notion that their work involved systematic reason. Mary Daly, for instance, declared that rationality itself was an instrument of patriarchal oppression: 'One of the false gods of theologians, philosophers, and other academics is called Method... under patriarchy, Method has wiped out women's questions so totally that even women have not been able to hear and formulate our own questions to meet our own experiences.' (Daly, *Beyond God the Father*, pp. 11-12) I think it plainly true that a narrow-minded use of rationality can restrict what questions can be asked, and limit the means to obtain answers. But Daly has a Method of her own, which includes its own set of questions, observations, arguments, and purposes, intelligently and reasonably applied. And so I think that contrary to her own assertion she was not abandoning rationality at all. She was liberating it from a long-established prejudice which mistook male thoughts for the whole of thinking itself.

I should wrap up this chapter by observing that not all feminist philosophy is pagan, and that not all pagan philosophy is feminist. But there is a large region of overlap between the two, and that region continues to produce interesting thinking. As we will soon see, the pagan movement in the 1970s was also intersecting with another activist movement: environmentalism. Feminism itself also intersected with environmentalism, resulting in a stream of thought called ecofeminism. Also, it's worth noting that in the late 1980s and early 1990s, feminist philosophy birthed a third wave. Taking into account the insights of postmodernism, the third wave rejected the gender essentialism of the second wave, and considered how ethnicity, class, and sexual identity affected women's experiences. It also considered the situation of other marginalized groups: people of color, people with disabilities, and gays and lesbians and transgendered persons. An exploration of third wave feminism is beyond the scope of this book. So let's turn to the other intersection that I mentioned: environmentalism.

§ 46. The Rise of Eco-Spirituality

Ancient paganism often worshipped deities who lived in the natural features of the world: mountains, lakes, trees, caves, the sun and moon, and so on. As observed by historian James Rives, ancient people sometimes worshipped the actual features of their natural landscapes too.

> The idea that different deities had different spheres of power is a familiar one... but Artemidorus includes in his list not only Poseidon but also 'the Sea itself': Poseidon falls into the

category of gods perceptible by the intellect, and the Sea into that of gods perceptible by the senses. In other words, he treats the Sea, the actual sea that people can see and feel and taste, just as much a god as Poseidon, 'the god of the sea'. And not only the Sea, but the Sun, the Moon, the Winds, the Rivers, and so on. (Rives, *Religion in the Roman Empire*, pg. 15-6)

Rives also notes that religious devotion to natural immensities wasn't just a figure of speech: 'Votive dedications to the Sun and the Moon, to Heaven and Earth, and to Storms and Winds indicate that people actually invoked these deities in prayer and believed that they responded.' (*ibid* pg. 16) And ancient people also worshipped abstractions in the same way. Fortune was treated as a divinity distinct from the Three Fates, the gods of fortune. And Love was a divinity distinct from Aphrodite, the goddess of love.

But by the late Roman period the eye of piety had mostly turned away from the earth. In the fifth century, the Roman philosopher Boethius wrote: 'Creation is indeed very beautiful, and the countryside a beautiful part of creation...' But we are not to take the beauty of Creation as an object of spiritual interest or worship, nor even of moral concern, because 'not one of these has anything to do with you, and you daren't take credit for the splendour of any of them... You are, in fact, enraptured with empty joys, embracing blessings that are alien to you as if they were your own.' (Boethius, *The Consolation of Philosophy*, pg. 66) And if one took too much interest in the natural world, then one might be accused of paganism, because 'the heavens are less wonderful for their foundation and speed than for the order that rules them.' (pg. 92) This remained the prevalent attitude toward the earth among philosophers for more than a thousand years.

Then Jean Jacques Rousseau happened, followed by the pantheists of the Enlightenment, followed by the Romantic poets, with their desperate longing for a new aesthetic of the immensity. And the prevailing attitudes about the moral and spiritual significance of the earth began to change. Then Emmerson, Thoreau, and Muir happened, and the whole company of American Transcendentalists. And the letters, speeches, and biographies of nineteenth century Aboriginal people like Chief Seattle, Chief Luther Standing Bear, and Chief Joseph were becoming more and more available in print. They expressed a respect for the earth which non-Natives were beginning to admire. Of course, this may have been because Aboriginal cultures no longer posed much of a military threat, and so it was 'safe' to think of them positively. The image of the 'noble savage', just then taking hold in the popular imagination, was just as false and patronising as the image of the 'wild west'. But the words and thoughts of Native people were now being recorded for posterity, and were gathering respect among those who felt that the destruction of Native culture was a terrible tragedy, however few those people may have been at the time.

Then Aldo Leopold (1887-1948), a professor of forestry, wrote *A Sand County Almanac: And Sketches Here and There* (1949; published posthumously) which expressed for the first time in Western philosophy a completely earth-centered moral world view. Others had already written of the moral importance of the natural world, as we have already seen; but Leopold was the first to make a definite moral case against the mistreatment of wild animals, plants, and landscapes.

> All ethics so far evolved to rest upon a single premise: that the individual is a member of a community of interdependent parts. His instincts prompt him to compete for his place in that community, but his ethics prompt him also to cooperate... The land ethic simply enlarges the boundaries of the community to include soils, waters, plants, and animals, or collectively: the land. (cited in Botzler & Armstrong, pg. 413)

And so Leopold calls for a transformation of people's attitudes towards the earth: 'In short, a land ethic changes the role of Homo sapiens from conqueror of the land-community to plain member and citizen of it.' (*ibid*.) The reason that Leopold says it is morally necessary to change our role in the world that way is because humankind already physically depends on the stability and integrity of the biotic environment, mainly through complex inter-connected food chains. 'Land, then, is not merely soil; it is a fountain of energy flowing through a circuit of soils, plants, and animals. Food chains are the living channels which conduct energy upward; death and decay return it to the soil.' (*ibid*, pg. 417) And given that human life and civilization depends upon the health of this circuit of energy, Leopold concludes with this startling and plain-spoken moral proposition: 'A thing is right when it tends to preserve the integrity, stability, and beauty of the biotic community. It is wrong when it tends otherwise.' (*ibid*, pg. 421) Leopold also speculates that the land of his native mid-western United States might not be capable of handling the changes imposed on it by transport, industry, and mechanized farming. This would confer on environmentalists a reputation for being against technology, against scientific progress, and against capitalism, and that reputation, deserved or not, still surrounds them to this day. Indeed a recent critic who felt that Leopold's holistic ethics was a threat to individualism, referred to The Land Ethic as 'not only nonsense, but dangerous nonsense'. (Sumner, Wayne, 1986. 'Review of Robin Attfield's The Ethics of Environmental Concern', *Environmental Ethics* 8:77)

A generation later in the United Kingdom, industrialisation and urban growth and the First World War inspired a literature that condemned English society for being culturally impoverished. Alienation from nature was blamed for this impoverishment. A kind of rustic country simplicity and innocence was seen as the solution: consequently, much of this literature was written for children. Henry Williamson, Kenneth Grahame, C.S.

Lewis, A.A. Milne, Arthur Ransome, J.R.R. Tolkien, and Rudyard Kipling are the most well known English authors who express this idea. Much Irish literature at the time, especially the collections of folk and faerie tales published by Ella Young, Augusta Gregory, and W.B. Yeats, shares the anti-industrial, pro-nature nostalgia. In a lecture that W. B. Yeats delivered in New York in 1904, he said: 'Whenever men have tried to imagine a perfect life they have imagined a place where men plough and sow and reap, not a place where there are great wheels turning and great chimneys vomiting smoke.' (Ellmann, *Yeats*, pg. 116) In Lady Gregory's *Gods and Fighting Men* (1904) there is a retelling of a mythological war between Fionn MacCumhal's Fianna and the army of the 'King of the World', representing a victory of 'nature' over 'civilization', as well as the hope for a politically independent Ireland. The Irish artist and mystic George Russell, writing in *The Candle of Vision*, declared with regret:

> After that awakening earth began more and more to bewitch me, and to lure me to her heart with honied entreaty. I could not escape from it even in that busy office where I sat during week-days with little heaps of paper mounting up before me moment by frenzied moment. An interval of inactivity and I would be aware of that sweet eternal presence overshadowing me. I was an exile from living nature but yet she visited me. (Russell, pp. 11)

Most of this literature can be characterized as 'sentimental' or as 'reactionary', depending on how charitable one wants to be. The excellence of its artistic merit is beyond doubt. Yet its impact on political will, at the time, was minimal. Philosophers, for their part, totally ignored them. So did Gerald Gardner and the other early architects of Wicca. Although their central ritual text identified the Goddess as 'the soul of nature', and although they sometimes performed their ceremonies outdoors, in secluded forest clearings, they generally treated their new religion as something best practiced in a temple.

That would change when the environmental activist movement began. Rachel Carson's *Silent Spring* (1962) is widely regarded as the first major published work to describe an environmental issue as a moral tragedy. In her case the issue was the widespread use of DDT as an agricultural pest-killer. The title referred to the possibility that in the future, a spring season might come without any songbirds remaining alive to herald it since the pesticides will have killed them. Two years later Ruth Harrison published *Animal Machines* (1964) which described factory farming as a morally outrageous exploitation of animals. Then Peter Singer published *Animal Liberation* and *All Animals Are Equal* (both in 1974) and the animal rights movement was fully underway. Charles Reich's revolutionary manifesto of environmental politics, *The Greening of America*, was published in 1970. It argued that an ecological consciousness transformation was in progress in American culture, and that this new consciousness will eventually change the political structure of the world. Meanwhile, scientific reports describing various forms of damage to the earth as a whole, caused by industrial activity, were beginning to reach the mainstream media. In 1971 an article published in *Science* magazine called 'International Environmental Problems – A Taxonomy' speculated that global warming might be a bigger problem than species extinction. (Russell and Landsberg, 'International Environmental Problems – A Taxonomy' *Science*, 25th June 1971, pp. 1307-1314) A second article was published in *Science* a few years later, entitled 'Climatic Change: Are We on the Brink of a Pronounced Global Warming?' (Broeker, W.S. 'Climatic Change: Are We on the Brink of a Pronounced Global Warming?' *Science*, 8th August 1975, pp. 460-463) To my knowledge those articles print the phrase 'global warming' for the first time. The Club of Rome's famous report on 'the predicament of mankind', *The Limits to Growth*, was published in 1972: it predicted that 'if the present growth trends in world population, industrialization, pollution, food production, and resource depletion continue unchanged, the limits to growth on this planet will be reached sometime within the next one hundred years.' (Meadows, *Limits to Growth* pg. 29)

Political activist groups such as Greenpeace, which was originally formed to protest against nuclear bomb tests, started paying close attention to this science, and to other threats to the environment besides nuclear war. And some of the people in these activist groups started to wonder whether there was something religious or spiritual about what they were doing. This curiosity about the spiritual side of environmental activism prompted renewed interest in Thoreau and the nineteenth century American nature writers. Thoreau's books, especially, inspired a 'back to the land' movement in which families and groups of friends sought to live simply and self-sufficiently on organic farming communes. Aboriginal ideas about the sacredness of the land loomed very large among those who saw environmental activism as a spiritual calling, perhaps because in rejecting some of the values of modern Western culture, they felt they had to embrace values from a non-Western culture. (It must be said, however, that they often took Aboriginal ideas without the consent of Aboriginal people.) Eastern ideas like Hinduism, Buddhism, and Taoism, some of which were popularized by rock bands like The Beatles, or soldiers returning from the Vietnam War, also fit this interest in non-Western cultural alternatives. Similarly, the new paganism of writers like Robert Graves and James Frazer offered an earthy pantheon of triple goddesses and dying-and-resurrecting gods who personified natural forces. And it offered a picture of the natural world crowded with spirits and demigods in every hill and river and rock and tree. This was a religious way to think about the interconnectedness of life as described by naturalists like Aldo Leopold. The new paganism definitely belonged to Western culture, but it did not appear to belong to *modern* Western culture – a very important distinction. (The discrediting of the stories of the Old Religion and the Burning Times had not yet escaped academia.) Thus pagan ideas appealed to these activists too. And activist ideas influenced the pagans in return.

An example of this influence can be found in the following ritual declaration which forms part of the standard liturgy of the Order of Bards, Ovates, and Druids. A ritual celebrant holds up a sword and says, 'Whilst this sword is unsheathed, promise you all that the Earth our home and mother shall be protected and illumined by the swords of our spirits and wills.' The other celebrants then place their hands on the sword blade and reply, 'We swear it.' (Nichols, *The Book of Druidry*, pg. 303) As another example, consider how the pagan understanding of magic and ritual had changed. In Crowley's day, magic was strongly characterized by what Starhawk would call power-over: Crowley defined it as 'the art and science of causing change in accordance with Will.' By the early 2000s, leading Wiccan authors such as Vivianne Crowley (no relation) defined it like in the terms of Starhawk's power-with, and Lovelock's Gaia Hypothesis:

Nature creates a biosphere – an interlocking, mutually dependent complex of organisms that cannot exist alone. When one organism becomes too dominant, the balance is lost, and so too is the world. Natural magic adds energy to what we do, but it is not a way to impose our will on the universe in an egocentric effort to make everything go our way... Natural magic is about learning to ride the wave, or as Chinese Taoists would say, traveling the way of the watercourser... Each of us has a purpose and a function, a role in the spiritual growth process of magic is to help us discover what that is. Tis is what some people call finding our True Will. (*The Magickal Life*, pg. 5-7)

The declaration of the first international Earth Day, on 22nd April 1970, is often taken as the occasion which prompted the contemporary pagan movement to re-discover its environmental roots. I don't think that is entirely true. Environmental consciousness had been growing in the minds of practicing Wiccans for at least the previous ten years, although admittedly, that growth was slow. Spiritual yet non-Christian, or only vaguely Christian, ways of thinking about the environment had been available in American culture since Emerson and the Transcendentalists. And Druids had been interested in the nature-based spirituality of pantheism since the time of John Toland. But it is true that the publicity surrounding the first Earth Day helped solidify the place of environmental consciousness in modern pagan thinking. Indeed Earth Day introduced to just about everybody the idea that the earth deserves protection from pollution and destructive forms of resource extraction. But I think a much stronger case can be made that the connection between paganism and environmentalism was made later, by the science of environmental biology, and by the Deep Ecology movement. So let's have a look at:

§ 47. The Gaia Hypothesis

In the early 1970s, the scientists James Lovelock and Lynn Margulis formulated The Gaia Hypothesis. This is a scientific theory which holds that organisms on earth and their physical environments evolve together. Organisms, by using the oceans and soils and atmospheres of their ecosystems to exchange organic compounds, alter those ecosystems to maintain an environment fit for their kind of life. At the same time the physical environment exerts evolutionary selection pressures on organisms. As Lovelock explains it in his own words:

> The Gaia Hypothesis said that the temperature, oxidation state, acidity, and certain aspects of the rocks and waters are at any time kept constant, and that this homeostasis is

maintained by active feedback processes operated automatically and unconsciously by the biota... Life and its environment are so closely coupled that evolution concerns Gaia, not the organisms or the environment taken separately. (*The Ages of Gaia*, pg. 19)

This idea prompted pagans to appreciate, albeit uneasily, the science of environmental biology. Pagans saw in it a solid scientific way to say that 'the earth is sacred' and deserves our respect and protection. Here's part of the story of how that happened. On 6th September 1970, Oberon Zell (b. 1942), the prominent American pagan teacher and the founder of the Church of All Worlds, had a spiritual vision of the Earth as a single organism, and in 1971 he published his thoughts about this vision in Green Egg Magazine, then the most widely circulated and influential American pagan periodical. Here are his words:

...we now realize that the being we have intuitively referred to as Mother Earth, The Goddess, Mother Nature, The Lady, is not merely a mythical projection of our own limited visions, but an actual living entity, *Terrabia*, the very biosphere of Earth, in whose body we are mere cells.... Thus we see that the Humanists are right: God *is* Mankind. Also correct are the Pantheists in their recognition that God is all Nature.
(Tim Zell, 'Biotheology: The Neo-Pagan Mission', *Green Egg*, Vol. IV, No. 41 (Lughnasad 1971), cited in Zell-Ravenheart, ed. *Green Egg Omelette*, pg. 29)

Terrabia, by the way, was Zell's word for the super-organism of the earth. In his article he seems to have thought that Terrabia could be conscious, or that we human beings are the consciousness of Terrabia. 'What, then, is the particular function of Neo-Paganism in the vast organism of Terrabios? As the only cells of the Noosphere yet to recognize the unity of our entire

Biosphere, we are inevitably in the vanguard of the advancing consciousness that will ultimately result in the awakening of the great planetary Mind.' (*ibid* pg. 31)

James Lovelock published his scientific idea in a newspaper about a year later, and followed it with various scientific articles. Zell started using the word 'Gaia', to avoid confusion. Then Lovelock published his first book-length treatments of the idea: *Gaia: A New Look at Life on Earth* (1979), and *The Ages of Gaia* (1988). And in the 1990s Lynn Margulis published her evidence that even at the microbial level, symbiosis (biological co-operation) is a stronger force than competition and aggression. The best of her books, in my view, is *The Symbiotic Planet* (1998). But Zell is wrong to say that he thought of the Gaia hypothesis first. Remarking on the history of the idea, Lovelock wrote:

> The idea that the Earth is alive is probably as old as humankind. But the first public expression of it as a fact of science was by a Scottish scientist, James Hutton. In 1785 he said, at a meeting of the Royal Society of Edinburgh, that the Earth was a superorganism and that its proper study should be physiology. He went on to compare the cycling of the nutritious elements of the soil, and the movements of water from the oceans to the land, with the circulation of blood. (Lovelock, *The Ages of Gaia*, pg. 10)

Actually, even Lovelock is partially wrong here: for as we have seen, John Toland put the idea in print back in 1720. But Toland wasn't a scientist, so the idea was generally ignored by scientists. And to be fair, James Hutton's statement of the idea was ignored for a long time too. But the claim that the earth is alive probably is as old as humankind. In pagan literature it appears in Homeric Hymns, *The Prose Edda*, as we have already noted. In oral traditions, the idea may well be older still.

It's worth emphasizing that Lovelock is a scientist and the

Gaia Hypothesis is a science. *The Ages of Gaia* includes a chapter on 'God and Gaia', in which he expresses his surprise that the theory was interpreted by the public as having to do with religion. He categorically rejects the suggestion that his hypothesis could serve as proof of the Design argument. 'I am happy with the thought that the Universe has properties that make the emergence of life and Gaia inevitable. But I react to the assertion that it was created with this purpose.' (pg. 205) But he accepts that thinking of the earth as a single living system can inspire religious feelings like wonder and celebration. He observes that 'theology is also a science, but if it is to operate by the same rules as the rest of science, there is no place for creeds or dogma.' (pg. 207) This is why, in the epilogue of the book, he states that 'there is no prescription for living with Gaia, only consequences.' (pg. 225) He revealed that his own religious background from childhood was 'an odd mixture, composed of witches, May trees, and the views expressed by Quakers, in and outside the Sunday school at a Friends' meeting house. Christmas was more of a solstice feast than a Christian one.' (pg. 204) But as an adult, his religion is a 'positive agnosticism', in which the idea 'that Gaia can be both spiritual and scientific is, for me, deeply satisfying.' (pg. 217) I think the most that can be safely drawn from this discussion is that it's fine to seek spiritual meaning in the Gaia Hypothesis, but it is probably too soon to declare that the hypothesis is a kind of 'pagan science'. (But I look forward to philosopher Michael Ruse, *The Gaia Hypothesis: Science on a Pagan Planet*, not yet published at the time I write these words.)

§ 48. Arne Naess (1912-2009) and Deep Ecology

Deep Ecology is a philosophical, spiritual, and sometimes political movement which holds, among its first propositions, that the earth and all its constituent ecological relations are inherently morally valuable. Therefore the earth and its ecological relations deserve protection from industrialization, pollution, destructive resource development, urban sprawl, and so on. The name was coined by Arne Naess (1912-2009), the Norwegian philosopher, political activist, author, and mountaineer. In 1973 he published 'The Shallow and the Deep, Long-Range Ecology Movement: A Summary' in the philosophical journal *Inquiry* (a journal which he founded), in which the term appears in print for the first time. But in that article he wrote as if the movement had been in full swing for many years already. I suspect that Naess simply put a name on a critical distinction between 'shallow' and 'deep' thinking about ecology which by then was already part of the regular vocabulary of environmental activists. In his words, the Shallow movement is the 'Fight against pollution and resource depletion. Central objective: the health and affluence of people in the developed countries'. But the Deep movement entails the 'Rejection of the man-in-environment image in favour of the relational, total-field image. Organisms as knots in the biospherical net or field of intrinsic relations.' (Naess, Arne (1973) 'The shallow and the deep, long-range ecology movement. A summary', *Inquiry*, 16:1, 95-100)

Deep Ecology also rests on a set of eight 'platform principles', which were put into their final form by Naess and several associates of his, notably George Sessions and Bill Devall. The eight platform principles are:

1. The well-being and flourishing of human and nonhuman life on Earth have value in themselves (synonyms: intrinsic value, inherent value). These values are independent of the usefulness of the nonhuman world for human purposes.

2. Richness and diversity of life forms contribute to the realization of these values and are also values in themselves.

3. Humans have no right to reduce this richness and diversity except to satisfy vital human needs.
4. The flourishing of human life and cultures is compatible with a substantial decrease of the human population. The flourishing of nonhuman life requires such a decrease.
5. Present human interference with the nonhuman world is excessive, and the situation is rapidly worsening.
6. Policies must therefore be changed. These policies affect basic economic, technological, and ideological structures. The resulting state of affairs will be deeply different from the present.
7. The ideological change is mainly that of appreciating life quality (dwelling in situations of inherent value) rather than adhering to an increasingly higher standard of living. There will be a profound awareness of the difference between big and great.
8. Those who subscribe to the foregoing points have an obligation directly or indirectly to try to implement the necessary changes. (Naess, 'The Deep Ecological Movement: Some Philosophical Aspects' *Philosophical Inquiry*, 8, 1-2 (1986))

Deep Ecology has an important foundation in several spiritual philosophies, and Naess felt that the principles of Deep Ecology are flexible enough to be derived from several world views. 'Those engaged in the deep ecology movement have so far revealed their philosophical homes to be mainly in Christianity, Buddhism, Taoism, Baha'i, or in various philosophies...' (*ibid*) And of those 'various philosophies' Naess especially credited the work of Spinoza, as well as twentieth century figures like Rachel Carson and Aldo Leopold. Naess observed that there was an 'intimate relationship' between Deep Ecology and the Buddhist principles of nonviolence and reverence for life, and so 'sometimes it is easier for Buddhists to understand and appreciate deep ecology than it is for Christians.' Naess also includes Taoism among its intellectual sources 'because there is some basis for calling John Muir a Taoist.' (*ibid*) Basically, the idea is that you can call yourself a deep ecologist if you accept the basic principle of the intrinsic moral worth of life on earth, and if you can see this principle rationally justified by your religious and spiritual world view, whatever that world view happens to be. In this sense Deep Ecology could be called a syncretic philosophy.

Yet Naess provided a world view of his own to support Deep Ecology, and he named it 'Ecosophy T'. The letter 'T' stands for Tvergastein, a cottage in the Hallingskarvet mountain range of Norway, where Naess wrote most of his books. This personal touch also opens the possibility that other supporters of Deep Ecology will have their own kind of Ecosophy. But here is how Naess explained his:

> Ecosophy T has only one ultimate norm: 'Self realization!' I do not use this expression in any narrow, individualistic sense. I want to give it an expanded meaning based on the distinction between a large comprehensive Self and a narrow egoistic self as conceived of in certain Eastern traditions of *atman*. This large comprehensive Self (with a capital 'S') embraces all the life forms on the planet (and elsewhere?) together with their individual selves (*jivas*)... Another more colloquial way to express this ultimate norm would be to say 'Live and let live!' (referring to all of the life forms and natural processes on the planet.) (Naess, *ibid*)

Notice the use of Hindu concepts in Naess' explanation of his own world view. Atman is the Hindu word for the higher cosmic self, which is identical with the Brahman, the soul of the universe, the unchanging highest reality. One's individual being, called the jiva, is only a reflection of the Atman, like light shining from a single facet on the surface of a great jewel. And the 'Self realization!' of Ecosophy T leads to important moral conclusions about how to relate to other living beings:

> ...the higher levels of Self-realization attained by any person, the more any further increase depends upon the Self-realization of others. Increased self-identity involves increased identification with others. 'Altruism' is a natural consequence of this identification. (*ibid*)

This line strongly reminds me of a passage in the *Bhagavad Gita*: 'He whose self is harmonised by yoga sees the Self abiding in all beings and all beings in the Self; everywhere he sees the same.' (6:29) Naess expressed admiration for this line and others like it in the Gita. For him, it expresses the proposition that all living beings are profoundly and irreducibly connected to each other through the natural world. Orthodox Hinduism interprets the passage very differently, of course. But Naess' use of it has precedents: Mohandas Gandhi, for example, also interpreted the passage in political terms. The idea is that if you find yourself spiritually at one with all other living beings on earth, and indeed one with the earth as a whole, then you will feel morally obliged to promote the flourishing of that life, and to protect it from attack.

I am quite convinced that global warming is real, and that it is not natural. It is caused by the things people and their corporations do which create pollution and which damage important climate-regulating ecosystems. The overwhelming majority of qualified scientists agree. Numerous studies of the temperature of earth's oceans and land-surface, such as that which was conducted by the Berkeley Earth Project in 2011 (which collated information from 40,000 weather stations around the world, going back 250 years), found that the earth is, indeed, getting unnaturally warmer. (Black, R. 'Global Warming 'confirmed' by independent study' *BBC News*, 20 October 2011; see also The

Berkeley Earth Project, at berkeleyearth.org) A 2012 study found 13,926 professional scientific articles in peer-reviewed academic journals which accepted the evidence that climate change is caused by human activity, and only 26 which rejected this evidence. (Powell, J. 'The State of Climate Science', *Science Progress*, 15th November 2012)

Allow me to address one of the biggest criticisms of environmentalism, which sometimes attaches to environmental ethics in general. The fourth of Deep Ecology's eight platform principles, the idea that, 'The flourishing of nonhuman life requires such a decrease' in human population, is obviously the most controversial. Now the idea that environmental problems could be solved by reversing the growth of human populations was not new when Sessions and Naess proposed it. Paul Ehrlich described it in a popular 1968 book called *The Population Bomb*. In a chapter called 'A Dying Planet', Ehrlich listed a number of threats to the stability and diversity of global ecosystems, and then concluded that 'the causal chain of the deterioration is easily followed to its source. Too many cars, too many factories, too much detergent, too much pesticide, multiplying contrails [from aircraft], inadequate sewage treatment plants, too little water, too much carbon dioxide – all can be traced easily to too many people.' (Ehrlich, *The Population Bomb*, pp. 66-7) This proposition remains part of the policies of some prominent environmental activist groups even to this day. For example, Dave Foreman, founder of Earth First!, wrote sixteen principles of ecological activism which included: 'A placing of Earth first in all decisions, even ahead of human welfare if necessary', and 'A recognition that there are far too many human beings on earth.' (Foreman, *Confessions of an Eco-Warrior* pp. 25-36) And a trace of it can be found in the same article in which Oberon Zell introduces the Gaia Hypothesis: 'At this moment, in the hour before Dawn, we find Terraba – our Earthly Biosphere, our Great Mother Earth Goddess – is already dying from cancer of the brain. And what is worse, we find that this cancer is ourselves – Mankind.' (*Green Egg Omelette*, pg. 31)

This skirts too close to the edges of misanthropy for my liking. Now the misanthropy is not in the claim that all life on earth is inherently valuable; and it's not that some environmentalists doubt the value of civilization. Thoreau, Muir, and Leopold, had raised such doubts before, without condemning humankind as a cancer. The misanthropy is in the reductionist belief that scaling back human population is *all that we need to do* to solve our problems. Now it's certainly true that the human population is huge, and growing. A prediction made in 2005 said that there will be 8.9 billion of us by the year 2050, and most of this population growth will be in the world's poorest countries. ('40% rise in world population by 2050' *Associated Press* 25 February 2005.) The problem with population as described by Ehrlich, Naess, Foreman, and others, assumes that every human being consumes the same volume of resources and energy. But that assumption is simply false. Rich countries consume more energy and resources per head of population than poor countries. So the problem is not simply how many of us there are. The problem is also the way resource demand and energy consumption is unequally distributed. So when people say all we need to do is reduce the human population, it is as if we just want to prevent people in poor countries from having too many children, so that they will thereby fix the problem for people in rich countries. Thus there's also a hidden element of race and class privilege inherent in this kind of thinking. To reduce it down to the stupidly simplistic problem of 'too many people' is to dress up a resentment of humanity in the fine clothes of environmental care.

But to be fair, these examples of misanthropy are twenty years old or more. Today, there are no disparagements of humanity in the policy statements or the arguments of any environmental organization known to me. And so let me return to the original narrative.

Deep Ecology is a world view which is both a topic of intellectual investigation for professional philosophers, and at the
same time a rallying cry for activists outside the academic
community. That pairing is a rather rare achievement. I've placed
it in this list of pagan philosophies because of the huge influence
it had on the contemporary pagan world view. Its vision of global
spiritual and ecological unity, and its syncreticism, appealed to
pagan pantheist and polytheist feelings. And now, modern
paganism is so deeply intertwined with 'green' thinking that the
two streams of thought are widely regarded as almost the same
thing. A columnist in Britain's *The Independent*, back in 1993, for
example, wrote that 'We're all pagans now':

> Nature, in other words, is the raw material of religion – the
> psychic fuel that powers the religious impulse. In the
> Christian era – which, with less than one-tenth of the
> population attending church, can be said to be receding into
> history – the majesty of nature was seen as reflecting the
> majesty of God, who remained outside the visible world.
> Fewer and fewer of us believe that: we find nature to have
> sufficient meaning in itself. The recent Gaia theory, the idea
> that the earth is a kind of organic being, is a sign of that
> change. What this means, in effect, is that we are all pagans
> now, whether we recognise it or not... (David Nicholson-Lord,
> 'Relax, we're all pagans now' *The Independent*, 20th June 1993)

I cite this example not because it is unique or outstanding, but
rather because it is typical. It represents a widespread
perspective about the nature of paganism which has grown in
influence enough to be very nearly mainstream.

Now the idea that one can derive spiritual inspiration and
fulfillment from a view of the earth need not be a theological
idea, in the sense that it need not have anything to do with God.

Nicholson-Lord observes as much: 'Fortunately, you do not have to be a paid-up member of the Christian ecologists or the ancient Order of Druids to derive pleasure – intense, life-enhancing pleasure – from a piece of woodland, a mountain view, or a wild creature. Nor, any longer, do you have to pretend it is something to do with God.' (*ibid*) This lends flexibility and inclusiveness to the idea. But at the end of the day, the reverence for the earth for its own sake, and the seeking of inspiration in the earth, is idolatry in Abrahamic eyes. And thus, *ipso-facto*, such reverence and seeking is pagan. Now Abrahamic seekers can certainly find ways to see the spiritual importance of the earth, and of activist efforts to protect the earth. Christian writers like Teilhard de Chardin, Bishop Hugh Montefiore, Matthew Fox, Thomas Berry, and Sean McDonagh, have done exactly that. But I think the pagan movement is better postured to understand the spiritual importance of the earth. For in pagan eyes, such reverence and such seeking is not idolatry. Rather, it is the whole point of pantheism. It is perfectly legitimate, and should be encouraged.

§ 49. Stewart Farrar (1916-2000)

Gerald Gardner published parts of *The Book of Shadows* in various forms in his lifetime. But there was no attempt to standardize the text until Stewart Farrar (1916-2000) and Janet Farrar published *Eight Sabbats for Witches* (1981) and *The Witches' Way* (1984). These two books, they claimed, made the entire text of the *Book* available to the whole public for the first time, along with their own commentary about its sources and possible meanings. Lest this create controversy from those who thought the contents of the *Book* should remain private or secret, the Farrars got written permission from Doreen Valiente; and Valiente herself contributed to the commentary as well. *The Witches' Way* included a chapter called 'The Rationale of Witchcraft' in which the Farrars reasoned about the world view presupposed by the spells rituals of the Wiccan path. They concluded that the rationale of Wicca 'rests upon two fundamental principles: the Theory of Levels, and the Theory of Polarity'. The first theory 'maintains that reality exists and operates on many planes', and the second 'maintains that all activity, all manifestations, arise from (and is inconceivable without) the interaction of pairs and complementary opposites – positive and negative, light and dark, content and form, male and female, and so on; and that this polarity is not a conflict between 'good' and 'evil', but a creative tension like that between the positive and negative terminals of an electric battery.' (pg. 106-7) The influence of Blavatsky looms large here, although she is not mentioned by name. Actually this way of thinking would later be satirized by Starhawk as 'attempting to measure a cloud with a ruler' (*The Spiral Dance*, pg. 154) Here is the Farrar's summary comment on the metaphysical world view of Wicca:

> In strict philosophical terms, witches are idealists; for while they believe that every entity or object on the physical plane has its counterparts on the non-material planes, they also believe that there are real entities on the unseen planes which do not have physical forms of their own... But to label witches as idealists, while correct, is perhaps misleading: maybe 'pluralists' would be better. For matter is very real to them; they are lovingly rooted in Nature, 'the Veil of Isis', vibrant with overtones of all the other levels. Tangible Nature is holy to them. (*The Witches Way*, pg. 112-3)

This 'theory of levels' is not a million miles from Plato, after all. But, with the additional claim that 'nature is holy', the correct name for what Farrar is describing here is panentheism.

I have only (briefly!) looked at some of the Farrar's metaphysical views. The text also discusses ethics, mostly in the mode of supporting the Wiccan Rede and the virtue-affirmations of the Charge of the Goddess. It also explores the religious and ritualistic importance of mythology and symbol, mostly leaning on the psychology of Carl Jung. Most of this material was written by Stewart, whose professional training was in journalism and not philosophy. That's probably why his intellectual method usually involved looking for explanations for Wicca's basic teachings, rather than calling those teachings into question, as a philosophy-trained writer might have done. But the range of sources he drew upon for his purpose is very impressive: the philosophies of Plato, Aristotle, Hegel, and Marx; the psychology of Freud and Jung; and of course the mythologies of numerous European and Middle-Eastern societies. The Farrar's early books represent the first serious attempts to reason about what Wicca inherited from Gardner, Valiente, Crowley, and company. And for probably twenty years the Farrar's books were the standard ritual sourcebooks in almost every modern pagan's library. So the reach of their influence is very long indeed.

§ 50. Isaac Bonewits (1949-2010)

The name and influence of Philip Emmons Isaac Bonewits dominated the American pagan community almost as largely as that of the prominent names in American feminist witchcraft. His earliest claim to fame was his reception of the first, and to this day the only, bachelor's degree in magic from an accredited public university. UC Berkeley, which granted him the degree in 1966, was at the time very open-minded about student-defined interdisciplinary programs. The university later enacted a policy disallowing degrees in magic or related fields ever again.

Two themes in Bonewits' works stood out to me as distinctly philosophical. One was his treatment of magic as a field of intellectual study. His bachelor's degree research, and several of his books including *Real Magic* (1972) and *Real Energy* (2007), attempted to raise the practice of magic to the status of an empirical science. In *Real Magic* he wrote that 'magic is predominantly a function of the mind and its thinking patterns'. (pg. 6-

7) He also compares it to natural forces like electricity (cf. pg. 117), so as to eliminate any moral dimension to its nature (i.e. 'white' and 'black' magic), and perhaps to make it more acceptable as an object of scientific study. As to the question of whether magic is 'real', he takes a pragmatic approach which would be familiar to readers of John Dewey: 'truth can be defined as a function of belief!' And therefore, 'if my belief in a 'real' Thor helps me to start a thunderstorm, then it is 'true' that Thor exists. Which may or may not help the theologians reading this.' (pg. 14) With lines like these, it is as if the logical strategy of his first book was, in part, to pull out the epistemic authority from other sciences, so that occultism and mysticism and magic could have just as much (non)legitimacy as other sciences. In *Real Energy* he consulted a number of professional physicists and chemists who reported unusual, as-yet-unexplained experimental results. This put his work on firmer ground, although for my part, I must admit, I remain skeptical.

The other major philosophical theme in his work which stood out to me was his argument that ethical dualism is the root of our social and political problems. By ethical dualism he means the idea that all things can be categorized into the mutually exclusive categories of 'good' and 'evil'. This theme began in *Real Magic* with his rejection of 'White' and 'Black' magic: 'the whole idea of White as Good and Black as Evil is purely the result of cultural bigotries.' (pg. 95) Yet Bonewits discusses the possible reasons why light became culturally associated with goodness and dark with badness: 'we cannot see in the dark', etc. (pg. 117)

Bonewits' committment to reason and rationality in the study of religion is perhaps best evident in his 'Cult Danger Evaluation Frame', which was published in the 1979 reprint of *Real Magic*. It is basically a kind of checklist of cult-like features of religious communities, and was intended for use by those who worried whether they, or others they cared about, were at risk of being harmed by a cult. Eighteen factors were on his list, including:

'amount of power exercised by leaders over members', 'amount of power exercised or desired over the world outside the group'. 'wisdom and knowledge claimed by or credited to the leader', 'emphasis on attracting new members', 'wealth desired or obtained by the group', 'sexual favoritism', 'censorship of information from outside the group', 'violence', 'dropout control', 'paranoia', 'surrender of will', and 'hypocrisy'. Users of the Cult Danger Evaluation Frame rank each criteria on a scale of one to ten, for the group they are worried about. Then users apply the same criteria to other mainstream groups that they were less worried about, and compare the results. Of course, he also warned that conservative fundamentalist Christian groups were likely to rank very high in his scoring system, perhaps much higher than most pagan groups!

But Bonewits's influence is mainly seen not in his writings but in the various organizations and communities he founded, especially including *Arn Draocht Fein* (A.D.F), which eventually became the world's second-largest modern Druid organization (only OBOD is larger). Here are his words in an essay called 'What is ADF?' (internally promulgated in 1984), which gives an idea of what he hoped the organization could accomplish.

Like our sisters and brothers in the other Neopagan movements, we're polytheistic Nature worshipers, attempting to revive the best aspects of the Paleopagan faiths of our ancestors within a modern scientific, artistic, ecological, and wholistic context. Like our predecessors and namesakes the Druids, we're people who believe in excellence – physically, intellectually, artistically, and spiritually. We're researching and expanding sound modern scholarship about the ancient Celts and other Indo-European peoples, in order to reconstruct what the Old Religions of Europe really were. We're working on the development of genuine artistic skills in composition and presentation. We're designing and

performing competent magical and religious ceremonies to change ourselves and the world we live in. We're adapting the polytheologies and customs of both the Indo-European Paleopagans and the Neopagan traditions that have been created over the last fifty years. We're creating a nonsexist, nonracist, organic, and open religion to practice as a way of life and to hand on to our grandchildren. We're integrating ecological awareness, alternative healing arts, and psychic development into our daily activities. Together, we're sparking the next major phase in the evolution of Neopaganism and planting seeds for generations to come.
(From the ADF web site, www.adf.org, retrieved 9th March 2013.)

As you can see, his project was ambitious! And as far as I am aware, this campaign for a more honest approach to the study of pagan history was the first of its kind in the modern pagan movement. Thus he was among the first prominent pagan leaders to accept that the story of the Old Religion and the Burning Times was a myth. Of course this did not stop him from using the story of the Burning Times as a rallying-cry for the activist pursuit of civil liberties for pagans. For better or worse, he also helped reduce Robert Graves' influence in the pagan community. In the 1990s, when I myself first entered the pagan community, Graves' ideas about the Triple Goddess and the Ogham Tree Calendar were widely assumed by most pagans I knew to be ancient historical truths. Bonewits was the (often solitary) voice pointing out that such ideas were not ancient at all, but Graves' original inventions, and that an 'authentic' modern Druidry should have nothing to do with them. (But to be fair to Graves, it wasn't entirely his fault that his readers made that mistake.)

Alas, Bonewits suffered from a disease called Eosinophilia-myalgia syndrome, which prevented him from doing as much as he might have wanted to do. It was a major factor in his decision to resign from the leadership of A.D.F. in 1990, less than fifteen years after the organization was founded. Certainly it prevented him from writing as many books as he wanted to write.

I met Isaac personally on a number of occasions. I found him irascible, playful, knowledgeable, and friendly. He was a strong supporter of my books, and acted as my literary agent for my first two titles. He had a great love of word-play and of off-color humor: sometimes this shows in his writings too! And although he was often strongly critical of the sillier things that modern pagans sometimes believe, he nonetheless loved the pagan community, and wanted it to flourish and prosper. I dare say the pagan community could not have asked for a more 'interesting' public figure.

Fifth Movement: Living Voices

Most of the people whose work I have looked at in this book have passed away, either centuries ago, or very recently. So in this last section I'd like to look at the work of people who, at the time I write these words, are still alive. This means that my treatment of their work must be incomplete: for I cannot cover books or essays that they have not yet written. But the bigger problem was choosing who to include here. For one thing, there are literally thousands of writers now, in fiction and nonfiction and poetry, producing books and essays and web-logs with interesting philosophical insights. But for another, some contemporary pagan writers will call their work 'philosophy' even though it is not, strictly speaking, philosophical at all. They don't address the big questions; they don't use systematic critical reason to support their claims; and they don't engage with the work of other philosophical writers. Such books are 'philosophical' in only the loosest and vaguest sense of the word. I therefore selected these living voices carefully. Even so, none of the people I contacted have university degrees in *philosophy* from a recognized public university. As far as I know, I am one of only two people in the whole world who are openly pagan and who have doctorates in philosophy. (In this sense, modern pagan philosophy is not yet in its infancy.) But the writers featured here are writing philosophically meritorious work, and that work is reasonably influential in the community. Although I may have reasons to be critical of some of them, nonetheless I find that their work is interesting and enlightening.

I also wrote direct letters to every writer featured in this section, and asked them to summarize their philosophical positions and projects. It seemed to me that having a record of their own thoughts about their own thoughts would be an extremely valuable resource for future generations who study pagan philosophy. I asked four basic questions: What ideas do you stand for? What are your most important questions? What are your answers to those questions? What reasons do you offer in support of those answers?

§ 51. Some Recent Trends in Pagan Ethics

Another difficulty with describing living authors in the pagan intellectual tradition is that it can be difficult to recognize what current trends in the tradition are important. It's not that there are no trends worth discussing. But it can be hard to predict which trends will turn out to last more than a few years, or which will influence future generations in a meaningful way. Here's one trend which stands out to me, and although I'm not sure how long it will last, it does seem philosophical: the revival of interest in pagan ethics, and especially pagan virtue. The name I'd like to give to the study of virtue is 'areteology': that is, a *logos* (an account, a speech, a rationale, etc.) of what is *arete* (excellent, praiseworthy) in human affairs. As I see it, areteology begins in the mythology of Bronze-Age and Iron-Age Europeans, as well as in the mythology of near-Eastern, Hindu, and Aboriginal thinking. In stories like the *Tain Bo Cuailnge*, the *Illiad*, the *Odyssey*, the *Eddas*, the *Epic of Gilgamesh*, and so on, we find models of human lives both heroic and wretched, presented to us both through praise and through criticism. Thus they often serve as teaching tools, imparting philosophical ideas through story-telling and literary narrative. Heroic Virtue is the oldest of all models of ethical thought; areteology, therefore, is also a study of the moral and philosophical ideas about human excellence that can be found in mythological storytelling. We can also expand the word to include the study of excellence in the arts, in sports and athletics, in craftsmanship and material productivity, in architecture and design, in education, in environmental stewardship, and just about any field of action in which judgments of moral and aesthetic value can be involved.

Among non-pagan professional philosophers, there is a long and well respected tradition of examining pre-Christian philosophical ideas, including the virtues. Most of the time this means examining the work of Greek and Roman philosophers. From the first half of the twentieth century there was a revival of Greco-Roman virtue ethics among non-pagan academics, started by the English philosopher Elisabeth Anscombe (it is perhaps significant that this revival was initiated by a woman). Thereafter the torch was carried forward by such authors as Iris Murdoch, Phillippa Foot, Rosalind Hursthouse, Charles Taylor, Alasdair MacIntyre, and John Ralston Saul. MacIntyre has probably done the most to promote this revival of virtue ethics. And although he is a Catholic, several of his books discuss in very positive terms our moral inheritance from Greek heroic and philosophical origins. *After Virtue* (1981) and *Whose Justice? Which Rationality?* (1988) are the best of them.

We should also take a quick look at John Casey, author of *Pagan Virtue* (1990). Casey argued that the four classical virtues of ancient philosophy – courage, temperance, prudence, and justice – are necessary for a worthwhile and flourishing human life. That much is a straightforward position taken directly from Plato and Aristotle. But Casey also demonstrates the important ways in which the values represented by pagan virtues are profoundly opposed to Christian values. Here is how he summarizes those differences:

> If there is any genuine way of distinguishing Christian from 'pagan' values it may broadly coincide with a different valuing of the 'irascible' and the 'concupiscential'. I understand the irascible as going with pride and shame, a sense of the noble, a certain valuing of courage and ambition. The concupiscential goes with sympathy and pity, and finds its highest value in love. One might indeed say that a 'pagan' system of values will consider honour to be a higher value

than love. (Casey, *Pagan Virtue*, pg. 212)

Casey also reminds us that in the pagan world view, it is not love, but fate, which makes the world go round: hence the central place that Homeric storytelling assigns to tragedy. And although Christian virtues do overlap with pagan virtues in several important ways, Casey also argues that the pagan virtues do a better job of defining what a good human life is really like. The pagan virtues are quasi-aesthetic: we admire people who have them not only for their moral goodness, but also for their expressiveness of artistic qualities like beauty and nobility. 'Nobility is something that can be presented directly to the eye.' (pg. 74) They are also deeply social: to successfully learn and practice them one must be embedded in a social environment where they make sense. 'Honour is something we give to others, and which others may choose to bestow upon us.' (pg. 84) And finally, the virtues also depend on practical advantages derived from luck and fortune. 'It is extremely difficult to imagine how a good life could be lived without these [classical four] virtues. Yet to exercise them requires the co-operation of Fortune.' (Casey, *Pagan Virtue*, pg. 210) I can think of very few books written by a non-pagan which express the pagan point of view on ethics so well.

The pagan feminists and the pagan environmentalists had been writing about specific political and social causes since at least the late 1960s. At the same time, practitioners of Asatru and Norse heathenism started building pagan communities of their own, mostly separately from those whose paganism derives from Gardner, Valiente, and Crowley. (Some northern heathens, I have learned, don't call themselves 'pagans', even though they clearly do pagan things like give offerings to pagan gods, and live by the teachings of pagan storytelling.) Norse heathens had been working on various statements of ethics which they derived from the study of texts like the two *Eddas*, and various Icelandic sagas. Such statements generally took the form of lists of character virtues. There are differing lists, although perhaps the most popular is the 'Odinic Rite' list: courage, truth, honor, fidelity, discipline, hospitality, self reliance, industriousness, and perseverance. In other lists, honor sometimes appears among the virtues, and sometimes appears as a reward for those who uphold the virtues. The latter position, in my view, more accurately represents the way it is represented in the sagas.

To the best of my knowledge, the Norse heathens are the first contemporary pagans to publish statements on ethics *in general*, and not just in relation to specific public issues – *other than* the Wiccan Rede. But their statements tended to be published in newsletters and (starting in the late 1990s) on websites aimed at other heathens, and so their ideas did not get much traction among other pagans until much later. Wiccans, Druids, eclectic pagans, and others whose communities are traceable to Gardner and Valiente did not give much attention to general ethics questions at the time. They tended to be more interested in questions about the existence of the gods, the possible scientific or supernatural basis of magic, whether mystical knowledge can be gained through ecstasy and trance, and so on. When they spoke of ethics, utilitarian views remained prominent, probably because utilitarian views already dominated the general over-culture of which the pagan movement is a sub-culture. This remains the case to this day. But due to the influence of the Norse heathens, virtue ethics is now emerging as a very strong alternative to the Wiccan Rede.

When, Why, ...If (1997), by the Tarot-deck designer Robin Wood (b. 1953) was probably the first book-length treatment of ethics written by a self-avowed pagan to be published in the trade-paperback market. Its argument consisted primarily in enthusiastic praise for the Wiccan Rede and for a utilitarian standard of moral reasoning. While it probably met the needs of the average non-academic reader, its thesis bore very little resemblance whatever to how ancient pagans thought about ethics. From the mid 90s onward, many books in the pagan trade-paperback market included single-chapters on ethics. The next major book on contemporary pagan ethics worthy of mention is Rabinovich and MacDonald's *An Ye Harm None* (2004). Both of these authors are professional academics: Rabinovich teaches anthropology at the University of Ottawa, and MacDonald (the pen-name of Sîan Reid) was at the time professor of sociology at Carleton University, also in Ottawa. While this title filled a need for a much more comprehensive treatment of pagan ethics, it also focused on practical affairs, and on the utilitarian side of the Wiccan Rede, and had little to say about historical models of ethics. Then Emma Restall Orr published *Living with Honour* (2008), which was the first complete book-length treatment of pagan ethics from a point of view other than the Wiccan Rede. My own book on heroic and classical ethics, *The Other Side of Virtue* (2008), was published three months later, and I followed it with two more works on related themes: *Loneliness and Revelation* (2010) and *Circles of Meaning, Labyrinths of Fear* (2012). But I apologize for blowing my own horn here.

The point of that short tour of pagan publishing on ethics is to show that contemporary pagans are addressing themselves to philosophically important topics, and contemporary philosophers are addressing themselves to pagan topics. And it is good that they are doing so. Modern paganism would become an insular and stagnated religious movement, justifiably ignored by the rest of the world, if it restricted itself to discussing spellcraft and ritual and its own internal problems.

With that said, let's focus on some individual pagan voices now, starting with the writer who did the most to understand political power from a pagan point of view.

§ 52. Starhawk (Miriam Simos)

Eclipsing the pagan movement's founders in terms of book sales, number of followers, and sheer name recognition, Starhawk is almost certainly the most influential pagan writer of the entire twentieth century. Her early work is a product of the intersection between modern pagan witchcraft and second-wave feminist political activism. She founded a community called Reclaiming, which sought to explore the ideas of American feminist witchcraft, and to put them into practice; this community now has thousands of members around the world. I imagine she thinks of herself as an activist more than as a philosopher; but as I'm a philosopher myself, I'll study her influence through her books.

The Spiral Dance (1979), Starhawk's first book, is part activist manual, part ritual magic manual, and part personal testament. It is written in a very accessible style, with numerous quotable proverbs and epigrams. Its purpose is mainly practical: Starhawk wants to get people to *do* things. Hence it is full of exercises and rituals. But it makes an important contribution to philosophy as well: it introduced a set of categories which help political activists distinguish forms of power which oppress from forms of power which liberate. They first appear in a discussion of the leadership of private groups of witches: in that group, 'Authority and power... are based on a very different principle from that which holds sway in the world at large. Power, in a coven, is never power *over* another. It is the power that comes from within.' (*The Spiral Dance* (2nd edition of 1989), pg. 51, emphasis hers.) In *The Spiral Dance*, Starhawk's use of the word power is almost interchangeable with her use of words like energy and ecstasy: it referred to something psychic as well as something practical. But in her next two books, *Dreaming the Dark* (1982) and *Truth or Dare* (1988) her categories of power would be defined more precisely, and more politically. The categories of power are:

- *Power-over*, which refers to authoritarian, hierarchical models of power in which one commands and another obeys: it 'comes from the consciousness I have termed estrangement' and is 'ultimately born of war and the structures, social and intrapsychic, necessary to sustain mass, organized warfare.' (*Truth or Dare*, pg. 9)

- *Power-from-within*, which refers to the confidence and proper pride that a mature individual may express as she pursues her ends: it is 'akin to the sense of mastery we develop as young children with each new unfolding ability.' (*ibid* pg. 10)

- *Power-with*, the third type of power, is 'the power of a strong individual in a group of equals, the power not to command, but to suggest and be listened to, to begin something and see it happen. The source of power-with is the willingness of others to listen to our ideas.' Power-with can only be exercised by someone who has learned to wield power-from-within, and who works in groups 'that do not depend on hierarchy for cohesion.' But 'in the dominant culture, power-with has become confused with power-over.' (*ibid* pg. 10)

Let's look briefly at term 'estrangement', which appears in the explanation of power-over. The idea is that when one is separated and divided (i.e. estranged) from others, such as by a hierarchical model of social order, then the only way to influence those others is by coercion and oppression. If, by contrast, one feels connected and related to others, one can influence them only with non-oppressive means, such as persuasion, co-operation, and trust. Starhawk first introduces her idea of estrangement in *Dreaming the Dark*, where she says:

I call this consciousness *estrangement* because its essence is that we do not see ourselves as part of the world. We are strangers to nature, to other human beings, to parts of ourselves. We see the world as made up of separate, isolated, nonliving parts that have no inherent value. (They are not even dead – because death implies life.) Among things inherently separate and lifeless, the only power relationships possible are those of manipulation and domination. (*Dreaming the Dark*, 1997 edition, pg. 5)

Spectres of the Marxist principle of alienation and alienated labor haunt these words: indeed, further down the same page Starhawk quotes Friedrich Engels in its support. Shades of Mary Daly and Carol Christ are also discernible here, as when Starhawk claims that women who look up to the image of the God of Abraham see an image that estranges them from themselves: 'Male imagery of God authenticates men as the carriers of humanness and legitimizes male rule.' (*ibid* pg. 6) Starhawk also says that the same experience of estrangement occurs to the black person who looks upon the image of God as a white man. By contrast, however:

The image of the Goddess strikes at the roots of estrangement. True value is not found in some heaven, some abstract other-world, but in female bodies and their offspring, female and male; in nature; and in the world. Nature is seen as having its own inherent order, of which human beings are a part... For women, the symbol of the Goddess is profoundly liberating, restoring a sense of authority and power to the female body and all the life processes: birth, growth, lovemaking, aging, and death. (*ibid* pg. 10-11)

This is the case because of what Starhawk seems to believe is the essential difference between feminism's Goddess and patriarchy's God. 'The symbolism of the Goddess is not a parallel structure to the symbolism of God the Father. The Goddess does not rule the world; She *is* the world.' (*The Spiral Dance*, pg. 23, emphasis hers.) That's a very pantheist thing to say. And the Goddess is the world because Starhawk and other members of the movement have willed Her so. 'I have spoken of the Goddess as a psychological symbol and also as manifest reality. She is both. She exists, *and* we create Her.' (*ibid* pg. 95) Combine these two propositions with Simone de Beauvoir's insight that the God of Abraham is a personification of male power, and you have the basic foundation of pagan feminist thealogy. By the way, the second proposition from Starhawk here reminds me of the third of Carol Christ's four implications of the symbol of the Goddess: the principle of will. And the appearance of will as a central theaological concept possibly derives from the influence of Crowley upon early pagan writers like Gardner and Valiente. As you can see, there's a continuity of thought growing, as multiple authors build upon each other's work.

Yet Starhawk also observed something else about this religious gender politics which, as far as I am aware, no second-wave feminist of her time had yet acknowledged. (There was, however, work being done by other feminists on colonialism, race relations, and the like.) She saw that the patriarchy which oppresses women also oppresses some men. 'Patriarchy literally means 'rule of the fathers' but in a patriarchy very few men are allowed to enact the role of the 'father' outside the limited family sphere.' (*ibid* pg. 110) And so she sought in the image of the Horned God an image of male power which does not oppress anyone. 'In the Craft, the male body, like the female body, is held sacred, not to be violated. It is a violation of the male body to use it as a weapon, just as it is a violation of the female body to use it as an object or a proving ground for male virility...' (*ibid* pg. 111)

In relation to that, please allow me a brief personal interlude. Since, alas, I am male and not female, it is perhaps unsurprising that these remarks about the Horned God were the lines in *The Spiral Dance* which excited me the most, when I first read the book as a starry-eyed teenager in 1992. Other parts of the text, such as the Womb Chant (pg. 146), were obviously not written for me, and back then I didn't know what to make of them. But even before I heard Starhawk's name for the first time, I had made up my mind that the Doctrine of Original Sin was false, and I was searching for an alternative. A high school guidance councilor lent me her copy of *The Spiral Dance* (and also Joseph Campbell's *The Power of Myth*) and I felt that I found that alternative. Starhawk offered acceptance instead of penance, original blessing instead of original sin, a male god who looked nothing like my father, and a female goddess who looked a lot like my friend. It's more than twenty years later now, and I've learned that just about everyone in my generation had a similar experience reading Starhawk at that age. I'm sure this is why Starhawk's work remains so well loved to this day.

§ 53. Emma Restall-Orr

Among the most influential pagan voices in Britain today is Emma Restall-Orr. She was the co-founder of two modern Druidic communities, the British Druid Order and the Druid Network. She also founded a cultural group called Honouring the Ancient Dead which campaigns for the respectful treatment of human remains discovered in archaeological sites. Her career as a writer began with books about Druidic magic and ritual, much like other pagan writers had done before her. (I can't hold that against anyone; after all, my first two books were similar.) In those books she interweaved straightforward descriptions of concepts and ideas together with narrative accounts of events in her life, and personal spiritual experiences; an unusual writing style which was widely praised for emotional honesty. Starting in 2008 she moved into more directly philosophical territory by publishing *Living with Honour* (2008) which was about ethics, *Kissing the Hag* (2009) which was about feminist issues, and *The Wakeful World* (2012) which was about animism, pantheism, and metaphysics. In each of these books she addressed herself to serious philosophical questions, yet continued to interweave her arguments with personal narratives in her distinctive, elegant style.

Earlier I wrote that *Living with Honour* was the first major published work written by a pagan to treat ethics from a pagan point of view. So let's have a look at what it says. First of all, Restall-Orr defines ethics as:

> ...the line we draw that articulates what is acceptable in terms of behaviour, and what is not, from a profoundly personal and individual standpoint. Putting aside any notion about where that line *should* be, more basically our ethics are an expression of our needs. Bluntly, they declare what we feel the world owes us and what we feel we ought to give in return. (*Living with Honour*, pg. 63)

Restall-Orr says she formulated this definition of ethics after discussing the matter with many gatherings of pagans over many years. This definition, therefore, may be interpreted as an account of the view of ethics which was generally accepted in Britain's pagan community at the time.

The title, '*Living with Honour*', suggests that the concept of honor will be a current theme throughout the text. Indeed this is the case, but before offering a direct examination of the concept, Restall-Orr takes the reader on a tour of the history of ideas in ethics. And this tour is a personal one; the relevance of each place where she takes the reader is demonstrated by relating it to a moment in the story of her own life. From there she introduces us to important canonical philosophers including a few we've already seen, such as Aristotle, David Hume, and Arthur Schopenhauer. The word 'honour', which appears in the title, is never defined directly, but there are a number of indirect associations which enable the reader to understand her meaning. She associates it with actions that preserve the dignity of a tribe (pg. 126), with the spiritual significance that old Celtic custom attributes to the human head (pg. 127), and with a person's sense of dignity and social standing. For her purpose, it seemed to me, is primarily to explain the relevance and the necessity of a 'tribal' model of ethics in the contemporary world. And her strategy for accomplishing this purpose is to deliver an intimately personal discourse, using narrative storytelling, internal experience, and even the occasional good joke.

May I respectfully submit a criticism: for Restall-Orr's understanding of honor is also strongly relativist. According to her account, relativism '...inspires tolerance, and indeed the attitude that steps beyond toleration into the celebration of pluralism. The ethical relativist is awake to the intricacies of difference, fully exploring circumstances in order to find understanding about a choice or action.' (pg. 76) She also implies that the only alternative to relativism is moral absolutism, which must be rejected since it does not respect diversity and can serve only to justify domination and oppression. (pg. 76) But I think this is a case of the fallacy of false dilemma. Restall-Orr states that relativism is 'traditionally unpopular with philosophers perhaps because the motivation of the thinker is so often to solve the untidy problems of nature's diversity.' (pg. 75) But the real reason relativism is unpopular among philosophers is because it is logically self-defeating, as any first-year logic textbook will tell you. Some of her discourse, therefore, holds a tension between statements of a relativist, individualist, or anarchist perspective, and statements asserting definite values (like honor) which derive their force from more than just individual relativist choices. In her discussion of medical issues, for instance, she says, 'In Pagan terms, the work of a doctor, a healer or carer is measured by the quality of peace, not in days of breathing.' (pg. 211) Well, I couldn't agree more. But against definite propositions like this, the relativism seems out of place.

The text is logically and philosophically much stronger when it confronts the way that 'honour' can sometimes motivate people to harm each other, and asks what can be done about that. 'With its historic connotations of pride and vanity, its provocation of irrational violence, how can the word have any ethical value in twenty-first century spirituality?' (pg. 127) Part of her solution is to treat humanity as a tribal species; therefore, however each person defines honor and ethics, it will in some way be associated with the history and the needs of one's tribe. The tribe she defines as 'any social unit within which we seek acceptance'. (pg. 64) She also treats honor as a compound idea, made of three inter-related virtues: courage, generosity, and loyalty. According to her account, these are the primary qualities of good character taught by the old Celtic tradition. (In research I conducted independently, my list of Celtic moral virtues was courage, generosity, and friendship, which is not so far different from hers.) So those who harm or even kill others in defense of their honor are people who have a false understanding of what honor truly is. Much of the second half of her book demonstrates how these three qualities can find expression in practical problems and realities: how to relate best to children, lovers, other adults in one's tribe, as well as to 'strangers', or 'others' who are not members of one's tribe. She also discusses environmental issues, topics in medical ethics such as euthanasia, and existentialist notions of freedom. It's a very impressive tour.

Since *Living with Honour* was published, Restall-Orr has branched out her work to cover new topics, notably animism. So I wrote to Restall-Orr to ask how she would describe her own philosophical views. Here is her reply:

Metaphysically, my philosophy can be described as a form of animism: the essence of nature is minded. It is this animism that informs my ethics, my politics, my theology and my religious practice. That within those sentences are at least eight, if not a dozen words, that can be defined in a number of different ways is in part what inspires and fuels my journeys of exploration, both those of language and of practical religious living.

Working as a priest, teacher and counsellor, within the landscapes of Britain, that exploration fell within my understanding of the word Druid. While I still consider my religious roots to be within Druidry, I no longer work as a priest, instead withdrawing into the life of a philosopher and mystic. As such, it no longer matters how I label my religion; of more interest to me are the words that effectively describe my beliefs.

Animism is, to me, a monist metaphysical approach. In other words, it rejects the dualism that declares a fundamental distinction between mind, soul, spirit, and matter, body, physicality. Instead, such an animism finds mindedness in every part of nature, including the wholeness of everything. Thus, pantheism is an inevitable element of this animistic perspective. Further, in acknowledging the mindedness of nature, we find minded beings whose presence is so affecting and influencing within our lives that it is wise to treat them with profound respect: these we might call the gods. So is polytheism also central to this monist animism.

It is not just the gods whom we must respect. Every action we take as human beings is based on what we need or desire, and what the consequences may be of satisfying those needs and desires. Such an animism challenges the dualist or materialist approach that declares there to be subjects who can feel, and objects that have no personal experience at all. Objects can be used, discarded, replaced: objects are things. Subjects have a different value. If all nature is minded, we are faced with questions about sentience, memory, inherent value, and a creature's right to thrive as itself for itself. We need to reconsider the notion of unnecessary harm, and allow our answers to guide us when we are thinking of care and sustainability.

Perhaps the key is to look at the nature of mind, and how

our human minds have constructed their sense of self. Releasing our grasp on the importance of the I, dissipating the survival instinct of the self, we can develop our living so as to be integrated within the greater minds of ecosystems, communities and gods. Perhaps then we may be able to start asking the really interesting questions.

§ 54. The Critique of Monotheism

Polytheism, the belief in many gods and not just one, has always been a major theme in paganism. Indeed it has always been a major plank of difference and sometimes conflict with the Abrahamic religions. Since the founding of Judaism, most philosophers in the Western tradition have assumed that monotheism is the only *rational* way to think about the divine. Where polytheism is discussed at all, it is often described as fraught with logical and moral faults which naturally lead to monotheism as the solution. A twentieth century example of this comes from H. Richard Niebuhr, author of *Radical Monotheism and Western Culture* (1963). Niebuhr acknowledged that 'our natural religion is polytheistic' because:

> ...though our religious and political institutions are officially monotheist ('one nation under god'), our social existence contains many values, many principles of being, many centers of worth. We give these 'gods' semi-personal names such as truth, beauty, justice, peace, love, goodness, pleasure, patriotism... (Niebuhr, pg. 121)

But Niebuhr believes this will lead to a kind of cognitive dissonance, because 'each god in turn requires a certain absolute devotion and the denial of the claims of the other gods'. (Niebuhr, pg. 121) These competing and irreconcilable claims, Niebuhr says, produce an unavoidable tragedy of divided loyalty which can be resolved by only one thing: monotheism.

Niebuhr assumes that polytheists worship their gods the same way monotheists worship their one god. But they don't. Lots of deities in historical polytheist cultures made requests, issued laws, sent people on missions, or even demonstrated models of human excellence for us to emulate, just as monotheist gods and their prophets did. But no deity in a polytheist culture demanded absolute unquestioning affirmation of his or her authority. And no present-day pagan community known to me requires its members to submit themselves to the will of their deities in a self-abnegating way. Polytheists generally relate to their gods the same way they relate to people in general: by loving them, talking to them, seeking their advice, giving them gifts, entering contracts with them, or following their example. Polytheists also get annoyed by their gods, criticize them, reprimand and chastise them, and even guard themselves from them, the same way they might treat strangers, or those who break their promises. And the polytheist world view generally assumes that the gods are usually content to ignore those who ignore them. Indeed polytheists worship their gods so radically differently from the way monotheists worship their one god, that polytheist worship probably shouldn't be called worship. We shall have to invent a new word for what polytheists do. Niebuhr assumes that all worship is the same, and so he fundamentally fails to understand polytheism properly.

But there is one part of Niebuhr's account of polytheism which is worth a closer look: the characterizing of polytheism as the natural religion of humankind, and the gods as centers of value. In one of the first serious book-length treatments of polytheism, American theologian David Miller, in a short text called *The New Polytheism* (1974) followed up Niebuhr's thought, but rejected the assertion that polytheism logically leads to the tragedy of divided loyalties. He wrote that 'monotheistic theology has all along been polytheistic at its base' (pg. 86) and that the 'real task' of theology is to recover that polytheist base:

The task rather is to rediscover the stories of the gods and goddesses, the theology of the people. It is to recover the varieties of religious experience lurking in the varieties of theological experience. The task begins in feeling and intuition, rather than in thinking. It probes the deeper functions of our Western philosophico-theological logics to discover the multifaceted richness lying in wait for the princely kiss of feeling. The task of a polytheistic theology will not be even begun until there is a sense for life in theology, a liveliness in understanding, a passion in thinking, a love of the gods and goddesses. A polytheist theology will attempt to recover the whole pantheon residing in our so-called monotheistic theological tradition. (Miller, *The New Polytheism*, pg. 89)

Similarly, In 1981 French philosopher Alain de Benoist published *Comment Peut-on être Païen?* 'On Being a Pagan' (English edition 2004 – by the way, I think a better translation of the title would be, 'What's it like to be pagan?'). Like Nietzsche before him, and on whom he relies, de Benoist's 'problem' is nihilism and postmodern malaise. His solution to the problem is pagan polytheism. Only the mythological spirit of the pagan gods of ancient Europe, he says, can effectively counteract those problems, and reinvigorate a failing sense of purpose and wonder. Not that he says we should swap Christ out and put the old gods back in: de Benoist does not consider himself a pagan. (I wrote to him and asked, and that's what he told me.) Rather, to de Benoist,

[Paganism] ...implies looking behind religion, and, according to a now classic itinerary, seeking for the 'mental equipment' that produced it, the inner world it reflects, and how the world it depicts is apprehended. In short, it consists of viewing the gods as 'centres of values'...and the beliefs they generate as value systems: gods and beliefs may pass away, but the values remain. (de Benoist, pg. 16)

Notice the casting of the gods as 'centres of values', as Niebuhr and Miller had done. It seems that it hardly matters whether the gods exist as actual thinking, living beings. It matters only that we contemplate what the gods stand for, and learn whatever lessons may be learned from their stories. de Benoist's understanding of paganism is also tightly bound to nationalism: one's nation is also a centre of value. But I leave that aside here.

This way of understanding the gods is a kind of pagan polytheist hermeneutics. The most recent scholar to study the gods this way is Edward P. Butler, in articles published in *The Pomegranate* (an academic journal of pagan studies) and in a self-published text, *Essays on a Polytheist Philosophy of Religion* (2012). But unlike the 'conceptual' approach of Miller and de Benoist, Butler's work is strongly Neo-Platonic. He argues that it's possible to understand the meaning and the message of the stories of the gods in a conceptual way without at the same time denying or suspending judgment about their personhood. He also rejects the syncretic claim that gods of different cultures who share the same spheres of concern are really the same god under different names. It's interesting stuff; but so far there's rather little of it, and I do hope he publishes more in the future.

In the past ten years, some historians and social critics are seriously suggesting that monotheism might have been a bad idea, and that polytheism is probably healthier for us. We already saw part of the argument against monotheism in the work of Friedrich Nietzsche, for whom polytheism represents diversity and monotheism represents conformity. And we have seen David Hume's argument that polytheism represents tolerance and acceptance of those who are different, and monotheism represents persecution of those who are different. The recent resurgence in such thinking is led by historians like Jonathan Kirsch, author of *God Against the Gods* (2004), and Jan Assmann, author of *The Price of Monotheism* (2010), and of course by various pagan writers. Assmann, although he claimed 'I am not advocating anything; my aim is rather to describe and understand' (pg. 13) nonetheless observed:

> ...the relationship between monotheistic and archaic religions is one of revolution, not evolution. My argument, then, is that the monotheistic shift... takes the form of a rupture, a break with the past that rests on the distinction between truth and falsehood and generates, over the subsequent course of its reception, the distinction between Jews and Gentiles, Christians and pagans, Christians and Jews, Muslims and infidels, true believers and heretics, manifesting itself in countless acts of violence and bloodshed. (Assmann, *The Price of Monotheism*, pg. 11)

Monotheism, his argument goes, does not emerge naturally from polytheism. It is, rather, an original development, and a definite break from the polytheist predecessor. And since that is so, it has a natural antagonism toward its predecessor, and to other faiths besides. Being naturally antagonistic toward other faiths, it has been used too often to justify too much suffering, violence, oppression, and cruelty. Therefore, according to Assmann, it is perhaps not so rational after all. (I hear the sound of Isaac Bonewits applauding from beyond the grave.)

Now a monotheist might reply by saying that not all pagans were necessarily peace-loving paragons of virtue. We have already seen, as an example, how the Druids could be learned astronomers and wise peacemakers, and at the same time practitioners of ritualized murder with the use of a Wicker Man. And the monotheist might also turn to the history of Christianity's first three centuries, in which it is said that Christians suffered terrible persecutions at the hands of Roman pagans. Actually, evidence is now emerging that these early Christians were *not* persecuted so terribly after all. It turns out that the story of the persecuted Christian was exaggerated from a small number of isolated incidents, and sometimes fabricated from nothing, in order to shore up the faith of the faithful, to silence dissenters and heretics, and to raise money for the early Church. Such is the argument of Candida Moss, professor of New Testament studies at Notre Dame University, in her book *The Myth of Persecution* (2013). In twenty-first century America, the myth of the persecuted Christian continues to be perpetuated for political gain by various conservative groups and political parties. But, as observed by Moss, the myth is based on no actual solid historical evidence at all. This point had already been noted by Edward Gibbon some three centuries ago, (cf. Kirsch, pg. 15) but Moss presents the most comprehensive study of the evidence. And as observed by sociologist Elizabeth Castelli, the myth is perpetuated by peer pressure and the constant repetition of slogans, and it totally ignores empirical evidence and rational argument. (Castelli, (2007) 'Persecution Complexes: Identity Politics and the 'War on Christians'' *Differences: A Journal of Feminist Cultural Studies*, Vol.18, No.5, pp. 152-180. See also Castelli, 'God and Country', in the same edition of the same journal.)

This critique of the myth of the persecuted Christian is perhaps tangential to the critique of monotheism in general. But it is relevant to those who say that Christianity was better because it was less violent. For the evidence tends to show that the very opposite is the truth.

Actually, the myth of the persecuted Christian goes back to a time long before the foundation of Christianity itself. To see how far back it goes, let's look at the Biblical book of Ezra the Scribe. The book tells the story of how Ezra was among those who led the Hebrews from their captivity in Babylon back to the city of Jerusalem. While rebuilding the Temple, a scroll was discovered in a foundation vault which turned out to be a record of the

Torah, the five books of Moses. Ezra ordered all the Jews to assemble, and then he proclaimed to them the re-discovery of the Torah, and read it aloud from start to finish for all to hear. On that day the Jewish people, having just reclaimed their homeland after years in captivity in Babylon, learned their history for the first time. They learned that Babylon was the second foreign nation to enslave them; the first one to do so was Egypt. They learned that they once lived in kingdoms ruled by wise men like David and Solomon. They learned about Noah and the Flood, and Moses and the Burning Bush, and even the stories of Adam and Eve, the first human beings. They learned about the covenant their ancestors made with God, and why they were God's chosen people, and why the other nations of the world hated them for it.

But let me introduce you to Lon Milo DuQuette. He's an American occultist, freemason, and probably the most important writer in the tradition of Aleister Crowley alive today. (He's also, by the way, a very entertaining musician.) In his book *The Key to Solomon's Key* (2010) DuQuette stated that the entire history of the Jewish people, prior to the time of Ezra and the captivity in Babylon (i.e. the sixth century BCE), has no foundation in empirical evidence. There are no documents and no archaeological remains older than the time of Ezra which could confirm that history. The implication is that *none of it actually happened.* Drawing upon on the work of prestigious historians and Biblical scholars like Thomas L. Thompson and Norman F. Cantor, DuQuette declared:

> The idea of twelve distinct tribes of the children of Israel with a past reaching back to the thirteenth century BCE was likely an ingenious concept fabricated in the sixth century BCE (or later) to provide a single cultural and religious identity to the descendants of a diverse assortment of people with no cultural memory whatsoever – people whose ancestors came

from a dozen or more regions conquered by Nebuchadnezzar – people whose real ancestors were thrown together by the fortunes of world events and who eventually had to be relocated when Babylon fell to the Persians. (DuQuette, *The Key to Solomon's Key*, pg. 90-91)

The provocative and perhaps incendiary claim here is that the stories of the kingdoms of David and Solomon, important Jewish ancestors like Abraham and Isaac and Joseph, and events like the captivity in Egypt, or the Covenant with God himself, are all works of fiction. These stories were sewn together by Ezra, or persons using that name, from a cloth of myth, legend, and folklore, and perhaps original (brilliant) invention. Then it was presented to the people as if it was history, in order to unite a band of former slaves and workers from Babylon into a single community. The conclusion DuQuette reaches is that 'the wars, the genocides, the hatreds and feuds that have cursed Western civilization for the last three thousand years have been (and continue to be) tragic arguments that began over nothing.' (pg. 92)

Monotheists certainly can find reasons to be tolerant and accepting of the differences of others, if they want to. And here we are on safer ground. The best statements of religious tolerance which I've ever read were made by Jewish philosopher Jay Newman (a former teacher of mine!) in books like *Foundations of Religious Tolerance* (1982), *Competition in Religious Life* (1989), and *On Religious Freedom* (1991). But a case can be made that the logic of monotheism itself demands violent competition in a way that polytheism doesn't. As noted by Jonathan Kirsch, the 'simple but terrifying logic that lies at the heart of monotheism' is that 'if there is only one god, [and] if there is only one right way to worship that god, then there is only one fitting punishment for failing to do so – death.' (Kirsch, pg. 2) This, according to Kirsch, explains why monotheists of varying traditions – Jewish,

Christian, Islamic – are sometimes capable of justifying terrorism in the name of religion, and polytheists are not. When polytheist societies went to war, they went to war for their own reasons and then entreated the gods for help afterwards. No god in a polytheist pantheon ever called for the deaths of the worshippers of other gods *for no other reason than because they worshipped other gods*. Yet precisely that demand appears in numerous places in the Bible and the Koran. The gods of various pagan mythologies might be vindictive, jealous, angry, or envious of each other, no less than human beings are of each other; but the gods never sought to exterminate each other, or each other's worshippers. Therefore polytheism is morally superior to monotheism – or so goes the argument, at least in broad strokes.

I should also mention that a critique of monotheism is also being carried out by a number of monotheists. American theologian Matthew Fox, author of *Original Blessing* (2000) is perhaps the best known of these. His theology does not exactly reject Original Sin. But he certainly downplays it in favor of a greater emphasis on other, more positive Christian messages, such as that we are all made in the image of God, and that God gave the earth to all humanity as a gift in common, and that God's creation is good. Canadian journalist and professor of New Testament studies, and Anglican priest, Tom Harpur, observed that absolutely all the important Christian teachings at least in Christianity's first three centuries, and all the important events in the life of Jesus Christ, were effectively copied and pasted from pagan sources almost verbatim. Some of those sources were already thousands of years old when the canonical Gospels were written. (Notice how different his position is from Jan Assmann's, in that regard.) We have already seen, in James Frazer's *The Golden Bough*, that there were plenty of dying and resurrecting gods in the ancient world before Jesus. In *The Pagan Christ* (2004), Harpur described in detail many more similarities between Christ and the Egyptian god Horus. Some of their titles like 'the Deliverer', 'The Light', and 'The Anointed One' are the same. Both are depicted as gods who 'descended' to earth and 'emptied' themselves in order to take on a mortal semblance. In that mortal semblance, both were born of royal family lines. Horus' ministry on earth lasted only one year; according to the Synoptic Gospels, Clement of Alexandria, and the Christian Origen, so did Jesus' ministry. Both had a transfiguration episode. Both raised the dead. Both used a donkey for their mount. And so on. Drawing on scholars like Godfrey Higgins (1771-1834), Gerald Massey (1828-1907) and Alvin Boyd Kuhn (1880-1963), Harpur concludes that there was almost certainly no historical Jesus, as most Christians believe. But that's okay, because what matters is that we recognize how the story of Christ plays out in all our lives. 'The myth itself is fictional, but the timeless truth it expresses is not.' (pg. 17) And the 'best proof of the authenticity of true Christianity' is not the historical existence of a person, but the 'inner experience of the presence and power of God as the Christ within our own consciousness.' (pg. 176) But when we read the events of the story of Christ as if it was a literal history, we miss the point completely, with consequences we all know.

> There is no doubt whatever that the Church of the late second, third, and fourth centuries scored a great triumph in winning over the uneducated masses. But by literalizing and making a pseudo-history out of the Jesus story... the Church turned that triumph into a pyrrhic victory of staggering proportions. Ignorance and an unquestioning faith were championed, frauds were passed for sacred truths, dissent of any kind was labelled heresy, and within a short time, all of Europe was plunged into the Dark Ages. Only a much later return to the so-called Pagans, Plato and Aristotle, injected sufficient ratio-nality and philosophy into Christian theology to keep it alive at all. (*ibid* pg. 179)

I praise and support Harpur's effort to save Christianity from itself in this way; but I also enjoy the irony of his use of pagan sources for that purpose.

By the way: Lon Milo DuQuette, who as we saw cast doubt on the historical existence of characters like Moses, Abraham, and King David, had similar thoughts about the meaning of their stories. The books of the Old Testament, he says, 'will forever offer real spiritual treasures to the sincere devotee, but to insist that they are also history is to invite their misuse by social and political entities, who are always ready to engender and perpetuate fear and hatred between peoples and cultures for their own interests.' (DuQuette, pg. 92-3)

Aside from DuQuette, there are other noteworthy pagan writers engaged in a critique of monotheism, and I'd like to turn to them now.

§ 55. John Michael Greer

One of the best known *logical* (not mystical) arguments in favor of monotheism over polytheism comes from William of Ockham (1288-1348), the Franciscan monk who invented the logical axiom now known as Ockham's Razor: 'No unnecessary replication of identicals', or more simply, 'the explanation with the fewest assumptions tends to be the truth.' Here's how the argument supports monotheism. Monotheists have claimed since at least the sixth century that God is an infinite being. (Notice the use of a mathematical term here.) Now one can certainly imagine that there are dozens or hundreds of infinite beings. But a dozen or more infinite beings would be *ex hypothesi* indistinguishable from one another: for if there were anything about them that distinguished them from each other, then they would not be infinite. So it is much simpler to imagine that there's just one. In the same way, it is possible to assume that there are ten thousand absolutely identical desks in front of me, and all of them are occupying exactly the same position in space and time. But it is simpler to assume that there's just one.

But just how well does Ockham's Razor support monotheism? John Michael Greer, the contemporary pagan writer who has arguably done the most to build an intellectual foundation for polytheism, says it doesn't necessarily support monotheism at all. 'Ockham's Razor cannot be used in advance of the evidence', and 'nor is Ockham's Razor a source of certainty.' (*A World Full of Gods*, pg. 46) The latter point is quite true: Ockham's Razor is a useful shorthand for most purposes, but it is an induction and not a deduction, and so it can tell you what is very probable, but cannot give you an indisputable truth. When we do actually look at the evidence, we may find, as the supporters of the 'teleological' or 'design' argument for the monotheist God claim to have found, that the laws of physics and chemistry render the world perfectly suited to the flourishing of life. That orderliness could not have happened by accident; it must have been designed that way by a creator God. Similarly, when we look at the evidence we may find that the morphological features of animals and plants and all life-forms are perfectly suited for their functions: wings for flying, hands for grasping, fins for swimming, and so on. That, too, cannot have been an accident; God must have been designed them that way. Supposing we accepted the initial premises of the design argument. There's no logical step that leads you to *necessarily* conclude that there was only one designer. There might have been many designers working together. Indeed, as Greer says, it may be better to conclude that 'the sheer diversity and complexity of the natural world could probably be used to argue that multiple intelligent designers are more plausible than a single one.' (pg. 49) There's a curious irony in the way Greer turns one of Christianity's best arguments against monotheism.

Greer also presents his own arguments in favor of polytheism, most of which rest upon the diversity of religious experiences. After presenting arguments for why religious experiences can be used as evidence that one or more gods might exist, he says:

> Even narrowing the focus to gods worshipped by existing religions and experienced by present-day worshippers, the diversity remains vast. Some gods are terrifying, others comforting, still others majestic, playful, fierce, impassive, maternal, passionately erotic – and such a list could be extended indefinitely. It's principally when religious experience is considered in the abstract, as it so often is, that these differences fade from sight, and this has simplified the task of theorists who argue that all religious experiences somehow work out to be experiences of the same thing. Attention to individual religious experiences is a crucial corrective to this sort of distortion. (*A World Full of Gods*, pg. 69)

Admitting that an experience of the monotheist God of Abraham is an actual religious experience that lots of people have, he places it as just one kind of experience among many. Thus Greer concludes that *'religious experience is inherently polytheistic'*. (*ibid*, pg. 70, emphasis his.) Greer also addresses himself in passing to atheists: in his view, their arguments amount to the logical fallacy of special pleading.

Greer's prose is terse without being cold: he gets to the point quickly and clearly. And he sometimes makes his point with good humor too: his parable of the five houses and three cats, which explains how people might come to believe in monotheism despite the evidence of their senses, was very entertaining. And there's no relativism here: Greer is completely convinced that polytheism stands up to the test of logic and evidence better than monotheism does. I appreciate that kind of confidence.

Greer is not a one-theme writer: polytheism is not his only interest. For example he's also an activist for an important public cause, 'Peak Oil', which is the campaign to draw public attention to the fact that the world economy will soon run out of petroleum. In the winter of 2013 I wrote to Greer to ask him to summarize his philosophical views in his own words. Here is his reply, in full:

> Like most people trained in traditional occultism over the last century or so, I absorbed an awkward mix of two philo-sophical traditions in the course of my magical education. The first of these is the Neo-Platonist tradition that had its source in Plotinus, Iamblichus, and the other pagan Neo-Platonists of the late classical period, and functioned as the core philosophy of Western magic straight through until the end of the Renaissance and the rise of modern culture. The second is the distinctive philosophical stance that Eliphas Lévi borrowed in modified form from Arthur Schopenhauer and made central to modern magic – the world as will and imagi-nation, to impose a Léviesque rephrase on the title of Schopenhauer's most famous book.
>
> Those two traditions clash in a galaxy of ways. To the Neo-Platonist, for example, the cosmos is an ordered whole in which meaning and value are objective realities and the human soul is an inseparable part of the Great Chain of Being. From within the philosophy Lévi brought to the magical revival of his time, by contrast, the universe is fundamentally unknowable in any objective sense, yet the will and imagi-nation of the individual acting together are capable of imposing form upon it – are, ultimately, the only things that can do so. Despite these difficulties, both philosophies are hardwired into the structure of contemporary magic, and attempts to do away with one or the other (such as the 'Chaos Magic' movement of the twentieth century's last decades) have not succeeded in embracing the full range of possibilities present in modern magical traditions.

The response to this clash toward which I have been working for some years now might, with a nod to Kant, be called critical Neo-Platonism. As E.R. Dodds noted in the foreword to his translation of Proclus' *Elements of Theology*, the core philosophical problem with Neo-Platonism is that it assumes that the structure of reality is identical with the structure of classical Greek logic. That criticism is valid, but it bears remembering that all we are capable of knowing as human beings are the modifications of our own consciousness – the sensations, emotions, thoughts, and other building blocks from which each of us constructs the universe of our experience.

Traditional Neo-Platonic philosophy in this light can be seen as a way to talk about the a priori structures of human experience, and how these relate to one another. Insofar as the world is the product of will and imagination, as Lévi proposed, will and imagination do not function in a vacuum. The underlying forms of our experience are given by the inherent structure of human experience, and we can no more step outside them than we can visualize a four-cornered triangle or a fourth primary color. Grasp those inherent structures and their interrelationships, and it becomes easier to use will and imagination in ways that are, quite literally, magical.

While my early books are fully (and rather unreflectively) embedded in the received traditions of modern occultism, everything I've written on spirituality and magic since *A World Full of Gods* (2005) has been informed by my work on critical Neo-Platonism, and I plan on working up a booklength treatment of it eventually.

§ 56. Michael York

Michael York is a retired professor of religious studies at Bath Spa University, best known for his *Pagan Theology: Paganism as a World Religion* (2003). Like Greer, York is among the scholars at the forefront of the critique of monotheism. A large section of his first chapter is devoted to criticizing scholars who treat polytheism as only a footnote in the history of religion, or who treat pagans themselves as mere target groups for Christians to evangelize. More interestingly, and more controversially, this text put forward the view that paganism is a world religion, a 'root' religion, elements of which can be found all over the world.

> In place of the increasingly obsolete but still entrenched position that doubts and rejects paganism as a religion, I argue that paganism is a 'root religion'... Historically, all other religions are offshoots and/or counterdevelopments of this root religion. And I even argue that if we wish to understand any religion, we must also understand paganism as the root from which the tree of all religions grow. (York, *Pagan Theology*, pg. 167)

I noted in the Overture how York understands the meaning of paganism: polytheism, animism, idolatry, and so on. In the course of his argument he refines the list down to essential features: '(1) a number of both male and female gods, (2) magical practice, (3) emphasis on ritual efficacy, (4) corpospirituality, and (5) an understanding of gods and humans as codependent and related.' (pg. 14) Overall, if I understand his position correctly: the more of these features one finds in a given religious tradition or practice, then the more reasonable it is to claim that it is a pagan tradition or practice. To that end York studies seven kinds of paganism including Chinese folk religion, Shinto, various Aboriginal traditions, Afro-American Spiritism, and contemporary Western paganism.

Actually, a lot of York's text involves identifying, defining, redefining more precisely, and further refining various categories of religious belief and practice. In that way, it seems to me, he can distill the idea of paganism down to its most essential elements, and having done so, recognize those elements when they appear in real-world religious practices, all over the world. Thus by the third and last division of the book, qualities like 'interactive', 'polymorphic' and 'tribal' entered the description of what it means to be pagan. Indeed York divides all the world's ideologies into four broad positions: Abrahamic, dharmic, secular, and pagan. (pg. 166) I would be tempted to criticize this process for being reductionist, or for committing too many sweeping generalizations, but his process for arriving at these positions is painstakingly careful. These four positions reminds me of the way American political scientist Samuel Huntington defined a civilization: 'The highest cultural grouping of people and the broadest level of cultural identity people have short of that which distinguishes humans from other species.' (Huntington, 'A Clash of Civilisations?' *Foreign Affairs*, Summer 1993) The reminder is strong for me since Huntington believes that it's religion which fills in one's cultural identity at that high and broad level. And that it's religion that causes all the conflict.

But even those four positions are not the last of them! For the Abrahamic and Dharmic traditions are both, in York's view, 'gnostic' at heart. Here's how his distinction works:

> If paganism is a theological ideal type, gnosticism constitutes another. In fact, the basic divide between all religions may be seen to rest upon pagan-gnostic distinctions... paganism posits the world or matter as real and valuable, while gnosticism sees the same as something to be penetrated, as something fictive or even evil. (pg. 159)

York's treatment of the category of gnostic religions is interesting because, according to his understanding of 'gnostic' noted above, the pagan traditions of Pythagoreanism, Neo-Platonism, and Theosophy, are not truly pagan at all! (cf. pg. 160) Yet historically, as York observes, paganism and classical gnosticism have become natural allies, because both were condemned by various councils in the early history of the Catholic Church. He also observes that these two categories describe 'ideal' types, and that it may be better to place a real-world religion not in one of the two hard categories, but rather in an appropriate field along a spectrum between the two poles. Even the Abrahamic traditions of Judaism, Christianity, and Islam have elements of both ways of thinking, and so may be very hard to locate on the pagan-gnostic spectrum. So these categories need not possess absolutely impermeable boundaries. York's last words on the distinctiveness of paganism are:

> If there is a single concept or practice that encapsulates the essential orientation and identity of paganism, it is celebration. If the basic notion of Eastern spirituality is release and that of Christianity is preparation or salvation, pagan celebration is a festive rejoicing that also embraces service because service is likewise an affirmation of humanity, the world, and divinity. Paganism views humankind, nature, and whatever the supernatural may or may not be as essentially divine. (pg. 167)

This final remark is very close to my own experience of what participation in the pagan community is like. Other religious traditions value celebration too, but that's okay, because paganism is the 'root religion', and its various concepts 'date back to the earliest stages of human encounter, to the time when everyone was pagan.' (pg. 168)

The value of York's work, I think, is that it mostly settles what is perhaps the most vexing and contentious question in the contemporary pagan movement: What is paganism? It is 'an affirmation of interactive and polymorphic sacred relationship by individual or community with the tangible, sentient, and nonempirical.' (pg. 162) I say that York 'mostly' settles that question, because as critics have noted, there are some important features of paganism to which he gives almost no attention: the role of female divinities, for instance. Also, as observed by religious scholar Melissa Raphael who reviewed the book in the *Journal for the Scientific Study of Religion*, 'many of the religions to which York ascribes paganism would disown it'. They might also reject the idea that their religion involves a *logos* of a *theos*, that is, a rational-philosophical account of the divine. And they might also reject the idea that they have anything in common with the other religious traditions that York classes as pagan. (Raphael, Melissa (2004). 'Review of Pagan Theology', *Journal for the Scientific Study of Religion* 43(4), pp. 556.)

But all this discussion of heavy categories represents the argument of only one of York's five major theological works. In early 2013, I wrote to York personally to ask him to comment about his own work. Here is his reply:

> My philosophical position is this worldly. I describe my own philosophy as one of enchanted materialism, pluralistic polytheism and humanistic pantheism. I reject panentheism because I hold that there is nothing beyond nature; nature is all there is. I reject any monotheism that is based on the jealousy of a single god as not being commensurate to the dignity of divinity and the essential thrust of democracy. Although I entertain and enjoy transcendental forms of mysticism, my paganism concentrates on the lives we have both personally and collectively.
>
> The ideas for which I stand are the following: (1) the expansion of freedom for every individual; (2) the protection and maintenance of environmental sanity, balance and sustainability as part of the context of that freedom, namely, a practical paganism that cherishes the earth as our mother, and as our mother, one who deserves mindful respect and appreciation. This translates for me into protecting the remarkable

ecology of the planet, the reduction if not elimination of pollution, and the establishment of an equable and feasible well-being for both the human/'earthling' community and the wider biodiverse forms in general that inhabit this planet; (3) the development of beauty as the flower of both the natural world and human freedom. With this in mind, I not only cherish nature but also see the artistic and technological as developments of the natural. To be healthy and viable, these must remain rooted in the organic to become its legitimate blossoms and not its annihilating anathema; (4) the valuing of the preternatural or 'co-natural' which, along with the gardening of the earth, the exaltation of the physical or corpospiritual and the contemplation of the mythological register, is not to be an escape from but rather a complement to dynamic being and the very mystery of the greater cosmos and life; (5) the re-examination and re-evaluation of the discipline of theology to emancipate it from Christian appropriation and historic dominance as part of the reclaiming of root/radical spirituality that begins with telluric desire and has no ultimate limit or end in astral reach.

The most important questions as I see them are: (1) in the face of the current corporate-military-financial hegemony, how do we awaken collective consciousness and the collective will to achieve a worldwide progressive equability? And (2) how do we attain liberation from the suicidal deadlock of 'disenchantment'? The answer to the first question I believe to be through education and the arts: education to raise people's awareness of the problems and possibilities at hand, and the arts to stimulate global and regional imagination along with the desire to be educated. An answer to the second question lies again with education and the arts as well as the need for passion and/or the passionate connection to the cosmos to which we are already integrally a part. One means for this last is to be found in the 'power plants' of nature that provide us with the possibility of recognising ever wider horizons and ever greater dreams. Yes, there may be dangers involved, but these might be mitigated through the re-establishment of initiatory mystery religions and the demand for governments of trust in place of those that operate by suspicion. The reasons I offer for the employment of education and the arts to achieve desired goals rest on their obvious constructiveness and economy in contrast to attempted solutions through war, destruction and waste. The reason for my advocacy of the natural physic is that, along with sustenance, it is yet again a great gift of nature and, as such, merits acceptance and gods-given use.

§ 57. Vivianne Crowley

Vivianne Crowley (no relation to Aleister) is one of the leading lights in Britain's pagan community. Trained in Gardnerian and Alexandrian lineages of Wicca, but also holding a Ph.D in Jungian psychology, she was praised by Ronald Hutton as 'the closest thing that Britain possessed to an informal successor to Alex [Sanders] in leading his tradition'. With her first book, *Wicca: The Old Religion in the New Age* (1989) she 'provided British witchcraft with a writer to match the spiritual power of Starhawk.' (Hutton, *Triumph*, pg. 373)

Each human being is unique and of value. When immersed in everyday life, it can seem that each of us is one of a mass; subsumed into the seething crowds that fill our city streets. If we look outward instead of inward, our perspective changes. When we look out into the night sky of myriad stars, we do not know if there are other conscious beings who are also wondering at the beauty of the universe; but given its vastness, we can assume that there are. Nevertheless, conscious life forms are relatively rare. Our planet has no immediate inhabited neighbours. To be a conscious life form in this wondrous universe of ours is therefore a special and privileged position.

We can believe if we wish that our planet and the wider universe are the result of a cosmic accident, but creation is purposeful. There is no rationale for why, but all around us life seeks to create new life. Each life form seeks to replicate itself, while evolving towards increasing complexity, diversity, and conscious awareness.

We can assume that our human existence is meaningless – or that it has meaning. Religions and philosophies create frameworks of meaning that enable us to cope psychologically with the paradox of being a conscious entity seeking to grow and expand in experience and consciousness; but at the same time subject to the finiteness of the human body. Often this paradox is rationalized by beliefs that human individuality has an independent existence beyond the body.

There are other ways of dealing with the reality of the finiteness of our existence. If we take the position that we are not separate and isolated consciousnesses but are part of a wider universe, then we can ask the question, 'Why does the universe create conscious beings?' rather than, 'Why do I exist?' Conscious beings are aware of the universe's existence and can appreciate and enjoy it. They can appreciate and enjoy one another. The function of human beings may therefore be to appreciate, enjoy and wonder at the universe and who and what it contains.

We do not need to know with certainty that our worldview is 'right'. Human understanding of the universe is limited. But if we take a position that our species is important, that the natural world around us is wondrous and beautiful – more beautiful than anything we human beings can create; and that the continuation of our species, each of whom is individual and unique, is of importance too, then this can be a starting point for living a life that reverences the universe around us and reverences each human being as an autonomous but interconnected centre of consciousness of the universe.

§ 58. Gus diZerega

Gus diZerega is an American political scientist, and author of *Pagans and Christians* (2001) *Persuasion, Power, and Polity* (2000) and *Beyond the Burning Times* (2009). Not long after completing his doctorate, he had a powerful spiritual experience which attracted him to Wicca and to shamanism. He is also among those at the forefront of pagan-Christian interfaith dialogue in the United States. I include him here as an example of an erudite pagan writer who expertly combines intellectual scholarship with personal spiritual revelations.

I entered paganism a newly minted PhD in Political Theory, believing in the scientific study of society, and torn by my strong pro-market leanings and my deep commitment to preserving wild nature and to living sustainably. Understanding and resolving these tensions as much as I could had long challenged me.

Then I discovered our world was conscious in a nontrivial sense, the Sacred was very real, shamanism was a genuine approach towards healing, the Gods existed and could contact us, and various phenomena written off as occult blitherings were quite real.

Decades later, how has my paganism changed my outlook?

First I have a vastly larger context within which to do my research, one where I know I will never be able to get the big picture. Consequently I adhere more lightly to my theories. When challenging information arrives I am more likely to think 'that's interesting, I wonder where it leads?' rather than 'that's a threat to my world view.' I think my spirituality has made me a better scientist in scientific terms.

My spirituality has enabled me to integrate the tensions I described above more than I ever thought possible. I remain an admirer of markets and am a solid liberal politically, a 'small d' democrat who while supporting markets as necessary for a free world emphasizes they must be embedded within rather than superior to civil society, which is the only large-scale human network able to encompass the full richness of human life.

My Jeffersonian political outlook has been deepened by appreciating the intrinsic value of the more-than-human world both in what we think of as nature, and far beyond it. Our world is alive in some sense all the way down, and we can access this aliveness. But in a world of many spiritual paths we have an obligation to try and make our case for how we should live in terms accessible to everyone of good will. Not just pagans.

I believe the spiritual values of love and compassion, trump every secular value. This is the context in which I believe we ultimately live our lives, and seek as best we can to embody these values. I do not always succeed. When we love the sacredness of the earth and the life on it, it is a daily challenge not to become filled with anger, despair, and even hate towards those who despoil it and their fellow human beings, and yet still oppose them wholeheartedly. In the secular world I see myself as a kind of warrior while seeking always to remember the larger context within which we all live.

Spiritually I am a devoted pagan, which also means I believe every spiritual tradition is but one more petal on an eternally unfolding flower through which spiritual reality expresses itself in the human world. What makes any petal spiritual is not its claims but rather how it enables and honors the heart and its expressions of love, care, and devotion. In short, now my understanding of our world is rooted in a context that privileges love, beauty and the heart as the most fundamental dimensions of duality.

§ 59. Janet Farrar and Gavin Bone

Stewart Farrar passed away in the year 2000, and his legacy was carried forth by his wife Janet, and her second husband Gavin Bone. I met them personally many times during the years I lived in Ireland: in fact a photo of me appears on page 222 of their first major work following Stewart's death: *Progressive Witchcraft* (2004). I found them to be knowledgeable, hospitable, and open-minded people. Herne's Cottage, their home near Kells, county Meath, Ireland, is a welcoming and comfortable little bungalow, with bad plumbing and no central heating. As some of the foundation stones were plundered from a nearby stone circle when the house was built fifty years ago, many visitors claim the house resonates with magical energy. At least a dozen cats come and go in the course of the day, comfortably sharing the house with the two-leggeds and happily chasing the field mice. And two pet goats live in a shed nearby. The interior is every inch a witches' house, with numerous works of art and sculpture adorning every available space on the walls and furniture. For research resources they have a library of hundreds of books, and Stewart's voluminous and meticulously archived correspondence with such pagan luminaries as Alex Sanders, Doreen Valiente, Ray Buckland, Scott Cunningham, and others. Stewart's presence is still palpable about the house, in features like the painted portrait of him that hangs in a hallway, the awards from the British Writer's Guild for his radio plays, and the many books he wrote which grace the shelves. An apple tree dedicated to him grows in the yard, bearing a carved plaque in his name.

Gavin has been accused of hijacking Janet and Stewart Farrar's reputation by becoming a co-author in their later books. But I think that claim is unfair. Gavin is a perfectly capable author in his own right, and for all of the books in which Gavin is co-author, it is he who does most of the initial research and who writes most of the first draft. *The Healing Craft* (1999), relied heavily on Gavin's own professional expertise as a nurse, for example.

I asked them to comment on their own philosophical views for the sake of this history. As you will see, their words show how Wiccans of the Gardnerian and Alexandrian lineages change their views over time in a manner that strongly resembles a developing critical tradition.

> We think it's fair enough to say that our philosophy regarding paganism and specifically Wicca has changed or, rather, evolved over the years. In the early days when we published our early works (*What Witches Do, Witches Bible* etc.) we, including Stewart, pretty much followed the given philosophical positions that Wicca offered. But even back then our belief structures were changing. Stewart and myself (Janet) realized after coming to Ireland that our practices had to reflect the land and culture we lived in; this is reflected in the rituals of *Eight Sabbats for Witches* (1980). We did not think we were involved in any way in a particular philosophical shift, but began to realize this was the case in the 1990s when we were exposed more and more to the international pagan community. It was travel that changed things for us. Exposure to varied pagan communities and traditional cultures (including Native American, Maori, and Leotho Sangoma), made us realize that the original philosophical teachings we had received in Wicca were quite restrictive and could easily lead to dogma. We began to realize that we were in fact following a more organic, evolving path, just as we had seen among the cultures we have visited around the word. We realized we had in fact been following this philosophy since the 1980s. To this day we stand by this philosophy, that by nature paganism must work on natural law and that includes

cultural (not social) evolution. It must evolve according to the cultures it is involved with and the land it is connected with. It is ludicrous, for example to do rituals to the death of the Corn King when there is no corn growing in the land you live in. Likewise it must continue to evolve into the twenty-first century, adapting to the cultural and technological changes that have occurred; the Wiccan Book of Shadows (BOS) has given way to the photocopied BOS, then the Floppy Disc of Shadows, the CD of Shadows and now the Smart Disc of Shadows! It is nice to adhere to romantic medievalism but even the rituals must change to fit the new millennia, and this includes same-sex handfastings, and even same-sex initiations (although anthropologically this is actually the norm), which include ones of a polarizing nature (which comes from a true understanding of magical energy). This has been Stewart's (and hopefully our own) legacy, that we were some of the first to openly adapt a neopagan tradition (Wicca) in this way, and therefore open the floodgates of change for the future.

Sixth Movement: A Commentary

You may recall from the overture that an account of the mere *survival* of pagan ideas into modern times was not my only interest. I also wanted to know if these ideas *flourished* as the bearers of a developing critical tradition, without the patronage of institutions. I now think it's safe to conclude, at the end of this road, that the answer is 'no'. To help an idea flourish in a big way, institutions are really, really helpful. For, as you can see in this book, a historical study of pantheism, Neo-Platonism, and pagan humanism is not really a study of the *development* of these ideas through history. It is merely the study of their occasional *reiterations, repetitions,* and *reappearances*. From the sixth century, when the Neo-Platonic philosophy schools were closed, to the middle of the twentieth century when the modern pagan movement began, we find pagan arguments and commentaries upon those arguments. But we do not normally find an ongoing exchange of argument, counter-argument, criticism, counter-criticism, improvement, adaptation, correcting of mistakes, and widening of application. In short, we tend not to find the signs of a fully fledged developing critical tradition. Without organizational support, ideas tend to take the form of strongly and/or poetically expressed propositions, and rather little else.

§ 60. A Developing Critical Tradition for Paganism?

The Abrahamic religions do have an ongoing critical tradition. Their core ideas remain recognizably consistent while their interpretation changes over time, as people investigate them more deeply, improve them, and apply them to changing circumstances or alter them in response to new scientific discoveries. Catholics once believed that hell was a definite place where the souls of wicked people are sent to be tortured in an eternal fire. Today, the Catechism of the Catholic Church says that hell is more like a psychological condition: 'the state of definitive self-exclusion from communion with God and the blessed.' (Catechism of the Catholic Church, 1033; c.f. also 1034-1037) And that's a much more rational idea. Similarly, Christians once believed that slavery was mandated by God, and various quotations from the Bible support that belief. Through the brave actions of evangelical Christians like William Wilberforce, and his humanist allies, the slave trade was abolished in the British Empire in 1807, and slavery itself abolished in 1833. These kind of changes come extremely slowly – perhaps too slowly for some people's liking – but they do come, as the social winds within such organizations blow back and forth between conservative and progressive directions. Now, I don't wish to assert a *causal* connection between Christianity's possession of institutions and the developmental progress of its ideas. But there is an undeniable *correlation*, and that correlation is thrown into the light when compared to the near absence of developmental progress for ideas that had little or no such organizational support.

Churches, schools, museums, businesses, governments, state-sponsored agencies, and so on, provide a kind of enormous laboratory in which people and material resources are concentrated and organized for specific purposes. In that laboratory, ideas and their associated practices are put to experimental variations, and to rigorous tests of reality. Unsound arguments are identified and dismissed; vague or elusive ideas are clarified; futile or immoral practices are abolished. This environment produces more than just tightened-up philosophical systems: it also produces literature and poetry, styles of art and music and architecture, models of social order and committed social activists and reformers working from within and outside of institutions, and much more besides. Without that intensification of people and resources, it is enormously more difficult to get those results. In fact I think it may be almost impossible.

Such laboratories are imperfect, obviously; they can also steer an idea into a retrogressive tangle of nonsense. Family Radio Network preacher Harold Camping's well-publicized prediction that the end of the world would occur on 21st May 2011, was such a tangle. So was his second prediction of October 21st of the same year. The institutionalization of an idea can also produce witch hunts, wars, oppressive political and economic orders, colonial takeovers of indigenous cultures, and horrifying acts of interpersonal violence. And those evil tidings can persist for generations, crystallized into the rules and traditions of institutionalized social structures which reward those who obey and punish those who rebel. That's why pagans don't like them. So, having an institution is no guarantee that ideas will progress for the better. But does this mean we must declare it forever immoral to create institutions? The answer is clearly 'no'. History shows us that organized ideas sometimes flourish and sometimes don't; but history also shows us that unorganized ideas almost never do. So we must ask the question: If you want your ideas to flourish, are you willing to get organized for their sake, knowing that they might degrade into something deplorable, but they might also blossom into something beautiful? In other words, are you willing to accept the risk?

The latter half of the twentieth century has perhaps been more kind to pagan thinking than any other time since before the fall of the Roman Empire. I think this is precisely because people who supported pagan ideas got organized. The various initiatory lineages of Wicca and witchcraft, the Order of Bards Ovates and Druids, the Covenant of the Goddess, the Reclaiming Collective, The Golden Dawn, the Order of Thelema, Arn Draocht Fein, the Wiccan Church of Canada, The Sisterhood of Avalon, and The Pagan Federation, are examples of pagans getting organized – I dare say they are examples of institutions. Gerald Gardner himself established institutions: not just his lineages of Wicca, but also his Museum of Witchcraft, in Castletown, Isle of Man.

Twentieth century pagans also made use of existing institutions to further their ends. They enrolled themselves as students in colleges and universities, to study paganism through history, social science, and the arts, under the tutelage of experts in those fields. Some rose high enough in the academic ranks to become professors themselves. Pagans also joined liberal and multi-faith churches like the Unitarian Universalist church, and they joined civil liberties organizations, and political parties. Thus they acquired the right to perform their own marriages and funerals, and the ability to resist legal discrimination. They started businesses such as publishing companies, music studios, and occult supply stores, and they rented or purchased land on which to host their festivals. These are all examples of pagans getting organized. And with the adoption of organized communities, signs of the beginning of a developing critical tradition started showing themselves.

I think the best example of such a sign is the way contemporary pagans began studying their own history more carefully, and then began revising their history when they found the evidence did not support their initial beliefs. The first generation of modern pagans believed that they emerged from an ancient neolithic matriarchy, which evolved into an organized witch-cult which persisted in Europe from the dark ages to late modern times: this is the myth of the Old Religion. But this religion was mostly destroyed by a series of persecutions in which secular authorities, supported by theological doctrines concerning the involvement of the devil in human affairs, punished its practitioners with death by fire or by hanging: this is the myth of the Burning Times. These myths were promoted by writers like Margaret Murray, Robert Graves, Zsuszana Budapest, and some of their associates. Indeed Gerald Gardner himself endorsed it. As he wrote in his book *Witchcraft Today* (1954):

The witches do not know the origin of their cult. My own

theory is, as I have said before, that it is a Stone Age cult of the matriarchal times, when woman was the chief; at a later time man's god became dominant, but the woman's cult, because of the magical secrets, continued as a distinct order. (pg. 43)

It's now widely accepted that there was no such witch-cult in the middle ages, and probably no such ancient matriarchy. A revised understanding of the evidence has mostly replaced the former beliefs with a new history. As summarized by Professor Ronald Hutton, the revised history goes like this:

Instead of a line of martyrs and embattled tradition-bearers, the immediate ancestors of [modern] Paganism became a succession of cultural radicals, appearing from the eighteenth century onward, who carried out the work of distinguishing the Pagan elements preserved in Western culture and recombining them with images and ideas retrieved directly from the remains of the ancient past, to create a set of modern religions. They can be regarded with the more pride in that they included some of the most celebrated, and generally admired, artists and authors in modern Western civilisation. In this model, Paganism is not something inherently different from mainstream society, and traditionally oppressed and persecuted by it, but represents an extreme, and courageous, distillation of some of its deepest and most important modern impulses. (Ronald Hutton, 'Revisionism and Counter-Revisionism in Pagan History' *The Pomegranate*, Vol.13, Iss. 2 (2011), pg. 231-2)

Nor is this the only example. While on one side of the Atlantic the myths of the Old Religion and the Burning Times were losing their footing in the evidence, on the other side of the Atlantic groups of feminist witches were producing important and original innovations, as we have already seen. And those innovations probably saved modern paganism from descending into fundamentalism or oblivion. They had to do with the acknowledgment of gender politics in one's spiritual identity, and also to do with environmentalism. As Hutton observed:

> American feminist spirituality had reinvested witchcraft with a pagan spiritual identity and invested it with a passionate ethic of world improvement and salvation through female liberation and conservation of the natural environment. It had given it a much larger and better-defined constituency of support, brought it out of the occult fringe into the mainstream of international cultural politics, and greatly enhanced its obvious relevance to contemporary issues and needs. (Hutton, *Triumph*, pg. 367)

Some might argue about whether Hutton's account of things got this or that small detail right or wrong. But there are two points I want to make here which we should not lose in the details. The first is that modern pagans have corrected and changed and enlarged over time their view of their own spirituality. Not that this process was easy or peaceful. As Hutton observed, American feminist witchcraft depended greatly on the stories of the Old Religion and the Burning Times. So those who questioned those stories risked being accused of betraying the sacrifice of their predecessors, or of 'defending patriarchy or betraying the great struggle to defend the planet'. (Hutton, *ibid.*) And while modern pagans were transforming their views, they might have looked like they were at war with each other. But that is precisely the way flourishing intellectual traditions function. Ideas are presented, either in words or in deeds, then they are subject to an almost endless process of criticism, counter-criticism, variation, experiment, and empirical test. This eventually leads to the selection and preservation of ideas that pass those critical tests, and the rejection of ideas that fail. It's like an alchemist's crucible that burns or boils away the dross until the substance within is pure. It's like an evolutionary force in which advantageous morphological novelty is transmitted to the next generation, and disadvantageous morphological novelty eventually falls away.

The other point I want to observe here is that pagan philosophy lost this dynamic process of development precisely when it lost the support of institutions. And it gained that dynamism back precisely when modern pagans started creating institutions again. Most pagans today associate the institutionalization of ideas with stagnation and with oppression. That view is perhaps one of the last elements of the myth of the Burning Times which is still widely accepted among pagans today. But the evidence does not support that view. In fact the evidence supports the very opposite view, which is that the *absence* of organizational support leaves ideas to stagnate, little-changed and little-grown, but merely repeated, for centuries.

So, where does this observation leave us? For one thing, my conclusion is surely about to be tested by the very same alchemical-evolutionary process I've just described. It might have supporters; it will certainly have critics. If my conclusion fails the test, it will be because my *method for reaching that conclusion passed the same test.* Because anyone who finds flaws in my argument will have examined the same evidence using the same kind of critical scrutiny. But if that is what happens, I should be grateful, rather than annoyed. For it would contribute something quite useful to the flourishing of the modern pagan community's intellectual life. When our faulty ideas are refuted, we are left free to pursue better quality ideas. And while we might feel sad to let go of faulty ideas that we were once emotionally attached to, or which we found politically useful, the benefit we gain from pursuing sound ideas is far better, and more than enough to outweigh the loss.

§ 61. Elemental Ideas

I have just rejected one of modern paganism's core beliefs, the belief that the institutionalization of ideas causes ideas to stagnate and become corrupt. But I think it would be wrong of me to leave it at that. I would like to replace that rejected belief with a new and better one. So let us ask this next question: if my conclusion is true, shouldn't ideas that lack organizational support just fade away? Why do some ideas keep coming back, even if only in the mode of repetition? I think the answer is that some ideas possess a great tenaciousness, a kind of staying-power, rooted in existential conditions. That is to say, ideas survive, even if only as mere repetitions, when they emerge from the contemplation of the world as we find it, and our way of being in the world as we dwell in it.

Consider the most basic, most universal, and most elementary of our ways. We human beings are born of a mother and father, and so our very existence on earth is already bound to social relations. We breathe an atmosphere shared and enriched by all other breathing organisms on earth, from insects to animals, from microbes to trees. We harvest and hunt the leaves and roots and flesh of other lives, and eat them, and thus we participate in a kind of circle of life. We drink and wash ourselves in water that moves in a circle of its own, that transports it from the deepest oceans to the highest clouds in the sky, and back again. We warm ourselves when we stand in the sunlight or sit by the fire, or lie in a shared bed with a lover. We fear the dark, we pound our chests with hubris, we fight each other, we compete for a bigger share of what wealth there may be, and we scurry for victory. We reveal our minds when we gaze upon each other, and speak, and listen; we reveal our hearts when we touch. And we drift into the autumn and then the winter, and we lean on walking-sticks and drink mulled wine, and close our eyes to sleep, perchance to dream, until the night we never open them again.

An elementary idea is an idea that emerges from the rational contemplation of everyday motions in the lives of one and all, such as these. In a sense, then, elementary ideas are there to be discovered by anyone who tunes their ears to the music of what happens. Pagan animism is an elementary idea in this sense. It emerges from our contemplation of the movements and apparent intentionalities, real or imagined, of the creatures and materials of the nonhuman world. Pantheism is elementary idea, because it emerges from the contemplation of the great inter-connectedness of all life on earth, through food chains and the cycling of organic compounds in the soils and waters and skies, and the turning of the seasons, and the movements of other natural immensities. Neo-Platonism is also an elementary idea, as it emerges from the nature of thinking and dreaming, and the whole of the interior life of the mind. And, finally, humanism is an elementary idea too. It emerges from our many great and complex psycho-spiritual pulses, especially including the will to know ourselves, and also the will to power. These things are broadly universal. Though some details change in accord with differing languages and climates, the overall principles of biology, physics, ecology, and consciousness remain generally the same, all over the world. Elementary ideas are in this way universal and eternal. It's not that the ideas have always existed, or that they are immortal. But the raw materials from which they are made are available every-where, to anyone, at any time. And the world remains ever open to our contemplations. So it should not be surprising to find pagan ideas resurfacing again and again, even after societies change and institutions are abolished and replaced.

Surely the rational contemplation of our way of being in the world is at least as good a source for our ideas as imagined histories of ancient societies that never existed. Surely it is at least as good as syncretic comparative generalizations drawn from the world views of disparate cultures. And surely it is at least as good as private mystical experiences. It is, after all, the 'original relation to Nature' that Emerson called for; it is the search for 'the soul of the universe' that Toland spoke of. And surely it is better than dogmatic claims about the supposed corrupting influence of institutions, or about the freedom and purity that supposedly follows from the absence of institutions!

Of course this does not mean elementary ideas are always sound, or that they are immune from criticism. Elementary ideas can be right or wrong, inspiring or banal, coherent or mistaken, the same as any more complex idea. The point is that they emerge from the contemplation of what things and people appear to be. And so their occasional resurgences are not mysterious, and perhaps to be expected from time to time. While I'm at it, it's possible that monotheism, hierarchical social orders, certain prejudices and stereotypes, or even the belief that the earth is flat, could also be elementary ideas. But again, the point is not whether they are sound or unsound. The point is that they recur. And when they recur, it is the job of systematic critical reason to develop, refine, correct, enlarge, or dismiss them, as may be necessary. And it is the job of a developing critical tradition to foster and support, and indeed to supervise, the work of critical reason, lest our ideas become stagnated. In that way, our elementary ideas are the seeds planted in the fields of our thoughts, though they are not necessarily the fruit which grows from those seeds, and which we finally harvest and eat. But that is not so bad after all.

Consider, as a possible example of pagan thinking in an unexpected place, this prayer, written by St. Francis of Assisi (1182-1226), and known as 'The Canticle of Brother Sun'. Now it might seem absurd to include a major Christian saint in a book about pagan thinking. But although it praises a transcendental God and not a pantheist one, there is little trace of the anthropocentrism which characterized Christian thinking at the time. Here it is, in its entirety, where you can see it for yourself:

Most High, all-powerful, good Lord, Yours are the praises, the

295

glory, the honour, and all blessing.

To You alone, Most High, do they belong, and no man is worthy to mention Your name.

Praised by You, my Lord, with all your creatures, especially Sir Brother Sun, Who is the day and through whom You give us light.

And he is beautiful and radiant with great splendour, and bears a likeness of You, Most High One.

Praise be You, my Lord, through Sister Moon and the stars, in heaven You formed them clear and precious and beautiful.

Praised be You, my Lord, through Brother Wind, and through the air, cloudy and serene, and every kind of weather through which You give sustenance to Your creatures.

Praised be You, my Lord, through Sister Water, which is very useful and humble and precious and chaste.

Praised be You, my Lord, through Brother Fire, through whom You light the night and he is beautiful and playful and robust and strong.

Praised be You, my Lord, through our Sister Mother Earth, who sustains and governs us, and who produces varied fruits with coloured flowers and herbs.

Praised be You, my Lord, through those who give pardon for Your love, and bear infirmity and tribulation.

Blessed are those who endure in peace for by You, most High, they shall be crowned.

Praised be You, my Lord, through our Sister Bodily Death, from whom no living man can escape.

Woe to those who die in mortal sin.

Blessed are those whom death will find in Your most holy will, for the second death shall do them no harm.

Praise and bless my Lord and give Him thanks and serve Him with great humility.

As you can see, the saint manifestly does *not* 'rule over the fish in the sea and the birds in the sky and over every living creature that moves on the ground.' (Genesis 1:28) Instead, he speaks of the elements in a highly personal way, not as mere 'things', but instead as family members. He positions human beings as but one creature among many in a world-wide family, neither more nor less important than any other creature on God's good earth. Now why does an apparently pagan idea appear in a testament of faith by a major Catholic saint? I think the answer is because the idea that the earth is a community is an elemental idea. It can be inferred by any thinking person who observes the world, and her place in it, with an honest and critical and loving eye.

Let's jump forward about six hundred years and have a look at everybody's favorite poetic testament of pantheism: *Lines Composed A Few Miles Above Tintern Abbey* (1798) by William Wordsworth.

And I have felt
A presence that disturbs me with the joy
Of elevated thoughts; a sense sublime
Of something far more deeply interfused,
Whose dwelling is the light of the setting suns,
And the round ocean and the living air,
And the blue sky, and the mind of man;
A motion and a spirit, that impels
All living things, all objects of all thought,
And rolls through all things. Therefore I am still
A lover of the meadows and the woods,
And mountains, and of all that we behold
From this green Earth...

Although Wordsworth praises a feeling, 'a motion and a spirit' that impels him from within, still he also praises the landscape of the Wye Valley itself, and loves it for itself. This might not be a pure-type example of pantheism, but it is a clear and unfettered exultation of the love of life and of being alive, the celebration of the earth and of the life of the earth. And that, as we have seen, is a pagan idea too.

Finally, here's a modern example of literary affection for a pagan god, in the flesh. It appears in Kenneth Grahame's *The Wind in the Willows*, (1908), in a chapter called 'The Piper at the Gates of Dawn'. In the story, the two animal-characters Rat and Mole, search for a missing child named Portly, the son of their friend Otter. In the late hours of the night, moments before sunrise, as they boat along a river searching for Portly, the sound of an otherworldly music draws them to an island.

'This is the place of my song-dream, the place the music played to me,' whispered the Rat, as if in a trance. 'Here, in this holy place, here if anywhere, surely we shall find Him!'... Then suddenly the Mole felt a great Awe fall upon him, an awe that turned his muscles to water, bowed his head, and rooted his feet to the ground. It was no panic terror – indeed he felt wonderfully at peace and happy – but it was an awe that smote and held him and, without seeing, he knew it could only mean that some august Presence was very, very near. With difficulty he turned to look for his friend, and saw him at his side cowed, stricken, and trembling violently. And still there was utter silence in the populous bird-haunted branches around them; and still the light grew and grew. Perhaps he would never have dared to raise his eyes, but that, though the piping was now hushed, the call and the summons seemed still dominant and imperious. He might not refuse, were Death himself waiting to strike him instantly, once he had looked with mortal eye on things rightly kept hidden. Trembling he obeyed, and raised his humble head; and then, in that utter clearness of the imminent dawn, while Nature, flushed with fullness of incredible colour, seemed to hold her breath for the event. He looked in the very eyes of the Friend and Helper; saw the backward sweep of the curved horns, gleaming in the growing daylight; saw the stern, hooked nose between the kindly eyes that were looking down on them humourously, while the bearded mouth broke into a half-smile at the corners; saw the rippling muscles on the arm that lay across the broad chest, the long supple hand still holding the pan-pipes only just fallen away from the parted lips; saw the splendid curves of the shaggy limbs disposed in majestic ease on the sward; saw, last of all, nestling between his very hooves, sleeping soundly in entire peace and contentment, the little, round, podgy, childish form of the baby otter. All this he saw, for one moment breathless and intense, vivid on the morning sky; and still, as he looked, he lived; and still, as he lived, he wondered. 'Rat!' he found breath to whisper, shaking. 'Are you afraid?' 'Afraid?' murmured the Rat, his eyes shining with unutterable love. 'Afraid! Of Him? O, never, never! And yet – and yet – O, Mole, I am afraid!' Then the two animals, crouching to the earth, bowed their heads and did worship. (Grahame, *The Wind in the Willows* (Simon & Brown, 2012) 91-2)

Here is a depiction of the Arcadian wild-god Pan, powerful yet approachable, imposing yet gentle. All the animals and plants and elements of the island are at peace in His presence. The pagan idea expressed here is not quite the natural communion of pantheism, although it is bound to the life of the earth. Nor is it the visionary auspice of Neo-Platonism, although we experience the same *mysterium tremendum*. And it is not the soul-raising affirmation of humanism, although the god we meet is in human form (well, mostly). Rather, the Piper at the Gates of Dawn embodies perhaps the very oldest and most elemental of all religious insights: animism, the idea that the things and creatures and elements of the world around us are home to a great panopoly of spiritual beings.

The Wind in the Willows was originally written for children, but its simple elegance and literary power, especially in this scene, was written for everyone. For when Rat and Mole heard Pan's music and found his island, we all got to see a little more of the world than what we normally see. And we got to remember – not forget – what life was like when we were children, and the world was full of amazing things. This, too, is an elementary idea. And it leads me to a second possible explanation for why pagan ideas resurfaced even after they lost the support of institutions.

§ 62. The Will to Dwell in an Enchanted World

Why do religious ideas continue to hold us? Well, they might hold us because they might be true. But the question is pressing because we now possess a veritable mountain of sound and solid ways to explain the world without recourse to the supernatural. In almost every historical disagreement between science and religion, science won. But religion did not crawl away defeated. And that is what prompts my question.

One type of answer can be discovered in science. A study by sociologist Gregory Paul found that religiosity (belief in a supernatural creator deity, belief in an afterlife, weekly attendance at religious services, etc.) is highest in countries that are poor, and it tends to decrease as a country becomes more prosperous and modern. (Gregory Paul, 'The Chronic Dependence of Popular Religiosity upon Dysfunctional Psychosocial Conditions' *Evolutionary Psychology* Vol. 7(3), 2009) In another study, he measured rates of violent crime, divorce, abortion, STD infection, teen pregnancy, etc. And he found that religiosity tends to be high in countries where rates of those social indicators are also very high. (Gregory Paul, 'Cross-National Correlations of Quantifiable Societal Health with Popular Religiosity and Secularism in the Prosperous Democracies: A First Look' *Journal of Religion and Society*, 7 (2005)) Correlation is not causation, obviously; but when asked by a journalist to explain his findings, he said that religion 'tends to be popular in societies that... have enough rate of dysfunction that people are anxious about their daily lives, so they're looking to the gods for help in their daily lives. It's not fear of death that drives people to be religious, and it's not a God gene or a God module in the brain or some sort of connection with the gods; it's basically a psychological coping mechanism.' (Kazi Stastna, 'Do countries lose religion as they gain wealth?' *CBC News*, 12 March 2013)

This answers much, perhaps most, but not all, of my question; for my question is not just sociological. It is also philosophical. Anyway, Paul's research doesn't explain why an educated and affluent individual might remain religious. And it says nothing about spiritual experiences. So to find an answer, let's remind ourselves of some of the ideas we have seen in this tour. There's the various Laws of Magic, and the Sacred King, described by James Frazer. There's the White Goddess that Robert Graves loved, and Doreen Valiente's Great Mother and Star Goddess, speaking with her voice when she draws down the moon. There's the intrinsically pleasurable and loving things that the Goddess asks us to do in Her praise: dance, sing, feast, make music, and love. There's John Toland's claim that the whole world is one's country, and Aleister Crowley's statement that every man and woman is a star. Here's Francis of Assisi's Brother Sun, Whitman's Song of Myself, the Druidic teaching that the soul is immortal, and the story of Rat and Mole meeting the Friend and Helper. Now what do these ideas really mean? Of course, on the surface, they mean exactly what they say they mean. Basic propositions can always be taken at face value. But to what world view do they belong? What must one presuppose in order to find them acceptable? What more and what else might follow from those presuppositions? And does the world view they proclaim make sense? And if yes, then why? And if not, then why not? And how can the answers to those questions help explain why pagan ideas survived without the support of institutions? Here's the possibility which, this evening as I contemplate it, I find the most reasonable. In various ways, these teachings presuppose that the world is full of supernatural beings, otherworldly presences, magical forces, sacred connections, and psychic possibilities – in short, that the world is *enchanted*.

Now, the will to dwell in an enchanted world is actually only a facet of a larger gem, and a single beat of a deeper, more pervasive pulse in the human spirit: the will to dwell in a world that is *interesting*. Now an interesting world is a world that is open to us. It permits questions; it invites exploration. But it also hints at what is still hidden, not yet explored, and perhaps soon to be discovered. A doorway or a gate suggests a space beyond it, that we might explore if we step forward. The shadows of a cave suggest treasures, and monsters, which might lie beyond the reach of the light. The thick blanket of snow that covers my country six months of the year suggests the green fields and gardens which will emerge to life again in the spring, when the snow melts away. I am taking a hint here from psychologist and druidic writer Philip Carr-Gomm, the current leader of the Order of Bards, Ovates, and Druids, for whom magic is 'the experience we have when something emerges into light from the darkness, from the unknown.' (Philip Carr-Gomm, *Beyond Belief*, presentation delivered at the Glastonbury Symposium, July 2009) By the same hand, a world that is interesting is a world that suggests that it is more than what it appears to be, and that deeper sounds may some day reach our ears. Its mysteriousness is not its hidden-ness: its mysteriousness is in the way that however much we discover, there is always more to discover. Its ineffability is not in its unspeakability, but in the way that however much we explain, there will always be more to say. In sum, an interesting world is a world with an inexhaustible supply of *revelation and immensity*. I think that people cannot live without something in the world that is interesting like this. I think the curious and imaginative mind needs an interesting world just as desperately as the hungry body needs food and air and water. As I have argued elsewhere, the notion of a good and worthwhile life depends greatly on finding or creating the right kind of social and ecological environment (and that there can be many 'right kinds' of environment). Here I'm adding that 'interestingness' is a quality of the right kind of environment. Without an interesting environment, the mind would be starved for wonder and hope, and we may as well be drones in a factory, with a life of mechanical routine.

A world that is *enchanted* is a world that is interesting in this sense because, by way of elementary ideas like animism and pantheism, it is deemed to be magical. For there might be nothing quite as interesting, in this sense, as a world that is full to the top of the sky with gods. These gods may or may not exist in actuality. But people look for them, try to speak to them and listen for them because that is one way the will to dwell in an interesting world can discharge itself. In *The Wind in the Willows*, for example, the great god Pan dwells on an island that is hidden because characters who visit there are magically compelled to forget their visit. But they know there's something special and magical about the island – they know it is the place of the song-dream – and this makes their world interesting.

The future will have its own animism and pantheism. For it will reach beyond our earth and touch a kind of interstellar ecosystem, in which great clouds of gas and dust condense to form stars and planets, and the stars eventually explode, producing new nebula, which produce new stars and new planets. And the future will have its own kind of Neo-Platonism and its own kind of humanism. With sciences like astronomy and quantum physics it will envision new infinities of time and space, beneath the veil of the visible, but contemplated by the mind. And it will elevate humanity to an even higher range of scientific knowledge and technological power. Soon we may discover whether the galaxy is full of life – and I think that will be the greatest revelation of all. There can be no end to discovery where there is life. The future will have these things because people shall continue to contemplate the world and their way of being in it, and they shall retain the will to live in an interesting world. With that heady combination, the future will have its pagan ideas too.

§ 63. An After-thought

Of my own philosophy, I shall say very little, and even this may be too much. I have no special teachings; I offer no new tables of the law; I make no demands; and I tell no one what to do.

I examine my situation, as a living human being, here at this place on earth, and at this time in history.

Things are so rarely what they appear to be on the surface. Everyone knows that; but few will tap upon the surfaces of things, to hear what realities echo back from within.

I find that I have these immensities before me: the earth beneath me, other people around me, my loneliness within me, and my death upon me.

And so I have these questions: how shall I dwell upon the earth? How shall I converse with all people? How shall I emerge from my loneliness? How shall I face my mortality?

And to find answers, I have all my relations: my body, my landscape, my animals, my food, my family, my guests, my friends, my lovers, my elders, my hometown, my arts, my possessions, my heroes, my mind, my teachers, my storytellers, my leaders, my healers, and my gods.

I find that every one of us has these same immensities, these same questions, and these same relations. In some sense, then, I find that we are one.

As I tap upon the surfaces of the immensities, I ask: which of my tuning-hammers makes music, and which ones only make noise? The best music, I have found, is made with humanity, integrity, and wonder. And I have found that everyone has these instruments ready to hand. Everyone, I affirm, although I also find that only a few of us take them up and play.

And to understand me fully, think of the many meanings of the word 'play'.

When I hear music, I share it; I hope that my people will listen with me. When I make music, I share it too; I hope that my people will celebrate with me and play along. When I make dissonant or offending sounds, I trust my people will warn me, so I can make amends.

This I do, not simply as a philosopher or a spiritual man; this I do as a human being, alive on earth, at this place and time.

Nothing more, perhaps, could be asked of anyone.

And, perhaps, nothing *less*.

Select Bibliography

Adler, Margot. *Drawing Down the Moon*, Revised edition (Boston: Beacon Press, 1986)

Apuleius, *The Golden Ass*, trans. Robert Graves (Penguin, 1950, revised 1990)

Aristotle, *The Metaphysics*, trans. Lawson-Tancred, H. (London: Penguin, 1998)

Aristotle, *De Anima (On the Soul)*, trans. Lawson-Tancred, H. (London: Penguin, 1996)

Aurelius, Marcus. *Meditations*, trans. Hammond, M. (London: Penguin, 2006)

Bade, (ed.) *Life and Letters of John Muir* (Houghton Mifflin, 1924)

de Beauvoir, Simone. *The Second Sex* (Vintage, 1989)

de Benoist, Alain. *On Being a Pagan* (Ultra, 2005)

Barnstone and Meyer, eds. *The Gnostic Bible* (London: Shambala, 2003)

Bede, *Ecclesiastical History of the English People*, trans. Sherley-Price, L. (London: Penguin, 1990)

Blavatsky, *Isis Unveiled*, Vol. 1. (Theosophy Trust, 2006)

Boethius, *The Consolation of Philosophy*, trans. Wats, V.E. (Penguin, 1969)

Bonewits, Isaac. *Real Magic* (New York: Coward, McCann, & Geoghegan inc., 1971)

Botzler & Armstrong, *Environmental Ethics: Divergence and Convergence*, 2nd edition (McGraw Hill, 1998)

Caesar, Julius. *The Conquest of Gaul*, trans. Handford, S.A. (Penguin: 1982)

Campbell, Joseph. *The Power of Myth* (Anchor Books, 1988)

Campbell, Joseph. *The Hero's Journey* (Princeton University Press, 1949)

Carr-Gomm, Philip. (ed.) *The Mount Haemus Lectures*, Vol 1, (Oak Tree Press, 2008)

Carter, Mark. *Stalking the Goddess* (Moon Books, 2012)

Cassirer, Ernst. et. al., eds. *The Renaissance Philosophy of Man* (U Chicago Press / Kessinger Publishing, 2010)

Charles, R.H. *The Chronicle of John, Bishop of Nikiu* (Evolution, 2007)

Chuvin, P. *A Chronicle of the Last Pagans*, trans. Archer, B.A. (Harvard University Press, 1990)

Cicero, *On the Good Life*, trans. Michael Grant (Penguin, 1971)

Cicero, *On the Republic, On the Laws*, trans. Keyes, Clinton W. (Loeb Classical Library, 1928)

Crowley, Aleister. *The Law is for All* (New Falcon, 1991)

Crowley, Aleister. *The Book of Lies* (Samuel Weiser, 1989)

Crowley, Aleister. *Magick*, eds. Symonds & Grant (Samuel Weiser, 1981)

Crowley, Vivianne. *The Magickal Life* (Penguin Compass, 2003)

Curd & McKirahan, *A Presocratics Reader* (Indianapolis: Hackett, 1996)

Daly, Mary. *Beyond God the Father* (Beacon Press, 1993)

Damon, S. Foster. *William Blake, His Philosophy and Symbols* (London: 1924 / Kessinger 2010)

Dodds, E.R. *Pagan and Christian in an Age of Anxiety* (Cambridge University Press, 1968)

Duddy, Thomas. *A History of Irish Thought* (Routledge, 2002)

DuQuette, Lon Milo. *The Magick of Aleister Crowley* (Weiser, 2003)

DuQuette, Lon Milo. *The Key to Solomon's Key*, 2nd Edition (CCC Publishing, 2010)

Dzielska, Maria. *Hypatia of Alexandria*, trans. Lyra, F. (Harvard University Press, 1996)

Ellis, Peter. *A Brief History Of The Druids* (London: Robinson, 2002)

Ellmann, Richard. *Yeats: The Man and The Masks* (Penguin, 1988)

Emerson, R.W. *Nature* (Boston: James Munroe & Co. / Cambridge Press, 1836)

Epictetus, *Enchiridion*, in *The Discourses*, Vol. II, trans. Oldfather,

W.A. (Cambridge, Mass, USA: Harvard University Press, 1961)

Eriugena, John Scottus. *Periphyseon* (Dublin: Institute for Advanced Studies, 1981)

Farrar, Janet & Stewart. *The Witches' Way* (Phoenix, 1984)

Frazer, James. *The Golden Bough* (Touchstone 1922)

Foreman, Dave. *Confessions of an Eco-Warrior* (Harmony Books, 1991)

Gardner, Gerald. *Witchcraft Today* (Magical Childe, 1991 (first published 1954))

Godwin, Jocelyn. *The Pagan Dream of the Renaissance* (Red Wheel Weiser, 2005)

Graham, William. *The Creed of Science* (London: Kegan Paul, Trench & Co., 1884)

Graves, Robert. *The White Goddess* (London: Faber, 1961)

Greer, John Michael. *A World Full of Gods* (ADF Publishing, 2005)

Gregory, Lady Augusta. 'Cuchulain of Muirthemney', in *A Treasury of Irish Myth, Legend, and Folklore* (NY: Gramercy, 1986)

Harpur, Tom. *The Pagan Christ* (Walker & Co., 2005)

Hecht, Jennifer. *Doubt: A History* (Harper One, 2004)

Heller, Erich. *The Importance of Nietzsche* (University of Chicago Press, 1988)

Hobbes, Thomas. *Leviathan* (Oxford University Press, 1996)

Hume, David. *The Natural History of Religions* (London: A. and H. Bradlaugh Bonner, 1889)

Hutton, Ronald. *The Triumph of the Moon: A History of Modern Pagan Witchcraft* (Oxford University Press, 2001)

Jacob, J.R. 'Boyle's Atomism and the Restoration Assault on Pagan Naturalism', *Social Studies of Science*, 8 (2), May 1978

Johnson, Oliver. *Ethics*, 7th edition (Orlando, Florida, USA: Harcourt Brace, 1986)

Kahn, Charles H. *The Art and Thought of Heraclitus* (Cambridge University Press, 1979)

Kaplan, Robert. *Warrior Politics: Why Leadership Demands a Pagan Ethos* (Vintage 2003)

Kelly, Fergus. *A Guide to Early Irish Law* (Dublin: Institute for Advanced Studies, 1995)

Kelly, Fergus (trans.) *Audacht Morann* (Dublin: Institute for Advanced Studies, 1976)

Kraemer, C.H. *Seeking the Mystery: An Introduction to Pagan Theologies* (Englewood, Colorado USA: Patheos Press, 2012)

Russell, Bertrand. *History of Western Philosophy* (London: Routledge, 1946)

Liebeschutz, J.H. *Continuity and Change in Roman Religion* (Oxford University Press, 1979)

Lovelock, James. *The Ages of Gaia* (Random House / Commonwealth Book Fund, 1990)

Marsch Wolfe, Linnie, ed. *John of the Mountains: The Unpublished Journals of John Muir* (Madison: University of Wisconsin Press, 1979)

Marlowe, Christopher. *The Tragical History of Doctor Faustus,* ed. Kocher, Paul H. (New York: Appleton Century Crofts, 1950)

Matthews, John. *The Druid Source Book* (London UK: Blandford, 1998)

Meadows, D., and 'The Club of Rome', *Limits to Growth* (Signet 1972)

Meyer, Kuno (trans.) *The Instructions of King Cormac Mac Airt* (Dublin: Royal Irish Academy, 1909; Todd Lecture Series, Vol. XV)

Meyer, Kuno (trans.) *The Triads of Ireland* (Dublin: Royal Irish Academy, Todd Lecture Series Vol. XIII, 1906)

Miller, David. *The New Polytheism* (Dallas, Texas: Spring Publications, 1981 (first published 1974))

Miller, Perry. *The American Transcendentalists* (Doubleday Anchor, 1957)

della Mirandola, Giovanni Pico. *Oration on the Dignity of Man* (Regnery Gateway, 1956)

Muir, John. *The Eight Wilderness Discovery Books* (London: Diadem Books / Baton Wicks, 1992)

Muir, John. *My First Summer in the Sierra* (Boston: Houghton Mifflin, 1910)

Muir, John. *The Yosemite* (WLC Books, 2009 (first published 1912))

Nichols, Ross. *The Book of Druidry* (Thorsons / Aquarian Press, 1990)

Nietzsche, Friedrich. *On the Genealogy of Morals* and *Ecce Homo* (omnibus edition) trans. W. Kaufmann (Vinage, 1967)

Niebuhr, H. Richard. *Radical Monotheism and Western Culture* (NY: Harper & Row Torchbook, 1970)

Nietzsche, Friedrich. *Beyond Good and Evil,* trans. W. Kaufmann (Vintage, 1966)

Nietzsche, Friedrich. *The Gay Science,* trans. Kaufmann, W. (Vintage, 1974)

Piggott, Stuart *The Druids* (New York: Thames & Hudson, 1975)

Plato, *The Republic,* trans. Grube, G.M.A. (Indianapolis: Hackett, 1992)

Plato, *Phaedo,* trans. Grube, G.M.A. (Indianapolis: Hackett, 1977)

Plato, *Symposium,* trans. Nehamas & Woodruff (Indianapolis: Hackett, 1989)

Plotinus, *The Enneads,* trans. MacKenna, S., abridged Dillon, J. (London: Penguin, 1991)

Rees, B.R. *The Letters of Pelagius and his Followers* (Boydell Press, 1991)

Regardie, Israel. *The Complete Golden Dawn System of Magic* (Falcon Press, 1984)

Reid, Sian. *Between the Worlds: Readings in Contemporary Paganism* (Toronto: Canadian Scholar's Press, 2006)

Restall-Orr, Emma. *Living with Honour* (O Books, 2008)

Rives, *Religion in the Roman Empire* (Blackwell, 2007)

Rousseau, Jean Jacques. *Reveries of a Solitary Walker,* trans. Butterworth, Charles. (Hackett, 1992)

Rousseau, Jean Jacques. *The Confessions,* trans. Cohen, J.M.

(London: Penguin, 1954)

Russell, Bertrand. *A History of Western Philosophy*, 2nd Edition (London: Routledge, 1961)

Russell, George William 'A.E.' *The Candle of Vision* (London: MacMillan and Co., Ltd. 1931)

Tacitus, *The Agricola and The Germania*, trans. H. Mattingly, revised. S.A. Handford (Penguin, 1970)

Schopenhauer, Arthur. *The World as Will and Representation*, Vol. 1, trans. Payne, E.F.J. (Dover, 1969)

Solomon & Murphy, eds. *What is Justice? Classic and Contemporary Readings* (Oxford University Press, 1990)

Spinoza, Benedict. *Ethics* (Wordsworth, 2001)

Starhawk, *The Spiral Dance*, 10th Anniversary Edition (Harper San Francisco, 1989)

Starhawk, *Truth or Dare* (Harper & Row, 1987)

Sturlson, Snorri. *The Prose Edda* trans. Byock, Jesse (London: Penguin, 2005)

Taylor, Thomas. *Eleusinian and Bacchic Mysteries* (New York: J.W.Bouton, 1875)

Thoreau, Henry David. *Walden* (Boston: Ticknor and Fields, 1854)

Toland, John. *Christianity Not Mysterious* (2nd Edition, London, 1696)

Toland, John. *Pantheisticon* (London: Sam Paterson, 1751)

Tyndall, John. *Address Delivered Before the British Association Assembled at Belfast, With Additions* (London: Longmans, Green, and Co., 1874)

Valiente, Doreen. *Witchcraft for Tomorrow* (Phoenix, 1978)

Waring, E. Graham. *Deism and Natural Religion: A Source Book* (Ungar, 1967)

Wittgenstein, Ludwig. *Philosophical Occasions: 1912-1951*, ed. Klagge J., and Nordmann A., (Hackett 1993)

Wittig, Monique. *Les Guerilleres*, trans. David LeVay (New York: Avon Books, 1971)

York, Michael. *Pagan Theology: Paganism as a World Religion* (New York University Press, 2003)

Zell-Ravenheart, ed. *Green Egg Omelette* (New Page, 2009)

Unnamed authors. *Manifesto: Positio Fraternitatis Rosae Crucis* (Grand Lodge of the English Language Jurisdiction, AMORC Inc., 2001) This is a privately circulated text, supplied to me by a person who used a pseudonym in correspondence.

Endnotes

1. Quotations from classical authors in this chapter are as cited in Matthews, *The Druid Source Book*, pp. 15-25, except as otherwise noted.
2. All fragments of Heraclitus cited here are from the Kahn edition, and numbered according to his arrangement.
3. I am grateful to Prof. J. Mitscherling, University of Guelph, for supplying me with an unpublished manuscript in which this argument is laid out in greater detail.

MOON
BOOKS

Moon Books invites you to begin or deepen your encounter with Paganism, in all its rich, creative, flourishing forms.